Free and Independent

FRANK SMALLWOOD

Free and

Independent

"That we will, at all times hereafter,

consider ourselves as

a free and independent state . . ."

Ira Allen, CLERK
The Westminster [Vermont] Convention
January 15, 1777

The Stephen Greene Press
Brattleboro, Vermont

This book has been produced
in the United States of America:
designed by R. L. Dothard Associates,
composed by American Book–Stratford Press,
and printed and bound by The Colonial Press.
It is published by The Stephen Greene Press,
Brattleboro, Vermont 05301

Library of Congress Cataloging in Publication Data

Smallwood, Frank.
    Free and independent.

    Bibliography: p.
    1. Legislators--Vermont--Correspondence, re-
miniscences, etc. 2. Vermont. General Assembly.
Senate. 3. Smallwood, Frank. I. Title.
JK3076.S6   328.743'092'4   75-41878
ISBN 0-8289-0272-0

76 77 78 79 80 9 8 7 6 5 4 3 2 1

Acknowledgments

I OWE a debt of gratitude to the many people who helped create this book.

First, I want to thank the many, many volunteers who assisted in my political campaign, most especially John Fieldsteel and the members of my family who worked very hard on my behalf.

Next, my respect goes to all legislators and other public servants in Montpelier, and to the many constituents scattered throughout Windsor County, who shared hopes and concerns that I have attempted to capture on these pages.

Also, I am grateful to a number of colleagues who reviewed different portions of my manuscript: Jim Epperson, Dick Winters, Bob Naka-mura, and Denis Sullivan at Dartmouth; Charles Morrissey, former Director of the Vermont Historical Society; Representative Norris Hoyt of Norwich; Jeffrey Pressman at the Massachusetts Institute of Technology; and Neil Kotler, currently on the Congressional staff of Rep. John Conyers, Jr. (Michigan).

Finally, I want to express my appreciation to four members of the Dartmouth staff—Chris Schile, Sheila Gallagher, Barbara Pryce and Virginia Darrah—for typing help, and to Janet Greene who served as editor of the manuscript.

A vote of appreciation to each for their interest and encouragement, with the understanding that final responsibility for any errors of fact or judgment are my own.   F.S.

Note

Since the account that follows represents an attempt to capture what I actually experienced in political life and the legislative process, all names and events described are real, not fictitious.

Obviously, my observations have involved subjective interpretations of a wide variety of activities which I have tried to report as fairly as possible. If I have inadvertently misrepresented any individuals, I offer my most sincere apologies.

Dedicated to

Susan, Sandy, David and Don

Who helped Ann take care of
the home front during my sojourn
in Montpelier

Contents

Where It All Begins

Open thou mine eyes, that I may
behold the wondrous things of thy law.
Psalm 119 : 18

E PLURIBUS UNUM. It's on every coin: "Out of many, one." That's how it all began. Thirteen colonies. A new nation.

Then, there was a fourteenth state—Vermont—followed by thirty-six others. The United States of America. Growing, always growing, into a big, restless, powerful giant with everything moving towards Washington, D.C., the home of all our trials and tribulations: Watergate, inflation, energy shortages, recession, tax loopholes, covert operations, unpopular adventures abroad. Woe is me! Whatever happened to all those states out there where it all began?

Watch every four years when they suddenly appear: Presidential primaries, party conventions, brass bands and banners—*Alabama* . . . *Alaska* . . . *Arizona* . . . *Arkansas*—the center of our political consciousness. But when all the hoopla is over, they fade away and go back to sleep until the next election.

Or do they?

Look again. Fifty different arenas full of noise and commotion. Fifty states chugging along, passing laws big and little that affect all sorts of everyday concerns: our children's education, the quality of our environment, the registration of our almighty automobiles, the protection of our lives and property, the jurisdiction of our cities and towns. Maybe everything isn't in Washington after all.

The states are big business now, bigger in terms of total employees (2.9 million) than even our national government (2.7 million). They spend mountains of money, over $100 billion each year. And, when you lump them all together, they nurture an incredible amount of political ambition in the form of fifty governors, 1,978 state senators, and 5,585 state representatives. This is still our political testing ground. Out where it all begins. Who are these people? What do they do? Where do they come from?

Tough questions. Analysis of any political body anywhere involves a challenging ordeal in subjective observation. A recent study in Utah, titled *The Dragon on the Hill,* referred to that state's legislature as "a creature so vast, sprawling and complex in construction that no one observer can have a final say on what it is." The study compares the trials of the legislative observer to "the confusion of five blind men describing an elephant based on a sense of touch—He's a rope; No, he's a tree; No, he's a great wall. From any vantage point, the view consists of only a fraction of the whole, and when one sees so little of all there is to see, myths spring up to fill the blanks in our vision."

Fair warning, well taken. My own political observations, set forth on the following pages, represent a personal view of one particular arena—the Vermont Senate—during a single two-year legislative session. After teaching political science at Dartmouth College for fifteen years, I took a sabbatical leave, made the political plunge, and, Lo and behold! managed to get myself elected as a state senator in the 1973–74 General Assembly.

What was it like? Well, first it was unlike other recent excursions into national masochism because I didn't develop a deep sense of despair over the American political process. Sure, I rubbed up against my share of wheeler-dealers, glad-handers, and power-brokers, but by and large I found the great majority of people out there to be refreshingly honest, industrious and dedicated. The American system of representative self-government is still alive.

Admittedly, the locale in which I worked is pretty small. In bare-boned statistics, Vermont ranks only forty-third in area (9,609 square miles) and forty-eighth in population (460,000 people) among the fifty states. It used to have more cows than people, but that isn't true any longer. The people population has grown during the past decade while the number of farms has dropped drastically. Today most Vermonters work in service trades, not agriculture, with slightly more than a quarter of the labor force engaged in manufacturing, followed by recreation and tourism. Much of the manufacturing is precision work (fabricated machine tools, computer components, etc.), since Vermonters are inventive and self-reliant. Tourism thrives because Vermont is a rural oasis in the Northeastern megalopolis, with two-thirds of its people clustered in small towns that average out to well under 2,000 inhabitants each.

What about the setting?

Thanks to its unspoiled rural character, Vermont is breathtakingly beautiful, a soft, rolling "Green Mountain" state (white in winter) with a patchwork quilt of pastures, meadows and small villages—all of which make it a very special place, a way of life. Many outsiders agree. They flock into the state during the summer, fall and winter months to escape the pressures of city living, to view the foliage, or to slip and slide down numerous ski slopes.

Because it has so much natural beauty to protect and preserve, Vermont has been very progressive in terms of legislative innovation, especially in the environmental field. It ranks as one of the pioneers (along with Oregon) in its attempts to wrestle with such challenges as state land-use planning, nondisposable bottle laws, a capital-gains tax on land speculators, and a host of related concerns.

Also, for better or worse (depending on who bends your ear at the local general store), Vermont has shouldered a remarkably heavy level of support for public services. Although only thirty-third among the fifty states in personal income per capita, Vermont ranks among the top five states in tax burden in relation to income and in per capita state debt.

In part, this strong public service commitment grows out of a long-standing tradition which Vermont's senior statesman, George D. Aiken, describes in his book *Speaking From Vermont*. Vermont did not join the original Union, remaining as an independent republic from 1777 to 1791, when it finally became the Fourteenth State. As Aiken explains, those early days were characterized by a twin belief in the ideals of liberty and liberalism to a point where Vermonters may have appeared to be "wild and undisciplined." The original Vermont Constitution, adopted in 1777, must have been "the most radical document of its day. It prohibited slavery in any form; it extended the right of suffrage to all men, regardless of property ownership; it recognized the subservience of private property to public need; and it specifically permitted freedom of speech and of the press."

Thus, from the beginning, Vermont, in the words of its 1777 Declaration of Independence, considered itself to be "a free and independent state." This is not to say that it cut itself off completely from the rest of the nation. In this same Declaration of Independence, Ira Allen, Clerk, recorded the rather brazen commitment that "we are at all times ready, in conjunction with our brethren in the United States of America, to do our full proportion in maintaining and supporting the just war against the tyrannical invasions of the ministerial fleets and armies . . . sent with express purpose to murder our fellow brethren, and with fire and sword to ravage our defenceless country." With this kind of heritage, it's hardly surprising that a century and a half later the State of Vermont declared war on Nazi Germany (the legislature called it a "state of belligerency") in September 1941, three months before Pearl Harbor!

That's the place. What about the legislative arena, with all those public servants milling around—thirty state senators and one hundred fifty representatives?

Although each state is unique, there are certain common political factors that cut across all levels. Anyone who has served in any legislative body has to: (1) get elected; (2) puzzle over, and pass upon, reams of nearly incomprehensible bills; (3) attempt to monitor an intractable governmental bureaucracy; (4) attempt to communicate with constituents; and (5) juggle a thousand and one other chores that come up in the course of the legislative day (or night).

That's what this book is all about. It is a firsthand account of how one academic wandered afield to find out what it was like out there in the everyday world of practical politics. It's written as a narrative, rather than a textbook, in an attempt to chronicle the ongoing dynamics of the political process, not only for students of government, but for anyone who is interested in a neglected, but important, aspect of political life in modern America. I hope it comes alive. At least the neophyte state senator who wrote it all down is still alive. And now, wish me luck as I start off on my trek into the political wilderness. Who says a watched pot never boils?

Frank Smallwood

Norwich, Vermont
1976

PART I

⊠ ☐ ☐ ☐

The Campaign

1

★ ★ ★ ★

The Decision

Our doubts are traitors,
And make us lose the good we oft might win
By fearing to attempt.
Measure for Measure

IT WAS a sparkling spring day. Almost perfect. Friday, May 5, 1972. I was driving down to the tiny town of Baltimore, Vermont, to meet Margaret Hammond. The road, twisting through the villages of Downers and Perkinsville, was bathed in warm afternoon sunlight that turned the fields into lovely soft green all the way to the base of Mount Ascutney, looming over the Connecticut River behind me.

The trip was exploratory. My objective was to talk to two retiring Vermont state senators whom I had not met before: Margaret Hammond of Baltimore and Olin Gay of Springfield. I wanted to sound them out on my possible candidacy for a Senate seat from Windsor County, a large geographical area that embraces twenty-four towns in east-central Vermont and has three senators. Both Senators Hammond and Gay were veteran Republicans who had represented the county for many years, and both were retiring, leaving two vacant seats. I was forty-four years old, by trade a political scientist who had taught at Dartmouth College for fifteen years, and (mercifully) was due for a sabbatical leave during the 1972–73 academic year. Although most sabbaticals are used for research purposes, circumstances—the two Senate seats suddenly vacant, the election coming up, my leave falling due—were conspiring to tempt me into making my first run for political office to find out what it was actually like out there in the world of *Realpolitik*.

Even though my car was dawdling along at a snail's pace, I almost missed a right turn into an old dirt road marked with a faded arrow saying *Baltimore*. Just after I made the turn, as I was bouncing along between ruts and the remnants of frost heaves on the approach to Senator Hammond's farmhouse, the first serious doubts began to creep into my mind about the nature of this unique excursion and its possible consequences. I realized it was a long shot for me to consider a fling into state politics. For one thing, I was an "outsider," a relative newcomer who had moved into Vermont only eight years earlier, although my ties with the surrounding area reached back considerably further. Initially, I had come to northern New England in 1947 to spend four years as a student at Dartmouth College. Following additional study at Harvard and a stint with the United States Government in Washington, I had returned to New Hampshire in 1957 to join the Dartmouth faculty.

It wasn't until 1964, however, that our family had finally moved over into Vermont to build a home on twenty-five acres of high, rolling meadowland in the town of Norwich, just across the Connecticut River from Dartmouth. A local farmer sold us the land for a very modest price with the proviso that he retain haying rights for the rest of his life. It was practically a gift. We used to picnic with our four young children at the top of the meadow, where our house now commands a spectacular view of the surrounding hills. The farmer had sold us the land because he felt it would be a nice spot for us to raise our family. He was right.

Yet despite our entire family's love for Vermont, the fact remained that I was a recent arrival in a closely knit state that harbored a traditional skepticism of outsiders. Perhaps this clannishness had resulted from the fact that there had been relatively few newcomers migrating into Vermont for more than one hundred years. Instead, the state had exported its talent to all points of the compass. The great exodus began in the middle of the nineteenth century with the loss of the Merino sheep industry to the vast grazing lands of the West. By 1860, more than 150,000 people had left Vermont. They fanned out into the frontier states to help found new communities with Vermont names such as Montpelier in Indiana; Vergennes in Illinois; Bennington in Michigan; and many others.

Eventually the situation stabilized, and Vermont settled down to dairy farming in its quiet corner of northern New England, unaffected by the booming urban growth south of its borders. It was not until the 1960's that Vermont showed its first significant immigration in over a century (the population jumped an amazing 14 percent, from 389,000 to 444,000 between 1960 and 1970). One of the key factors that attracted the more recent newcomers was the clean, unspoiled beauty of a state which hadn't been opened up to large-scale tourism until the interstate highway system carved its way north to the Canadian border. The new highways brought new people, who brought a host of political challenges with them. By the 1970's, Vermont was pioneering with environmental protection laws and many related concerns designed to accommodate the new growth and keep it under control.

My personal involvement in this flurry of activity had grown out of my service on the Board of Trustees of the Vermont State Colleges. Philip Hoff, Vermont's first Democratic Governor in over a century, had appointed me a trustee in 1967, despite the fact that I was a Republican. As we wrestled with the problems of constructing new campuses to hold the influx of students, it became obvious to me that we had to establish a more co-ordinated statewide higher education system. In 1971 I had chaired a commission which drafted a bill to accomplish this objective, but the measure had been badly beaten in the previous legislative session. This particular experience constituted a key reason behind my potential interest in running for the Vermont Senate: I figured that maybe I could make a contribution to higher education in the state if I could get elected.

Still, the fact remained that I was without any real background at all in Vermont party politics. Both the retiring state senators I was planning to visit, on the other hand, had a wealth of practical experience. Margaret Hammond, who was seventy-two years old, had served in the state legislature for twenty-eight years. Olin Gay, even more elderly, had twenty years of legislative service. The purpose of my trip was to sound both of them out, to get some idea whether they felt it made any sense at all for a political unknown like myself to run for one of their seats in the Senate.

Finally, Margaret Hammond's farmhouse came into view. I parked out front near a big mud puddle, drew a deep breath, and took my first hesitant steps into the Vermont political arena.

My visit with Senator Hammond went quite well. When I arrived I found her standing on the top rung of a high stepladder, hanging wallpaper in her living room. A strong, handsome woman, she joined me at the kitchen table for a long conversation that involved a fascinating excursion through numerous diaries she had kept of her legislative experiences. We had a good talk. At the end of an hour she indicated in a friendly, but alarmingly open, fashion that she hoped I would run for the Senate, although she couldn't support me in the primary election in September because she was already committed to other candidates who were planning to run. She did say, however, that she would be glad to circulate one of my nominating petitions among her friends in order to help me get my name on the ballot. True to her word, two months later she sent me back a petition with twenty-five signatures from residents of Baltimore.

After I left Margaret Hammond, I headed five miles south to Springfield, the home of Senator Gay. Springfield is by far the largest town in Windsor County, with more than 10,000 people. The Springfield area is often referred to as "Precision Valley" because of its major machine-tool factories. It stands as a symbol of Vermont ingenuity, having produced a host of inventions including the combination lock, the adding machine, the breech-loading rifle, the steam shovel, the jointed doll, the "Taylor mop," and a variety of sophisticated machine tools, "the machines that make machines."

Senator Gay, a remarkably spry and alert man despite his eighty-five years, greeted me at the front door before leading me into a large living room where I was formally introduced to his wife, who was sitting with a lapful of sewing.

Following a few introductory pleasantries, Senator Gay began to probe into why I wanted to reverse the usual order of candidacy and run for the Senate without first running for the House of Representatives to gain political experience. He told me that Lee Davis, one of Springfield's representatives, was going to run for the Senate, and he was planning to support him partly because of Lee's previous experience in the House.

I explained that Norwich's representative, Allen Foley, was running for his fifth term in the House. Foley, an extremely popular legislator, had encouraged me to try for the Senate since, with two vacancies opening up, I might have a chance to win one of the three Windsor County seats.

Senator Gay remained skeptical. His wife, busy with her sewing, didn't pay much attention to our conversation, which, quite frankly, appeared to be going exactly nowhere at this point. I considered whether I should leave quietly, primarily because I didn't know what to say. Casting around for something to fill the void, I mentioned that I knew Senator Gay's young grandson. He looked surprised. Mrs. Gay looked even more surprised. It was as if an electric current had gone through the room. I had obviously struck a responsive chord. "Do you really?" Mrs. Gay exclaimed. "How do you know young Olin?"

I replied that my elder daughter, Susan, a freshman at the University of Vermont, had served with Olin as a counselor at the Rock Point Episcopal Summer Camp north of Burlington. Mrs. Gay left her sewing, and pulled up a rocking chair to join the conversation. Senator Gay nodded pleasantly, and began to reminisce about the old days in Vermont.

"You know," he remarked, "it's interesting to think about our younger people like my grandson and your daughter. I've seen a lot of changes in my day. That's right, young man, I've seen a lot of changes. I was born in Tunbridge 'way back in 1886, and I moved to Cavendish in 1888. I've seen a lot of changes in my day."

A dam had burst. Senator Gay told me about his early career as a woolen manufacturer in Cavendish and Ludlow; about his marriage to Mrs. Gay on Christmas Eve in 1913; about his children and his grandchildren—which brought us back again to young Olin.

"You know, Olin is in the Navy now. Somewhere in the Pacific. Do you think he will be all right?" Mrs. Gay asked me.

"I hope so," I told her. "Vietnam is basically a ground war. I think he's safer in the Navy than he would be in the Infantry or the Marines."

She nodded thoughtfully. I prepared to leave, but Mrs. Gay would have none of that, insisting that I stay for coffee and cake, and Senator Gay wanted to show me his study. After we toured the first floor of

the house, he took me over to a lighted work area in the basement that
was stacked high with legislative journals bound in different colors.

"I won't be using these any more," he murmured. "You should take
them back to Norwich and read them over."

After staggering out to my car with a huge load of documents I returned to the kitchen for a cup of coffee. During the ensuing discussion, Senator Gay indicated that he was going to remain noncommittal
until he found out who else was going to run in the primary, but he
hoped I would consider entering the race. Mrs. Gay asked me to visit
again the next time I was in Springfield. I finally left by the kitchen
door, waved goodbye, and headed back to Norwich.

I turned on the car radio a few miles north of Springfield, in time
to hear the local news broadcaster report that Representative Lee Davis
had announced his candidacy for the Vermont Senate that afternoon.
Another candidate, William Tufts of Bethel, had announced the
previous day, and the third incumbent senator, John Alden of Woodstock, had indicated that he probably would run again. It looked like
there were already three candidates for the three Senate seats. The
long drive back to Norwich gave me plenty of time to weigh the pros
and cons of entering the race. Both Senators Hammond and Gay had
been courteous, but reserved. With three candidates in the field, I
was obviously going to face a battle in the primary. In the light of
the odds, I wasn't at all sure it would be worth the effort involved.

¶My FORAY into the field to meet Senators Hammond and Gay came
at a time when I was swamped trying to keep on top of my job at
Dartmouth. I had served as Dean of the Social Science Division for
two years, and during the spring of 1972 I was filling in as Acting
Dean of the Faculty while Dean Leonard Rieser was on a research
leave abroad. It was a very tough period, an endless series of faculty
committee meetings, coupled with a real push on "affirmative action"
hiring of women and minority-group faculty members. And the Vietnam situation was flaring up again.

Tuesday, May 9, was gray and rainy. The preceding night President
Nixon had announced a blockade of Haiphong harbor in a nation-
wide television address. I looked out my office window, and through

a spatter of raindrops I could see the outlines of a student-faculty protest forming on the College Green. Shortly after lunch a group of faculty members entered my office to hand me a petition requesting a faculty meeting to discuss the "rapidly deteriorating Vietnam situation." After a telephone discussion with President Kemeny, we agreed to hold a meeting in Webster Hall the following afternoon. It turned out to be an orderly, although heated, exchange. That evening, President Kemeny felt events were steady enough on campus, and he left for the West Coast to fulfill a speaking engagement.

The rest of the week turned out to be a nightmare. The very next morning the Hanover police arrested thirty-two demonstrators at the U.S. Army Cold Regions Laboratory, a mile north of the college. In addition to numerous protests and arrests, frantic efforts were underway to locate the body of a young Dartmouth student who had drowned in the Connecticut River over the weekend; and the college's popular Dean of Freshman, sixty-two-year-old Albert Dickerson, had suffered a fatal heart attack during the same weekend.

I was worn out when the week was over, but I had to go over to Randolph Center on Saturday morning to chair a meeting of the Vermont State Colleges Trustees. It was a beautifully clear day. After I returned from the trustees' meeting I took our younger son, twelve-year-old Donny, over to Hanover on a shopping trip. All during the afternoon two helicopters kept circling overhead, searching the Connecticut River for the body of the young student who had drowned. On the way back to Norwich, Donny and I were startled to see that the river had been drained of much of its water, exposing high mudbanks and numerous sodden tree trunks. We parked the car, got out, and walked along the Vermont bank of the river for a considerable distance. We could see a number of search and rescue boats crisscrossing the center of the shallows south of us toward Wilder Dam, which had been opened to lower the river.

During our walk I realized that Donny was troubled. I suspected it was a natural reaction to the tragedy surrounding the drowning. After a long silence, he asked me about death, and why people had to die. We had a long talk, but I didn't feel I provided very satisfactory answers. Then Donny abruptly changed the subject. He knew I was considering running for political office, and asked me if I was serious about entering politics. I told him I really didn't know at that point—which was a perfectly honest answer since I was having a hard time juggling all the different problems I was trying to handle.

Then he said he hoped I wouldn't become involved. I asked him why. "Because I will miss you," he replied quite matter-of-factly. "But if you really want to do it, I think you would be good."

I smiled and reached for his hand. We didn't speak again as we walked slowly back to our car.

The next afternoon I drove up to Montpelier to discuss the situation with an old friend from prep-school days, State Senator William Doyle. Bill, who had been in the legislature for four years, was the only active Vermont politician I knew really well.

Again it was a lovely spring day, but I hardly noticed the scenery because I was in the throes of another bout of introspection. During the preceding twenty-four hours I had thought a lot about Donny's question. Was I really going to run for the Senate? I tried to weigh all the alternatives as objectively as possible. (Come on, Frank, you're a college professor; let's be totally rational about this. O.K. Let's see: What is your motivation? What are you attempting to accomplish? What are your chances for success? Will it be worth the effort involved?) I evaluated a number of considerations. They all seemed to come out negatively.

First, motivation. Although I definitely was interested in co-ordinating Vermont's higher education system, I could hardly classify myself as a deeply driven ideologue, powered by a passionate desire to change the world. On the contrary, as an academic I had attempted to maintain a certain detachment from politics in the belief that this would protect my "objectivity." As a result, I questioned whether I had enough ego drive—enough real hunger and zest for political office —to survive the rough and tumble of political combat. I wasn't at all sure I wanted to plunge into crowds of strangers at shopping centers, trying to glad-hand everyone, and tell them that I had the answers to all their problems.

Second, personal factors. My family was lukewarm, at best, to the idea of my entering the political arena. We had a nice home and a comfortable life in Norwich. My wife, Ann, valued our family privacy very highly. Neither she nor our four children had any deep interest in seeing me become involved in politics.

Well, so far it's one great big Zero, I concluded. I turned to more practical aspects, trying to evaluate my possible chances of winning. The results seemed even more dismal. I rapidly ticked off umpteen reasons why I couldn't get elected.

One. As a fairly recent newcomer, I was an "outsider." This was a potential liability that I had already analyzed in detail during my trip to Baltimore. (And all out of proportion, because, in the end, I think the fact that I was a fresh face may have constituted my single strongest asset.)

Two. Aside from Bill Doyle, I had virtually no strong contacts in the world of Vermont politics.

Three. I was a college professor, hardly the most charismatic of political launching pads. With the exception of a four-year federal government stint in Washington during the 1950's, my entire professional career had been spent in academia where the political images were hardly very attractive: eggheads, long-hairs—all No-no's.

Four. I lived in Norwich, Vermont, and worked across the Connecticut River at Dartmouth College in Hanover, New Hampshire. Unless the United States Constitution was amended to permit cross-state voting, many of my closest friends and colleagues wouldn't even be able to cast a ballot for me.

Five. Norwich is a small town of less than 2,000 people tucked away in the very northeasternmost corner of Windsor County, quite remote from the larger population centers, particularly Springfield, which was in the southeast corner of the county forty miles away.

Good Lord! I thought, why continue?

Scarcely overconfident, I arrived in Montpelier, where Bill Doyle strongly encouraged me to enter the race. On the way back home I decided it was time to fish or cut bait. Doubts, doubts, doubts. Damn, damn, damn. For the rest of my life was I going to sit on the sidelines—the great American spectator sport—or was I going to make the plunge?

To hell with the odds. I decided to run for the Vermont Senate.

The reaction was hardly overwhelming when I announced the big news at the family dinner table that evening. I hesitated for quite a while before I said anything, looking first at Ann and then at each of the four children: Susan (eighteen), Sandy (sixteen), David (fourteen), and Donny (twelve).

"Quiet, please. I have an announcement to make." I raised my hand in a sign of peace. "Yesterday Donny asked me a very interesting question: Am I going to run for the state Senate? The answer is Yes. I shall throw my hat into the ring."

The silence was deafening.

"What hat?" David finally broke the ice. "You don't wear a hat, even in the winter."

"Come, come, young man. Be serious," I retorted in gentle but statesmanlike tones. "This is a significant occasion of momentous historical importance."

"Dad, do you think you can win?" Donny was next in line.

"That's a very good question," I said. "To be completely honest about it, I think it's a long shot; a very long shot indeed."

"Does it make any sense to run if you can't win?" Sandy piped in.

I paused a moment before replying. "Sandy, in the classical words of Euripides, 'Thou hast heard men scorn thy city . . . Go forth, my son, and help!' "

Sandy looked mystified, and Susan joined the fray.

"Come on, Dad, it's your turn to be serious," she smiled. "In the first place, you're not a son, you're a father—almost forty-five years old. In the second place, Vermont isn't a city, it's a state. But even more important, what's the point of going through all the agony of running for an office if you can't even win?"

The forcefulness of her remarks set me aback. I recalled an admonition from Stimson Bullitt's book *To Be a Politician:* "Having children and trying to answer their questions is good preparation for a politician who must deal with many things he does not understand."

After another pause I answered her, albeit defensively. "It will be a great experience. I will meet a lot of interesting people. And even if I lose I could write another book, one about running for office. It will be a very challenging way to spend a sabbatical leave from the college. Out there on the firing line. Right in the middle of all the flak. Onward and upward into the fray."

"Good grief, write a *book* about it!" Susan groaned. "I can see it now. Right on top of the national bestseller list: 'How to Lose in Vermont Politics with Your Dignity Intact,' by Professor Smallwood, Ph.D., Dartmouth College. Good grief! I can see it now."

When the commotion subsided, Ann entered the conversation. "Come on. Tell us the truth. Are you really going into this thing? And, if so, why?"

I hesitated again, this time groping for a convincing reason to justify my decision. Then a light flashed on.

"Actually, my motives are threefold. First, I want to test myself to see what I can contribute. I've been lucky enough to have had a good education in political science. I want to go out to see what I can offer; to see if I can make any real difference.

"Second, quite frankly I'm curious about the challenge involved. I think too many of us have been content to sit around and point fingers, rather than to risk getting roughed up by dealing with the tough problems we face. I've taught about the political process, and I've written about politics, but I've never really participated in any deep way. It's time for me to get off my duff and take part in the action.

"Third, right now Vermont faces some extraordinary political problems. We're trying to respond to a great deal of pressure and change. Some big issues are coming up during the next two years. The state land-use plan, reorganization of the higher education system, a lot of others. I think Vermont is an ideal spot to try some creative innovations."

Ann nodded. We all lapsed back into silence.

"Look, let's face it," I said, "If you want to know the truth, I'm not sure this makes very much sense. It really is a long shot, and my chances of winning are pretty slim. Maybe I'm crazy, but perhaps I can accomplish something useful. I'd like to give it a try. I guess it's as simple as that."

"Well, kids, it looks like your Dad really is serious," Ann said. "I don't know whether it's the right decision, but we should all try to help him in every way we can."

I really appreciated the reassuring smile she gave me across the table. Although none of us realized it at the time, this was the start of a great adventure: exciting, exhausting, exhilarating, frustrating, hilarious, zany, and deeply moving.

On May 24 I issued a press release announcing my candidacy. A couple of days later I received my first two fan letters. One from retiring Governor Deane C. Davis, which commented on my work with the Vermont State Colleges, was the height of optimism: "Three cheers! You will be a tremendous influence in the Senate."

The other, from a less enthusiastic admirer, expressed outrage over "loose morals" at these same institutions, with the writer attributing such licentiousness directly to my service on the Board of Trustees: "I intend to launch a big attack . . . and your candidacy gives me the opportunity . . . The taxpayers of Vermont are not going to subsidize and promote houses of prostitution even though it is free."

My campaign was off to a flying start.

CHAPTER

2

★ ★ ★ ★

Getting Organized

If one were to flatten Vermont, it would be
as large as Texas. . . . Vermont is a land
of ups and downs.
Frank M. Bryan
Yankee Politics in Rural Vermont

ANY CANDIDATE running for political office anywhere must come to grips with at least four key challenges, or tests, in order to have a reasonable chance of success. Once I had decided to run for the Senate, I concluded simultaneously that I would make an all-out effort to respond to each of these challenges. The act of decision, itself, had a catalytic impact on me: I was no longer a bundle of self-doubts.

My first challenge was the Knowledge Test. I knew a lot about higher education in Vermont, but not very much about other issues. I had to learn a great deal about the state in general, and Windsor County in particular—its problems, its potential, its people and their aspirations and concerns, my political opponents and their stands on the issues. In short, I had to do a lot of homework; as much as possible, as fast as possible.

It didn't take me long to recognize several basic facts that were going to pose very great difficulties for me in meeting the remaining challenges. One was the fact that the Republican primary in early September was the key to the entire election. In some states a primary election is a pushover, but as more and more Republican candidates announced for the three Windsor County Senate seats, it became obvious that this would be a horse race. Although the Democrats had been making serious inroads into Vermont politics during recent elections, Windsor County was still pretty solid Republican territory. Hence a major problem was one of timing. It was already early June,

15

to Montreal

CANADA

FRANKLIN

*Newport

ORLEANS

GRAND ISLE

N. Hero

*St. Albans

ESSEX

LAMOILLE

CALEDONIA

Guildhall

*Winooski
*Burlington

CHITTENDEN

*Stowe

WASH~
INGTON

St.
*Johnsbury

★ Mont~
pelier

Barre

ADDISON

ORANGE

Middle~
bury

*Randolph

Middle~
bury

WINDSOR

Norwich

RUTLAND

Rutland

Woodstock

Dartmouth
College

Windsor

Spring~
field

Manchester

Bellows
Falls

THE COUNTIES
OF VERMONT

BENNINGTON

GREEN MOUNTAINS

WINDHAM

to
Albany

Benning~
ton

Brattle~
boro

to
Springfield

MASSACHUSETTS

NEW YORK

LAKE CHAMPLAIN

NEW HAMPSHIRE

CONNECTICUT RIVER

CONNECTICUT R.

N

which gave me only three months to organize and run my entire primary campaign despite the fact that I was holding down a full-time job at Dartmouth until August first.

This problem of time was compounded by another major difficulty: most of Vermont is sparsely populated. It is more intensely rural than any other state except Alaska. In the 1970 census, 67 percent of its 444,000 people lived in rural areas. Windsor County's percentage was even higher, with 87 percent of its 44,000 people classified as rural.

I realized immediately that this kind of dispersed constituency placed an especially rough burden on a political unknown. How was I going to communicate with such a scattered population in the limited time available to me? The more I analyzed the situation, the more difficult it looked. There was an awful lot of territory out there in Windsor County; 963 square miles to be exact, which made the population density average out to only 46 people per square mile, spread out through numerous communities, mostly little villages. Twenty-one of the county's twenty-four towns contained less than 3,000 residents, and twelve towns contained less than 1,000 residents each. The only sizable population clusters in the entire county were Springfield (10,000) in the southeast corner; Windsor (4,150) midway up the Connecticut River; and Hartford (6,500), which contains White River Junction, in the northeast corner.

Windsor County's scattered population patterns forced me to turn quickly to my second political challenge: the Organization-Recruitment Test. It was obvious that my campaign was not going anywhere unless I got some help in a hurry. The area was too large, and the population too dispersed, for me to cover alone. I had to recruit volunteers who would be willing to share the workload with me.

The third challenge followed on the heels of the second. This was the Resource-Strategy Test. Once my campaign team was assembled, it was necessary for us to make key decisions about how to use the limited resources at our disposal. This is a critical problem in politics. In his study "The Job of a Congressman" (in Wolfinger's *Readings on Congress*), Lewis Anthony Dexter sums it up nicely:

> The one thing a Congressman cannot do is all things. He must choose among them. The reason he must choose is the scarcity of resources. Re-

sources are various; they include time, money, energy, staff, information and good will. All these have one common characteristic—there is never enough.

The fourth challenge, and the culmination of the other three, was the Public Test. The objective of a political campaign is to communicate effectively with people—lots of people—in order to get elected. This involved two questions: How could I expose myself to as many people as possible so they would be aware of my existence? How could I present myself to these people as effectively as possible in order to gain their support?

My sabbatical didn't start until August, so each of my difficulties was compounded by the fact that I was still swamped with responsibilities at Dartmouth. During June the campus was crowded with visitors and alumni attending commencement and class reunions. The Vietnam protests finally died down as the students headed for home, and the search teams finally located the body of the drowned student, but the college was still going full steam ahead, and I was flat out trying to handle a thousand and one assignments.

Because my severest limitation at the beginning of my campaign was lack of available time, I decided to concentrate my efforts on the first two challenges: gaining knowledge, and recruiting volunteer help. Every night after work I read state and county reports, marked local newspaper articles for my children to clip and file, and accumulated any other information I felt would be useful. I pushed hard on this because I was anxious to prepare a simple one-page campaign flyer that would outline my positions on key issues I would raise when I finally had time to get out on the road during the summer months.

The work involved in preparing the leaflet indicates the role that volunteers can play in a political contest. The graphics designer at Dartmouth gave me a preliminary sketch, and the college photographer took some informal pictures of me wearing a casual sweater in a woodsy setting—no cap and gown, since I wasn't about to run as a college professor. Fortunately our golden retriever, Brownie, jumped into one of the family pictures, and this one we used on the back of the flyer. Later, a number of people told me that they had voted for me because they liked the looks of our family dog.

The pictures turned out well, but finding a catchy campaign theme proved to be much tougher. A number of faculty members tried to help, but with miserable results. A member of the Classics Department, who wanted a dignified theme, suggested a line from Pericles' Funeral Oration to the Athenians: WE MAKE OUR POLIS COMMON TO ALL. After this was quietly laid to rest alongside Pericles and his fallen colleagues, another professor (History this time) pushed for a more aggressive theme: WINDSOR COUNTY CAN STILL BE SAVED. I rejected this on the grounds that I didn't think the county was being lost, so an Economics Professor advanced another idea: LET'S MOVE WINDSOR COUNTY AHEAD. Although better than the others, it didn't really click with me. I finally chose the theme I had wanted all along: LET'S FACE THE ISSUES.

I think it reflected a streak of perversity on my part, because a number of my political science colleagues told me that modern elections were becoming less issue-oriented, and suggested that I should run on my personality!

Just when I was in the middle of the flyer go-around, I received a totally unexpected telephone call from the third senator from Windsor County, John Alden. A thirty-six-year-old incumbent (and the youngest man in the Senate) who ran an insurance business in the town of Woodstock, he told me he was planning to run again. Of even more significance, he indicated he wanted to help me get elected because he felt a person with my kind of background would make a good colleague. You could have knocked me over with a feather. I certainly appreciated his support, which proved to be invaluable during the campaign.

His telephone call illustrated another important ingredient in the political process: the need to be flexible enough to adjust to unexpected opportunities. Specifically, he was a member of the Woodstock Rotary Club, and he invited me to speak at a Rotary luncheon on Wednesday, June 7. I hadn't planned to deliver any speeches at all during June because I was busily trying to research the issues before going out on the road. However, when opportunity knocks—well, to make a long telephone call short, I accepted the invitation immediately.

The Rotary meeting was held at the Woodstock Inn. Woodstock is an important town in Windsor County, not necessarily because of its size (only 2,600 people), but because of its influence and wealth. To use the academic jargon, it has "high socioeconomic status." Laurence Rockefeller owns a home there, and the Woodstock Inn, financed by the Rockefeller interests, is a quietly sumptious hotel that Donald Riegle described in his book *O Congress,* after attending an international conference there with Henry Kissinger and a lot of other big power-brokers.

As I drove down the picturesque main street of Woodstock on June 7, I tried to picture how Dr. Kissinger might handle this particular situation. Obviously, diplomacy was in order, but I was unsure what to expect since I had never been to a Rotary meeting in my life. All I knew was that John Alden had told me to keep my talk short. Because I didn't have any time to prepare a speech, I decided to discuss the problems of higher education in Vermont—hardly a jazzy topic, but it was the only subject I could talk about on such short notice.

John Alden greeted me at the door of the inn and escorted me downstairs to a luncheon room to meet numerous local dignitaries: insurance and automobile dealers, lawyers, bankers, medical practitioners, various civic officials, and the like. Finally, the Rotary vice-president, a retail fuel-oil dealer, banged a big bell at the head table, and we all sat down to eat lunch.

I was seated at the head table, where I kept sneaking glances at my notes to make sure they were in order. Finally lunch was over, and I braced myself to get up to deliver my speech. However, the vice-president banged the bell again, and asked for a few songs from the Rotary songbook, ending with a rousing "All Hail to Rotary" to the tune of "Anchors Aweigh." After the singing I braced myself again to deliver my speech, but the next order of business was the ritualized introduction of visiting Rotarians.

I was fascinated with the proceedings but increasingly nervous about my speech. It was already after one o'clock, and I had been instructed to stop at one-thirty sharp, with plenty of time for questions. But the next items on the agenda were reports on the club auction and on a program conducted by the Woodstock Brass, followed by a debate over whether club members should accept an invitation to play golf at a nearby resort development.

At last, at ten after one, the vice-president banged the bell once again and introduced me to the audience. I rushed up to the podium and launched into an eight-minute oration on the problems of higher education in Vermont. Following instructions, I left time for questions. The curve balls were immediately served up from the floor: What did I plan to do to halt spiraling property taxes? How did I feel about Common Sense Associates, a newly organized lobby group for economic and business development? How did I propose to halt the rapid growth in state government employment? What was my position on the Equal Rights Amendment for women?

Mercifully the one-thirty deadline arrived, and the vice-president bonged the bell for the last time. I felt as if I would dive off the head table if he hit the thing again, but he simply said, "Thanks for a fine talk." John Alden walked up and asked me to drop by his insurance office before I drove back to Norwich.

Waiting with him in his office was Harry Ames, a young Dartmouth graduate who had established a computerized real-estate listing business in Woodstock. Both men were enthusiastic.

"Congratulations. You made a short speech—very short—and you handled the questions beautifully," Ames said.

"My God, what questions," I complained. "Not a single one about education. Why did they ask such tough questions?"

"Because I told them to," said Ames. "I planted the questions because John said you looked like a good candidate. I wanted to see how you would stand up under pressure. Four questions. Four home runs. Socko! Right out of the ball park. You can't do any better than that."

"Thanks a lot," I muttered.

"Seriously," he went on, "you're in business, a real live candidate for a seat in the Vermont Senate. But, for Lord's sake, you've got to stop talking about education, and you've got to go out and meet the people. No one knows you. You're Frank Woodsmall as far as John Q. Public is concerned. Your job during the next three months is to get

your name known—Frank Smallwood, Frank Smallwood, Frank Smallwood—so that the voters will remember who you are when the primary election rolls around on September twelfth. That's all there is
to political campaigning. Getting people to know your name. Period."

"Thanks a lot," I said again. "I appreciate your interest."

I thought about Harry Ames's advice on the way back home, won-
dering how I could ever possibly get 44,000 people in Windsor County
to know my name. Then I suddenly realized that I had completed my
first public test, and according to both Harry and John I had passed
with flying colors. I guess I should have been elated, but I kept thinking about all those other people out there, and I couldn't help won-
dering whether I would really be able to pull this thing off.

About a week later, when I was back at my job at Dartmouth, I became involved with Test Number Two—recruiting—although it occurred quite accidentally as far as I was concerned.

John Fieldsteel came in to visit me at my office just before noon on
Friday, June 16. John was very anxious to see me, but I couldn't
imagine why. He had taken one of my courses during the fall term
and had graduated from Dartmouth only the previous Sunday. He
was wearing a pair of faded blue overalls that were covered with streaks
of fine white powder.

"Hi, John, what can I do for you?"

His answer was abruptly direct. "I understand you're running for
political office. I want to work for you this summer."

"That's very nice," I told him, and I meant it; "but I'm afraid I
don't have any money to pay you."

"I don't want any money," he replied. "I'm taking off a year before
I go to law school. I want to get some practical experience this summer working on a political campaign."

His response was so unexpected that it caught me off guard. Changing the subject temporarily, I asked him what he had been doing since
graduation.

"I'm operating a jackhammer for the college's Buildings and
Grounds crew, knocking down brick walls in one of the dormitories.
Since Dartmouth is going into a year-round co-educational program,

we're converting some double rooms into triples to accommodate the extra students they expect next fall. My God, the job is terrible. I can't stand the noise and the dust much longer. It's really dreadful."

I asked him to sit down. He seemed a little shaky. I couldn't tell whether it was the effect of the jackhammer or whether he was simply nervous. He agreed to work as a full-time campaign assistant without pay, on the understanding that I would try to give him something at the end of the summer if I could scrape up enough money.

John was the beginning of a permanent campaign team: a marvelous group of volunteers who worked long and hard during the summer months of 1972, a group which grew in size as I later went out onto the road to meet more volunteers in various Windsor County towns. Politics is a tiring, but strangely rewarding, business. It never occurred to me that so many people would care whether or not I won a seat in the Vermont Senate.

In addition to recruiting a staff, the other resource I had to go after right away was money. Politics involves money. Big campaigns involve big money, but even little campaigns involve some money.

When I first decided to run for office, I concluded on purely subjective grounds that I would limit my total campaign spending to a maximum of $1,000. I had no idea whether this was too little or too much. It simply struck me as a pretty sizable amount, so this was all I was prepared to spend. Since I planned to invest $500 of my own in this effort, I decided to approach some close friends to see if they would be willing to provide some financial support to launch my fledgling political career.

Following my talk with John Fieldsteel, my secretary, Barbara Roka, came into the office on her free time on Saturday morning to type twenty-five letters requesting funds, which two college friends agreed to send out for me. The response was phenomenal. The letters brought forth twenty-five contributions totaling $945. My campaign budget was covered almost overnight.

I turned the money over to Carolyn Miller, the campaign treasurer who kept track of my major expenses: flyers, postage for mailings, plus some newspaper ads and radio spots just before the primary election.

It wasn't a lot, but, as Lewis Anthony Dexter pointed out, you never have enough resources. Actually, I was glad I didn't have any more money. It helped me to make disciplined decisions. If I had had unlimited funds at my disposal, I might have wasted a lot on unproductive and even foolish endeavors.

This danger was driven home to me rather forcefully much later when I was astonished to hear Jeb Magruder testify before the Ervin Committee that the Nixon forces had so much money in the 1972 Presidential campaign that they didn't know what to do with it. As a result, they were throwing money all over the place on all sorts of bizarre projects.

In light of the 1972 Nixon campaign disclosures, I couldn't help going back over my files to see how I had handled my own campaign finances. I had a very strange feeling in the pit of my stomach when I looked over copies of the letters my secretary had typed for me that Saturday morning in the office. Thank the Lord I hadn't tried to raise too much money: all twenty-five letters were dated June 17, 1972—the day of the Watergate break-in.

¶By LATE JUNE the primary campaign was falling into shape. A total of seven Republican candidates were running for the three Senate nominations: incumbent Senator John Alden of Woodstock; Representative Lee Davis of Springfield; former State Senator Donald Arnold of Bethel; George MacKnight, the Republican County Chairman, from Royalton; William Tufts, a member of the Republican County Committee from Bethel; Herbert Ogden, the owner and operator of a cider- and gristmill in Hartland; and last, but (I hoped) not least, yours truly from Norwich.

The blossoming of this large field confirmed my belief that the summer primary campaign would be the key to the entire election. Although the Republican stranglehold on Vermont politics had been broken back in 1962 when Philip Hoff, a Democrat, was elected Governor, Windsor County was still Republican territory. Thus I was anxious to size up my primary opposition at our first candidates' meet-

FRANK Smallwood
FOR STATE SENATOR

A LEADER AS

* Chairman
  Vermont State Colleges Trustees
* Chairman
  Vermont Committee on
  Higher Education Planning
* Veteran, U. S. Army
* Vestryman, Norwich Church Parish
* Organizer, Town Community Forum
* Director
  Public Affairs Center Dartmouth College

VOTE SMALLWOOD FOR VERMONT SENATE

REPUBLICAN PRIMARY
Tuesday, 12 September

LET'S FACE THE ISSUES

1) Tax Reform and Controlled Development

"We pay a higher proportion of our personal income in state and local taxes than the residents of any other state. Spiraling property taxes are forcing Vermonters to sell their land to out-of-state developers. We should tax speculative profits derived from rapid turnovers of Vermont land and return these tax receipts to our local communities to help reduce property taxes."

2) Full Employment

"Springfield and many other Windsor County communities are in tough shape economically. The key to our future economic health lies with our own people. Vermont is the only state that has no comprehensive planning for education beyond the high school. We must create new jobs and provide the training necessary to enable our labor force to fill these jobs."

3) Services for Our Senior Citizens

"Almost half of Vermont's senior citizens over age 65 have annual incomes below the minimum federal standards. Property tax relief is needed now for our senior citizens. We must also provide opportunities for better transportation and social services for our elderly."

I need your help, and your vote, to achieve these goals.

VOTE SMALLWOOD FOR VERMONT SENATE

REPUBLICAN PRIMARY
Tuesday, 12 September

ing, which was to take place in Damon Hall, Hartland, the evening of
June 27.

I picked up John Fieldsteel at seven o'clock and we drove down to
the meeting, arriving at Hartland fifteen minutes ahead of time. There
weren't many automobiles around, so we strolled into the hall together and chatted casually with Senator John Alden while we waited
for the crowds to gather. Although the meeting was scheduled for
eight o'clock, only twenty people had shown up by ten minutes after
eight. Seven of these were the Republican candidates running for the
Vermont Senate. The remaining thirteen people consisted of John
Fieldsteel and two of the candidates' wives, plus ten local Hartland
residents, clustered in two lonely groups amidst what seemed like a
sea of wooden chairs arranged in neat rows.

By twenty after eight, when it was obvious that no more people
were coming to the meeting, the master of ceremonies got up. After
thanking the audience for turning out to hear the senatorial candidates who were participating in this vitally important political contest, he proceeded to introduce each speaker, allowing us ten minutes
apiece for our remarks. He started off with John Alden, and worked
his way down the list until he came to me, the seventh and last candidate.

By the time I got up to speak, virtually everything possible had
been said about the economy, the environment, taxes, the need to
control crime, the need for clean air and clean water, clean government, plus sundry other subjects. So I simply indicated who I was,
why I was running for office, and what I hoped to accomplish if the
ten resident voters in the audience sent me to the State House in
Montpelier.

During my remarks a bearded young man stomped noisily into the
back of the hall. As soon as I had finished, he jumped up and asked
me what I planned to do to halt the construction of nuclear power
plants in Vermont. I told him I hadn't really studied the state's long-
range electrical energy needs, but I felt that nuclear power plants
could be risky, so they had to be handled with extreme caution.

The young man wasn't at all satisfied with my answer. He stated that
he was flatly opposed to any nuclear power plants in Vermont. He

warned me that if I wanted his support, I had better join him in opposing any nuclear power plants at all.

I replied that I really didn't know enough about the subject to give a categorical answer. Under the circumstances, I was afraid I was going to have to lose his support.

One of the other candidates, George MacKnight, immediately jumped up to defend me, and Representative Lee Davis of Springfield, another of my opponents, also supported my position that we had to adopt a practical approach to our long-range power needs, since the cost of energy in Vermont was very high. At this point all seven candidates entered the fray. By the time we got through agreeing with, and contradicting, each other, we had left the ten local Hartland residents in the audience in a state of utter bafflement and confusion.

Finally the master of ceremonies stepped in and said that it had been a wonderful discussion, but it was approaching ten o'clock; because many of the Senate candidates faced long trips home, he thought we should call it a night.

On the drive back, John Fieldsteel was very complimentary. He told me that my remarks were excellent. He felt that, due to my college background, I was the best prepared and most articulate of all the candidates.

"Good Lord, John," I replied irritably, "in the classic words of Pudd'nhead Wilson, 'Cauliflower is nothing but cabbage with a college education.' There were only ten people in the audience. Even if I gave the greatest speech in history, all I could have picked up was seven or eight votes, and I'm certainly not going to get any support from that fellow on the nuclear-power-plant issue."

John fell silent, and I apologized. Actually, the meeting had been valuable, because it had given me a chance to meet the six other candidates who would constitute my opposition in the primary campaign.

I explained to John that I was a little jumpy because the primary was crucial.

"We've got to figure out some way to meet a lot of people between now and September, John. Windsor County is Republican territory. The three candidates who win the September primary will be almost assured of winning the general election in November. Indeed, it isn't even clear whether the Democrats are going to nominate any Senate candidates at all this year. Our problem is time. We've only got a little over two months. We're sunk unless we use our time wisely."

John nodded his agreement, and lapsed back into silence. I thought about the Hartland meeting the rest of the way home. Strangely enough, I liked all the other candidates, and I was particularly impressed when a number of them had supported me on the nuclear power issue. If it was necessary to have a "killer instinct" to succeed in politics, I was going to be in deep trouble.

On the last day of June I stopped by the printer's in White River Junction to pick up my campaign leaflets. I had a sinking feeling as soon as I ripped open one of the brown manila packages. The things were a disaster, an utter catastrophe. All 3,500 copies were printed in a vomitose yellow that was nothing like the lovely soft forest green that had been specified. The photograph of my face was much too dark, and the paper was so thin that the print showed through from one side to the other, making it difficult to read anything at all.

I was so upset I demanded to see the manager of the press, who checked over my order before nodding his apologies. There had been a mistake as a result of the confusion surrounding a flurry of orders they had received in connection with upcoming Fourth of July festivities. They would reprint the leaflets in green on paper of a heavier weight.

As I drove back to Norwich I reflected on the first month of my campaign. It had been virtually all background-organizational work with some pretty good results. I had learned a great deal about Windsor County and its politics (Test Number One). I had recruited the beginnings of a solid volunteer staff, and raised some money (Test Number Two). I had even done reasonably well in the few public appearances I had time to attend (Test Number Four). Things were finally easing up at Dartmouth. I hoped it would be possible to get out on the road much more within the next couple of weeks. It looked as if everything was in pretty good shape.

Or so I thought. Somehow, though, I had completely overlooked Test Number Three. I had no over-all strategy, no plan whatsoever, to make maximum use of my limited resources, especially my own time. This lesson was driven home to me with a vengeance a week later when I finally managed to shake loose from the office to spend my first full day on the campaign trail.

3

★ ★ ★ ★

The Primary Race

We invested every gram of energy and
imagination in the campaign—a blur of
shaking hands . . . speeches, brochures.
Donald Riegle
O Congress

AMID THE SOUND of blaring trumpets and the roll of drums, I picked up
John Fieldsteel early on the morning of July 10 to begin our first all-
day sojourn on the road. Our destination was the towns of Rochester
and Stockbridge, about sixty miles away in the northwest corner of the
county. Since only ten people had shown up at Hartland to meet the
candidates, I explained to John that it was necessary to seek out constituents on their home ground in order to get the votes I needed to
win the primary.

"The organizational work and planning are finally completed,
John," I enthused. "Now we go out into the political vineyards to
reap our rewards."

The drive from Norwich to Rochester makes a long, lovely swath
across the northern border of Windsor County. Interstate 89 follows
the White River valley, climbing dramatically beyond Sharon to provide spectacular aerial views of South Royalton just before the Bethel
interchange. After passing through Bethel, we turned west again on
a high dirt road that climbs over a mountain gap before coasting down
to the Rochester village green, nestled in a valley on the eastern border
of the Green Mountain National Forest.

It was nine-thirty when we arrived. The green was utterly deserted.
So was Rochester's main street—a stretch of State Route 100, the fa-
mous "skiers' highway." The entire town was serenely quiet. It was a
little eerie. The only living soul I could see was a middle-aged man

perched on a high extension ladder, painting the white framing around some second-story windows. I debated whether I should yell out my arrival to him (Hi, I'm Frank Smallwood, here to solve all your political problems), but I decided this probably wasn't a dignified way to shatter the town's trancelike morning silence.

John and I began a casual walk down Main Street, eventually entering a hardware store devoid of customers. I introduced myself to the clerk, who looked suspicious but reluctantly agreed to take some leaflets to leave on the counter. We entered a few more stores, but again they lacked customers, so we chatted with still more clerks before walking across Route 100 to a new supermarket on the northern edge of town.

My heart sank as soon as the automatic doors hissed open. With the exception of two check-out clerks, there wasn't a soul there. After a while a young man appeared in the breakfast-cereal aisle, about halfway between the stacks of Wheaties and Cheerios. He wore a pin labeled *Assistant Manager*.

I walked over to him and extended my hand. "Hello, hello," I bubbled, trying to sound enthusiastic. "I'm a candidate for the Vermont Senate. Would you mind if I left some flyers at your check-out counters?"

He frowned. "I'm sorry, but it's against company policy. Nothing personal, but if you do it for one, you have to do it for all." After an awkward silence, his face lit up. "Say, have you seen our mural? It's beautiful. Governor Davis came to Rochester last year to dedicate our mural. He gave a wonderful talk about community spirit. You should have been here then. Lots of people," he chuckled cheerfully as he led us to the back of the store.

The mural covered the entire back wall of the store above the frozen-food cabinets. It was extraordinary. Really charming. In the bottom lefthand corner were big yellow block letters: THE FOUR SEASONS IN ROCHESTER BY THE EIGHTH GRADE '71. The first season was winter, with many swirling snowflakes painted on a black sky dominated by a yellowish-brown, Van Gogh-like sun. Just to the right of the black sky, the mural exploded into a riot of colors. Skiers and snowmobilers in the winter were followed by precise depictions of houses, stores, cars, trucks and people, all standing out against a soft green background of spring and summer. On the far right, over the frozen-meat display, the sharp yellows, oranges and reds of fall brought the mural to a blazing climax.

"What an incredible sight," I gasped. "I've never seen so many happy people. Do they all live in Rochester?" (Deep dark thought: And if so, where the hell are they hiding on this steamy summer day?)

The assistant manager was delighted. "Oh yes, yes, it's a local scene. Painted by the eighth-graders in the Rochester school last year. There was a blank wall over the frozen foods when we built the new store, so the eighth-graders decided to paint the mural as a class project." He beamed from ear to ear.

John and I thanked him. I bought a couple of small containers of chocolate milk as a token of our gratitude. When we were back out on Main Street I suggested we had better start off for Stockbridge. Although we had met only about eight people in Rochester, it was approaching eleven o'clock, and the day was becoming extremely hot.

We almost missed Stockbridge at the point where Route 100 takes a sharp turn to the southwest. Just as we whizzed by, John spotted a little sign saying *Stockbridge Green*. We turned and drove up a hill. When we reached the top I was flabbergasted, utterly flabbergasted. There was nothing there! Well, not quite nothing. There was a house on the right with a lovely colorful flower garden. There was also a very handsome plain white church that faced the northern end of the green, and a fairly large cemetery to the west of the church. That was it. No stores. No town hall. Nothing else at all to break the ghostly silence.

We got out of the car and walked across the green to the church. There was a large painted sign above the righthand door:

JESUS IS LORD

STOCKBRIDGE

UNION   CHURCH

WORSHIP

SUNDAY   9:30 A.M.

"I guess we got here on the wrong day," John muttered.

I was despondent. What a fiasco.

I walked over to the cemetery and started looking at the gravestones. Many of them were weathered. Some were almost impossible to read. I lay down before a grave with a faded American flag, and looked up toward the sky. Then I looked at the inscription:

Col. Robert Lyon

Died

March 17, 1844

John came over and lay down beside me. There was a long silence before he spoke.

"Professor Smallwood, I'm not sure we're going about this in the right way. I don't want you to misunderstand, but I'm not sure we can meet many people in places like Rochester and Stockbridge. I checked the census figures last night. Rochester has a total of 884 people, and Stockbridge has only 389 people. I sort of wondered why you wanted to start off here."

Drawing upon my years of academic research, I explained to John the geopolitical-time dimensions of campaigning.

"Campaigning is a mixture of geography, timing, issues, energy, exposure, and hard work," I stated.

"And common sense, plus luck," John added.

"That's right," I acknowledged, then continued: "Now, John, the reason I decided to begin my campaign in the far northwestern reaches of Windsor County is really quite logical. My geographical thrust is keyed to timing. I'm starting in the less populated outer edges of the county before working in to the more populated Connecticut River towns so that my campaign will gain a gradual sense of momentum. This is where timing comes in. Timing is crucial in politics. It will be bad if I peak too fast. It's necessary to build up support slowly, in order to finish with a rush. Since I feel it's important to visit all the Windsor County towns, I decided to start out here in the smaller ones first, and then build up to a crescendo just before the primary election."

John rolled over on his side to face me more directly. He looked mystified. A soft breeze blowing off the Green Mountains to the west provided some relief from the muggy noonday sun.

"I don't know," he said after a moment. "President Nixon tried to visit all fifty states in the 1960 election, and it wore him out. I'm not sure we should try to meet everybody in Windsor County."

I was impressed with the fact that John knew about Nixon's 1960 Presidential campaign, since he must have been only about ten years old at the time. I don't think he learned that in my course. I was quite impressed.

"O.K.," I said. "What do you think we ought to do?"

"Well, we've got to figure out a way to meet some living people. We can't keep looking at murals and lying in cemeteries. I think we should get out of this cemetery, and go back to Norwich right now to figure out how to use our resources most economically. After all, you told me on the way back from Hartland that time is your most precious commodity. I'm not at all sure you should use up this much time on a geopolitical-peaking thrust. Theoretically, it may make sense; but practically, it's a disaster. Let's develop a strategy to use your time more productively."

I thought about John's advice. I decided he was probably right. Good Lord, he was obviously right. The round trip between Norwich, Rochester, and Stockbridge was about 130 miles. We had met only eight people. Coupled with the ten people from the Hartland rally, we'd met a total of 18 possible supporters in two outings. I wasn't going to get elected dogcatcher at this rate. John had put his finger on Test Number Three: strategy. I needed to develop a strategy to guide my campaign.

When we arrived back home in midafternoon, John and I went to work. First, we checked the county's total population: 44,082 people. Next we checked the total number of registered voters: there were 24,225. Then we checked the results of the 1970 Republican primary election: for the three Senate seats, John Alden had come in first with 3,679 votes, followed by Olin Gay with 2,975 and Margaret Hammond with 2,751. Alden had led the primary by polling only 8.3 percent of the county's total population and only 15 percent of the total registered voters.

So I didn't have to meet 44,000 people. I had to meet only a fraction of these people *if* I could persuade the ones I met to go to the polls and

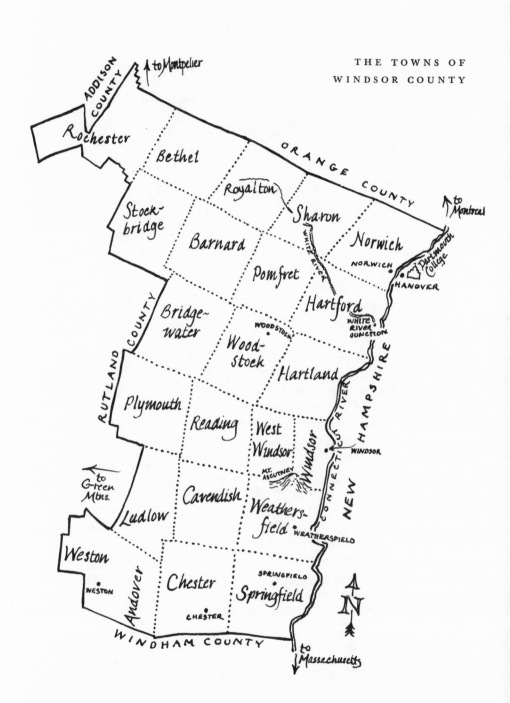

THE TOWNS OF
WINDSOR COUNTY

to Montpelier

ADDISON COUNTY

Rochester

Bethel

ORANGE COUNTY

Royalton

Sharon

to Montreal

Stock-
bridge

Barnard

Norwich

NORWICH

Dartmouth College

WHITE RIVER

Pomfret

HANOVER

Bridge-
water

Hartford

RUTLAND COUNTY

Wood-
stock

WOODSTOCK

WHITE RIVER JUNCTION

Hartland

NEW HAMPSHIRE

Plymouth

Reading

West
Windsor

Windsor

CONNECTICUT RIVER

WINDSOR

to Green Mtns.

MT. ASCUTNEY

Cavendish

Weathers-
field

WEATHERSFIELD

Ludlow

Weston

Andover

Chester

SPRINGFIELD

Springfield

N

WESTON

CHESTER

WINDHAM COUNTY

to Massachusetts

vote for me. This was the key. How could I motivate a relatively small number of people actually to go out and vote for me in the primary? We discussed an appropriate target figure before deciding that I could probably win one of the three Senate nominations with only 3,000 votes, about the same number that Olin Gay had received two years earlier. This became the target. What strategy should I follow to get these 3,000 votes that I felt I needed to win in the primary?

We decided on a threefold coalition strategy that was designed to focus our limited resources on specific groups.

The first group in the coalition would consist of people I actually met face-to-face. To do this, I would visit as many towns as possible, but I would concentrate on the larger towns, and only after I had lined up someone from each locality to escort me through the community and introduce me to key people. Also, I would try to speak to all seven Rotary clubs scattered throughout the county. In this way, I figured I could talk directly with perhaps 1,500 people, about half the total in our target figure.

The second part of our coalition strategy involved direct mailings to selected groups. John suggested that he make up a list of all persons who signed my nominating petitions so I could send them a personal note of thanks, while urging them to go to the polls on primary election day. He also suggested making up lists of other key groups— prominent town leaders, plus school teachers and the like—with the understanding that I would send to individuals in each group a note dealing with an issue of special interest to them. We guessed I could reach maybe another 1,000 people through these direct mailings.

Finally, I would try to use the news media as effectively as possible in an effort to communicate with all those other people out there who were not reached in the two coalition groupings above. This meant preparing a well-researched press release each week for the dozen daily and weekly newspapers in the county, plus appearing on all available noontime radio interview shows on six different radio stations that blanketed different communities. I had no idea how many people I could reach in this manner, but hoped they would raise the grand total to the 3,000 votes which John and I felt were necessary in the primary.

Following our long strategy session we got a late sandwich supper before settling down in the living room in front of the television set. The Democratic national convention had started in Miami that evening, and the major credentials challenges were under way. We watched the floor maneuvering with considerable fascination. Just after eleven, the California challenge came up. The clock ticked past midnight as we were caught up in the drama, until, at twelve-fifty, McGovern won back the full California slate.

McGovern was riding on top of the world. Or was he? I seemed to be going nowhere. Or was I? The vagaries of politics are wondrous to behold. The McGovern forces were about to begin a week of disastrous, cataclysmic mistakes.

And I was finally about to get myself organized.

¶It wasn't until later in July that I had my first big opportunity to put our new coalition strategy to its initial road test in a speech to the Windsor Rotary Club. John Howland, a prominent local business leader, had invited me to speak. I had written him one of my target letters advising him that I was running for the Vermont Senate. He had responded with a telephone call, asking me to give a nonpartisan talk at a Rotary luncheon in his town. It was a very nice gesture, a real act of faith on his part, since he really didn't know who I was or whether I could speak at all.

I drove down to Windsor before noon for a get-acquainted visit that went well. We then drove out together to the luncheon, which was held in the clubhouse of the Windsor golf course, just north of town.

Windsor is an interesting community. The town prides itself as the "birthplace of Vermont" because the first state constitutional convention was held there in 1777. During the nineteenth century, Windsor was a highly successful industrial community, and it contains many fine historic homes. Today the town is still quite industrial. It also served as the home of the antiquated Vermont State Prison, which had been a source of unending concern and controversy due to an almost constant stream of breakouts by its inmates.

When my host and I arrived at the Country Club, we walked out to the dining area on the porch, a large pleasant place enclosed by storm windows now wide open to the balmy July weather, and here I met numerous local businessmen and dignitaries before the luncheon. As soon as we sat down at the head table I began to think about my talk. I had followed the advice given me in the postmortem on my maiden political speech before the Woodstock club some four weeks earlier. Instead of talking about higher education again, my topic was Vermont's Changing Economy. I had spent almost a week gathering material for my presentation.

My main pitch was that Vermont, and Windsor County, had become "service" economies. Only 5,500 (32 percent) of the county's work force was employed in manufacturing, and only 588 (or 3 percent) in agriculture, leaving more than 60 percent of the jobs in Windsor County in the service sector. I planned to talk about the implications of our changing economic base in terms of future employment opportunities in the county.

Following lunch there were the club's ritual announcements and songs before I was introduced to the audience. I thanked my host and launched into my statistical oration, first covering statewide employment trends. Then, just as I was about to zero in on the Windsor County situation, I heard a loud noise outside the open window immediately behind me.

A garbage truck had pulled up in the driveway. It seemed to stop precisely below the window at my back. I paused for a few moments in the hope that the driver would have enough good sense to turn off the engine.

The damn thing remained on a rather noisy idle, however, so I returned to my talk, speaking quite forcefully now in order to reach the tables at the far end of the porch.

Almost immediately I was interrupted by a series of thuds and smashing glass as the driver began to throw buckets of debris into the rear of his truck.

The situation was deteriorating rapidly. I didn't know whether to plow ahead, or hold off in another play for time, so, in an act of desperation, I decided to time my sentences to see if I could use the periodic explosions outside the window as exclamation points to drive home my message:

"Windsor County has fifty-five hundred people employed in manufacturing——" *Smash!!!!!*

"On the other hand, we have just a little more than one-tenth that
number employed in agriculture——" *Bam!!!!!*

I seemed to be getting away with it—although my voice was taking
on a shrill, shouting quality—when an incredible grinding and wheezing erupted. The truck driver had turned on the compacter, which was
crushing the glass and other trash into a solid mass.

It was obvious that I was never going to get to the service sector of
the economy. I turned to John Howland, who smiled weakly. I
couldn't control myself any longer and burst into a roar of laughter.

The fifty assembled Rotarians and their guests all seemed to share
my hilarity, since I could see most of them shaking and slapping their
knees, although it was impossible to hear anything at all above the din
of the garbage truck.

At last, after a few more minutes of wheezing and grinding, the
ruckus stopped. The driver gave the garbage truck a full head of
steam and rumbled off down the driveway.

I had difficulty getting back to Vermont's changing economy, but
I think I managed to reach some semblance of a conclusion. There
wasn't much time for questions, thanks to the garbage truck's inter-
ruptions, but a number of Rotarians told me afterwards that I had
"done very well under the circumstances."

John Howland drove me back down into Windsor. He was ebullient.
He apologized for the garbage truck, but said he thought my speech
was "first-rate, very thoughtful and informative." He offered to help
in any way he could.

Before heading back to Dartmouth, I walked across Windsor's Main
Street to visit with Ray Osgood, a Windsor selectman who ran a
printing shop in town. After I had written him a letter, he had asked
me to stop by to see him when I was in Windsor. I walked into his
shop, introduced myself, and asked him if there was anything I could
do for the town of Windsor if I was elected to the state Senate.

"I'm very interested in your candidacy," he replied. "It looks like
you have a very strong background. I think you could help us on a
serious problem we have here in Windsor."

"What's that?"

"Here, come to the door. It's right there," he pointed his finger, "right there across the street. That building used to be the movie theater, but it hasn't been used in years. It's completely run down. The roof leaks. It's an eyesore; it's dangerous; it could collapse any day. There it stands, an ugly symbol of Windsor's decay, smack in the middle of Main Street. The selectmen have contacted the state for advice on condemnation proceedings, but we can't get anybody to do anything."

We walked out of Osgood's shop and made a circle tour around the offending building. We peered inside and saw plaster falling down everywhere. It really was a mess, a great big white elephant right in the heart of Windsor. I told Ray that I didn't have any immediate ideas, but I would get in touch with him after I had thought about it.

"Anything you can do would be welcome," he told me. "We would be most grateful."

I got in my car and was driving north on Main Street, when, just as I was leaving the village, I noticed the historic-site marker on the left:

CONSTITUTION HOUSE, WINDSOR

THE BIRTHPLACE OF VERMONT, 1777

The idea didn't germinate slowly—it simply burst out full-grown, right there in my mind's eye:

WINDSOR, THE BIRTHPLACE OF VERMONT

1777–1977

The state was heading for its own bicentennial celebration only five years in the future. I had read in papers about a group of Windsor residents who had recently organized Historic Windsor, Inc., to save a landmark Greek Revival building on Main Street known as Windsor House. There had been an article about it in *The New York Times*. The group had received a $20,000 grant from a foundation, plus a $1,000 grant from the National Trust for Historic Preservation.

There was obviously a strong interest in preserving the historic legacy of Windsor. The derelict theater block could be the touchstone for the revival of the entire town. It could be demolished, and con-

verted into a handsome Constitution Park, or Constitution Plaza, right
in the heart of the shopping area.

I raced back to Norwich to ask a friend who was a professional town
planner what he thought of the idea. He was encouraging, and suggested there might be federal funds for such a project. I called John
Fieldsteel, telling him to meet me at Dartmouth's Baker Library.
There we went into the Documents Room and poured over recent
federal statutes. Finally we found it—*Public Law 91–609,* authorizing
funds for federal assistance for historic open-space preservation.

As soon as we left the library I called Ray Osgood to tell him I
would like to meet with the Windsor Board of Selectmen about the
decaying theater. He invited me down for the next meeting, where
John and I presented our Constitution Plaza idea to the board. The
selectmen were enthusiastic, especially when we mentioned the possibility of federal funds for the project. They asked the town manager
to follow up on this with us.

After the meeting, members of the press asked me to walk over to
the decrepit building for some pictures. I invited the Republican
state representative from Windsor, Ed Conlin, to join the tour. The
press coverage the next day was fantastic. The Springfield paper played
up the story on the first page, while the Rutland *Herald* gave it a big
inside story with a four-column headline:

SENATE CANDIDATE FRANK SMALLWOOD OFFERS SOLUTION
TO DILAPIDATED THEATRE ON WINDSOR'S MAIN STREET

The local weekly, the Windsor *Journal,* gave the story the biggest
spread of all, with a nice front-page picture.

There was also a second story in the bottom lefthand corner on my
Rotary speech, starting off with the statement that "Frank Small,
Republican senatorial candidate for Windsor County . . ." They
didn't even get my name right! Oh well, I thought, you can't win
them all.

Although I made occasional forays into the field during July, my
campaign really didn't get into full swing until I officially began my
sabbatical leave from the college on August 1. From then until the

September 12 primary election it was a blur of continuous nonstop activity.

The job of collecting names on nominating petitions had become a major preoccupation from the time I dropped off my first petition sheet with Senator Margaret Hammond back in the first week in May. According to Vermont law, candidates for county offices must get nominating signatures from "not less than two percent of the total number of votes cast for the candidate receiving the highest number of votes for the office at the last preceding election."

The "last preceding" election had not been the 1970 Republican primary, but the 1970 General Election when John Alden had led the Windsor County senatorial ticket with 11,800 votes. This meant I had to obtain 236 signatures to place my name on the primary ballot in 1972.

The real name of the game, however, is to get as many signatures as possible. It's an effective way to expose one's name to the general public, to stir up interest in one's candidacy. Also, I hoped many of the people who signed my petitions would take the time to vote for me, since I planned to follow John Fieldsteel's suggestion and send a personal note of thanks to each of them.

I worked very hard to line up people in various towns to circulate petitions for me. By mid-July more than forty different people were carrying my petitions throughout the county. They were a wonderfully diversified group: housewives, lawyers, grocers, doctors, dentists, newspaper dealers, hairdressers, insurance agents, farmers, teachers, stockbrokers, and factory workers. Fourteen were close friends from Norwich, but I also had ten workers in the Springfield-Ludlow area, five in the Windsor-Hartland area, eight in the Woodstock-Pomfret area, three in the White River Junction area, and a scattering in the smaller towns.

The first petition arrived back in my mailbox in early June. It was from Tony Romano, who had run a corner newstore in White River Junction. I was very excited, trying to read the twenty-five signatures, mostly indecipherable, of people who had signed my petition.

Afterwards I began to keep a running account. By mid-July I had received over 400 signatures, considerably more than the 236 required;

by July 24 the list had grown to 640, by July 28 to 776 signatures. On August 2, the deadline, 815 voters had signed my petitions.

As the cut-off date approached, I developed a fixation about signatures. It produced some odd and disturbing results. I always carried a spare petition in my pocket. When I would see some friends in Dan & Whit's General Store in Norwich, I would pounce on them with pen in hand to obtain their signatures. As the petitions began to pile up, I would add to totals nightly—a bizarre ritual that threatened to make me think of people as sets of numbers rather than as living, breathing human beings. Numbers became an obsession. Let's get 500 signatures, then 600 signatures, then 700 signatures. It was a heady and alarming engrossment, intoxicating and dehumanizing.

If the petition signatures were having an odd psychological impact on me, they were driving John Fieldsteel to the edge of blindness. Every day I would hand him one or two newly signed petitions, and he would begin the laborious process of translating twenty-five nearly illegible scrawls into names and addresses on 3-by-5-inch file cards— a ghastly task that he carried out with remarkable diligence.

As the load grew heavier, John got another Dartmouth student assistant to help with the address files. At John's suggestion we added the names of members of all seven Rotary clubs in Windsor County to our burgeoning mailing list. Then John added addresses of school superintendents, school-board members, and teachers.

In addition, Representative Allen Foley agreed to send letters supporting my candidacy to all Dartmouth alumni living in Windsor County; the head of the labor union that staffed Dartmouth's Buildings and Grounds department signed letters to all college service employees; a Dartmouth librarian signed letters to college staff employees; and a doctor sent letters to medical staff at the Mary Hitchcock Hospital, in Hanover, who lived in Windsor County.

After these letters to residents of my county were mimeographed I signed each one of them by hand, and then we held an addressing party, an all-day-long affair, on our porch. Huge stacks of envelopes were addressed by all six members of the Smallwood family, plus a group of nine volunteers which included the ever-faithful John Fieldsteel.

All in all, I signed well over twelve hundred letters, while Al Foley and the union leader, the librarian and the doctor signed another three hundred. The 1,500-plus letters we sent out constituted more than half the number of votes John and I figured would be necessary to secure one of the three Senate nominations in the primary.

¶IT WAS MID-AUGUST. The weather was really hot now, surprisingly so for Vermont, and the signs of late summer were already apparent in the fields tall with corn for the cattle.

Every morning I would drive out to visit another town, where local supporters took me around to meet people at the weekly news-papers, the stores, the town offices, the police and fire stations, the post offices. In this fashion I was introduced to voters in Ludlow, Chester, Brownsville, Hartland, White River Junction. I toured the far corners of Weathersfield in a Jeep on one of the hottest days of the summer. I looked at the thermometer on the wall of Barton's Garage as the proprietor and I posed for a news photograph: it registered 96 degrees Fahrenheit. On the way back to Norwich I stopped to visit with my brother and sister-in-law, Bill and Nancy Smallwood, at their summer home off the Weathersfield Center road. The water in their swimming pool was gloriously cool.

Occasionally I would take one of the children with me on an all-day trip. Susan accompanied me to Bridgewater and Plymouth, where another Susan—Mrs. Susan Webb—introduced us to local townspeople in Plymouth's various small villages. Mrs. Webb was running (successfully, as it turned out) for a seat in the Vermont House of Representatives. My other daughter, Sandy, was a little reluctant to campaign, but she finally agreed to spend a day with me visiting Woodstock, where John Alden, my remarkably helpful Senate opponent, escorted us through numerous stores before we headed for Pomfret and Royalton. The boys, David and Donny, seemed to enjoy the road trips the most. They accompanied me to the southern part of the county—to small towns like Andover and Weston, plus a visit to Radio Station WCRF in Springfield, where I appeared on a noon-time interview show.

It was fun to go out on trips with the children, but I usually traveled alone. I had a lot of time to think as I crisscrossed the lovely, often lonely, back roads of Windsor County.

The most remarkable political greeter I encountered during the entire primary campaign was Representative Charles Johnson of Springfield.

Charlie ran a taxidermy business in his home, but before that he had operated a general store for thirty years, during which time he had managed to join every conceivable community organization in the Springfield area: the Boy Scouts, the Grange, the Veterans of Foreign Wars, the American Legion, the Loyal Order of Moose, the Springfield Boosters Club, the Springfield Humane Society, and, since he served on the House Fish and Game Committee, an endless series of local and regional sportsmen's clubs. Every time I had gone to Springfield I was advised to "meet Charlie Johnson because he knows everybody."

It wasn't until the middle of August, though, that I could call him to arrange a morning meeting at a motor lodge off the Springfield exit of Interstate 91. He told me he would be sitting at the breakfast counter wearing a red shirt to make it easy for me to spot him.

"Hi, Smallwood," he greeted me. "I've been hearing some good things about you, but I always like to meet people firsthand so I can make my own decisions."

I ordered a cup of coffee and we chatted amiably for a few minutes before Charlie started to probe.

"Tell me, what's your position on veterans' legislation?" he asked casually.

"I'm a veteran," I replied noncommittally.

"You're a veteran—that's good!"

"I don't want to mislead you. I'm not a combat veteran," I explained. "I was too young to serve in World War II. I only turned eighteen in June 1945, just as the war was ending, so I wasn't inducted into the Army until after the war was over."

"That's O.K. You did your job. That's very good," Charlie nodded. Then: "Tell me, what's your feeling about the deer herd?"

This time the question was posed with considerable intensity. I hesitated before answering, well aware that management of the deer herd is a potentially explosive issue in Vermont politics, because there is constant bickering in Montpelier over whether the legislature or the Fish and Game Department should handle this awesome responsibility.

"Well, to be perfectly truthful about it, Charlie, I don't have a position on the deer herd," I finally answered. "I'm not really a hunter. I like to fish—trout fishing, preferably dry flies. I guess I would have to look to people like you on the House Fish and Game Committee for advice if this issue comes up again in the next legislative session."

For a moment he looked thunderstruck. "That's incredible." He bit his lip. "That's really incredible." He shook his head. "You're the first politician I ever met in Vermont who doesn't have a position on the deer herd. For God's sakes, never admit that in public. It's dynamite, murder, political suicide. They will cut you to pieces."

Charlie kept shaking his head so hard he started to spill his coffee all over the counter. I figured I had blown this one completely. Good grief, the perils of the deer herd in Vermont politics!

Suddenly Charlie interrupted my thoughts with an unexpectedly enthusiastic outburst. "Smallwood, you look like an interesting candidate to me. Quite frankly, I admire your honesty. But, for God's sakes, never make statements like that about the deer herd in public. I will be more than happy to advise you on the issue in private." He nodded sagely before continuing. "I think you can get elected, but there's only one way to do it. You've got to meet people, lots of people.

"Say, that gives me an idea: how would you like me to take you down to the shopping center to meet some of the fine folks of Springfield?"

Phew! That was a close one. I indicated my agreement, and we drove down to the shopping center in Charlie Johnson's car, a four-wheel-drive vehicle plastered with campaign stickers urging votes for John Alden for the Vermont Senate and for a host of other Republican candidates. Even the spare tire on the rear had a political sticker neatly pasted on a diagonal slant. RE-ELECT REP. CHARLIE JOHNSON.

We parked near the entrance of the supermarket. It was jammed with people.

"Friday morning. Good crowd. Give me some of your brochures," Charlie shot out, beginning an endless series of short commands. We were off to the races.

"Molly, I want you to meet Frank Smallwood, candidate for the Vermont Senate. A really fine fellow. Here, have a brochure.

"Sally, how are you? How's John? Did young Tommy get his hand fixed up? I want you to say hello to Frank Smallwood, our next county senator. Take one of his brochures. Tell your friends about him.

"Hello, Danny. How's the new job going? Meet Frank Smallwood, candidate for the state Senate. A good man. Have a brochure.

"Hi, George. What's the story with the football team this fall? This is Frank Smallwood. He's going to represent Springfield in the state Senate. Take a brochure."

I could hardly believe it. This single human being—this walking political whirling dervish—seemed to have every name in Springfield stuffed away in a computerized memory bank.

"Good Lord, Charlie," I remarked in amazement, "you know everybody in Springfield."

"Lived here a long time. Was born here in 1919. Lived here all my life. You can't live here any longer than that," Charlie roared as we strolled down the sidewalk promenade, constantly meeting and greeting more and more people.

When we reached the end of the plaza we turned around to begin our stroll back to the supermarket where Charlie had parked his car. It was the same thing all over again: "Hello, Tom—Hi, Clara—What do you say, Roger?" We greeted whole new groups of people as they emerged from the stores.

It took us another thirty minutes to work our way back to our starting point. It was remarkable, fascinating, exhilarating. Until I noticed a disturbing sight: some of my leaflets had ended up face down in the gutter!

"Charlie, look at that," I blurted. "They're throwing my things into the gutter!"

"Forget it." Charlie waved his hand reassuringly. "That's politics. As long as they remember your name, you don't have a worry in the world. Say, this was fun. Let's do it again next week. Wednesday afternoon. Double green-stamp day! Wait till you see the crowds then."

During the next two weeks Charlie Johnson and I made three more trips through the Springfield shopping center, where I encountered more people than I met in all the other twenty-three Windsor County towns combined.

"There's only one way to get elected. You've got to meet the people," Charlie kept telling me. It was a little more complicated than that, however. As Stimson Bullitt noted in his memoir of campaigning in his home state of Washington, "to enjoy politics one must enjoy people . . . yet be numb to their rebukes." Bullitt had made this observation after he had exchanged a handshake and brochure with an individual who had driven off in a truck with his opponent's sticker on the bumper. He recalled the incident vividly: "I smiled and pointed to the bumper as he drove by. He waved and smiled back."

It was pretty exciting to go to the Springfield shopping center, but I couldn't help thinking about handfuls of my leaflets lying face down in the gutter every time I finished one of my excursions with Charlie Johnson.

My feverish activities in the Springfield area continued through August. One of the most delightful events of all was an evening reception given for me by Leland and Ruth Lawrence at Old Colonial Farm. The party was another act of faith on the part of my host and hostess, who had never met me before. It was a very successful evening. All four of Springfield's Republican candidates for the House were there, along with Senate candidate Lee Davis. Retiring Senators Margaret Hammond and Olin Gay came, as did Joseph Johnson, the former Governor, also from Springfield.

I was introduced to so many people that I had a terrible time trying to remember names. Carol Fellows, a local reporter for the Rutland *Herald,* asked Ann and me to pose for a picture with Olin Gay. While we were waiting for Carol to adjust her flashbulb, Olin told us this was a very special occasion—his eighty-sixth birthday; he had been born August 16, 1886.

Two days after the reception a marvelous three-column picture of the three of us appeared in the *Herald*. Ann looked radiant, Olin had a big smile on his face, and even I looked good. Later the chief *Herald* correspondent in Windsor County told me I was lucky as hell: it was the best group picture Carol had ever taken for the paper. My campaign was gaining momentum.

Several days later I received a postcard from a friend in Montpelier:

> That was a teriffic [sic] picture in the Herald—much bet-
> ter than all that issue garbage. I feel that with a little luck
> you can turn it over. Shalom!

The "issue garbage" my admiring friend referred to resulted from a series of speeches I had delivered to Rotary clubs all over Windsor County. By late August I had managed to wangle invitations to speak to six of the county's seven Rotary groups, and since there had been no coverage of my first Woodstock talk, I decided to write my own press releases on issues I discussed at the service-club luncheons.

The first releases were a disaster. Single-spaced, difficult to read, too pedantic. Yawn. Yawn. But they shaped up as I gained more experience. By the end of the campaign, I even drafted my own head-lines, which were often picked up intact by the smaller weekly papers. I remembered the advice Harry Ames had given me after the first Woodstock Rotary meeting back in May: *Get your name known.* Hence it was always SMALLWOOD URGES THIS or SMALLWOOD PROPOSES THAT, etc. Although I never seemed to be able to fit "Frank" into the headlines, I sure worked like crazy to highlight the word *Smallwood*.

It was early September.

John Fieldsteel and I made our last all-day campaign trip to the same two towns we had visited at the outset: Rochester and Stock-bridge. It was a sentimental journey, but this time the response was different because we were escorted through Rochester by a very special local resident, Professor Henry Roberts of the Dartmouth History Department. Henry was highly respected in Rochester, having dis-charged a host of civic responsibilities including service on the town library committee. He introduced us to all the people we had not met on our first visit, all of whom had a warm feeling for Henry. They told me that if I was a friend of his, they would be happy to vote for me.

Just one month later Henry Roberts died of cancer at the age of fifty-six. I was really stunned. I never even suspected he was suffering from a terminal illness when he took so much time to show us around Rochester on that lovely, clear September morning.

We left Rochester at noon and headed for Stockbridge, where the chairman of the town Republican Committee, Stanley Miner, had arranged a luncheon for us. I had received a letter from Stan earlier in the summer, following our first disastrous trip to the Stockbridge cemetery. Before he retired to Vermont, for many years he and my father had commuted together to New York City from my old home town of Ridgewood, New Jersey, and they were good friends. The Miners had invited about twenty friends to meet me at a buffet lunch on the porch, followed by an hour-long question-and-answer session.

I couldn't handle all the questions, but I think I did O.K. When I drew a complete blank, I answered with a simple "I don't know." This can be a surprisingly effective political statement on occasions, because a number of people later told me they voted for me because I didn't pretend to know everything about everything.

John and I had a long talk about the campaign on our way back to Norwich. We were both impressed with the large number of people who had helped out. I told him about a study Professor Lester Milbrath made for his book *Political Participation,* where he divided the American public into three roles: "apathetics," "spectators," and "gladiators." According to Milbrath:

> About one-third of the American adult population can be characterized as politically apathetic or passive . . . and . . . another 60 percent play largely spectator roles in the political process; they watch, they cheer, they vote, but they do not battle. In the purest sense of the word, probably only 1 or 2 percent could be called gladiators.

Our trip back from Stockbridge marked the end of an exhausting effort. We felt we had run a pretty decent campaign, thanks to the large number of "gladiators" who had volunteered to help us during the summer. I dropped John off in Hanover and returned to Norwich just in time for supper. As I pulled into the driveway I looked at the speedometer of the new little car I had bought the day I made my first political speech—the one to the Woodstock Rotary Club—back in June.

After three months of campaigning around Windsor County, it clocked 7,144 miles.

4

★ ★ ★ ★

Election Night

Politics is a zero-sum game.
Anonymous

PRIMARY DAY, Tuesday, September 12, was gray and cloudy. After voting at the Norwich Town Hall in the morning I tried to keep busy by splitting a new load of firewood that had been delivered to us the previous weekend.

Despite the physical exertion, I couldn't keep my mind off the election. According to well-known academic terminology, politics is a "zero-sum game." One side ends up winning everything (+1); the other side ends up losing everything (−1): the results cancel each other out. Therefore the sum of the game is Zero—which is a fancy way of saying that politics is a winner-take-all struggle. You can work to the point of physical and emotional exhaustion, but if you lose by only one or two votes, you lose it all.

We had invited a small group of friends over to the house in the evening to follow the primary returns, so I drove down to the store before supper to pick up some supplies for the party. While I was shopping, a number of people told me that the voting in Norwich was very heavy. I took this as a good sign. If I could do well in my home town, it might help offset some of the vote in the larger communities in southern Windsor County, where I was less known.

I was reasonably optimistic about taking one of the top three spots on the Republican ticket, specifically the third spot. There were some good omens. Only four of the seven local newspapers had endorsed specific candidates, but all four of them had endorsed me along with

John Alden. According to my guesstimates, John was a cinch to run first. I also felt that Representative Lee Davis would probably run second because of a big local vote in his home town of Springfield.

The third place appeared to be up for grabs between Herbert Ogden and me. Herb hadn't campaigned formally, but for years he had been writing a lot of "letters to the editor" of local papers. More immediately valuable, though, was his devotion to the cause of getting railroad-passenger service restored to Vermont. He had set up AMTRAK booths at all the summer fairs in the county, and the announcement of AMTRAK service came through in late August—at the perfect time to give his "noncampaign" a very important boost. The three other Republican candidates—Don Arnold, George MacKnight, and Bill Tufts—hadn't campaigned as hard as I had. I figured that the key to whether Herb or I took third place would be the voter turnout. I kept my fingers crossed, hoping that the 3,000 voters I had tried to reach would now take the time to go to the polls.

Our guests began to assemble about eight o'clock. There was a real air of "election night" excitement because we all felt I was a cinch to win in the general election in November if I could take one of the three Republican nominations in the primary.

We spent the first hour in casual chatter, since no returns were in. It takes a long time to hand-count ballots in the small towns. A little after nine o'clock the phone rang in the kitchen. It was John Alden:

"Frank, I've just gotten the returns from Cavendish. You came in fifth: Alden 107, Davis 87, Ogden 58, Arnold 41, Smallwood 32, Mac-Knight 27, Tufts 17. Not a bad showing, but it's obviously too early to tell anything. I've got people calling in from the different towns. I'll ring back when I get some additional results."

Not a bad showing! I was stunned. Cavendish is in the Springfield area, so I had expected Lee Davis to do well. But for me to come in fifth!—'way behind Herb Ogden, and behind Don Arnold as well. I had spent a lot of time in Cavendish; the town manager had escorted me around town; I had made two additional visits there. Good Lord, why didn't I spend more time in Cavendish during the campaign? Only 32 votes! I couldn't believe it.

Before I could report the results to the group in the living room, the phone rang. It was John again.

"Frank, the second town is in—Hartland. You did very well considering it is Herb Ogden's home territory. Alden 236, Ogden 233, Smallwood 138, Davis 73, Arnold 70. I'll call back."

Thank the Lord for Nancy Klevana, who had escorted me around Hartland four weeks earlier. She was in our living room with her husband, Leighton, and I was ready to run in and kiss her. I added up the totals for the first two towns to report: Alden, 343; Ogden, 291; Smallwood, 170; Davis, 160; Arnold, 111; with both George MacKnight and Bill Tufts running further behind.

I walked casually into the living room and announced:

"Two towns are in. I'm running third behind John Alden and Herb Ogden."

A huge cheer went up from the group. The children were very excited. David jumped up, took a deep bow, and intoned, "I want you to meet my father, Senator Frank Smallwood." Everybody laughed.

I told them to calm down. Only two towns out of twenty-four were in so far. It was going to be a long evening.

Another hour went by. We couldn't pick up any results at all from the nearest radio stations, which are located across the Connecticut River and therefore were focusing on the New Hampshire primaries. The Springfield station, forty miles to the south, was too weak to do us any good. But a little before ten John Alden called again:

"Hello, Frank. John again. I've got quite a few results now: Barnard, Bridgewater, Pomfret, Rochester, plus some of the bigger northern towns. Let me give you the bigger towns first. You did O.K., running third in each. In Hartford: Alden 437, Ogden 331, Smallwood 299, Arnold 185. In Windsor: Alden 421, Ogden 326, Smallwood 236, Davis 185. In Woodstock: Alden 668, Ogden 470, Smallwood 377, Arnold 221.

"Personally, I'm disappointed with the Woodstock results," John added. We should have done better by you. Also, I'm a little surprised with Windsor after all the work you did on the Constitutional Plaza idea. Oops, there goes the other phone. Let me give you the grand

totals with nine towns reporting: Alden 2,316, Ogden 1,635, Smallwood 1,328, Arnold 841, Davis 685. Don't worry. You're running a
strong third. Say, is there anything in from Norwich?"

"No, John. I've asked them to call me as soon as they've counted
the ballots. It was very heavy turnout. I'll let you know as soon as I
hear anything."

"O.K., thanks. Don't worry. You look good at this point."

I hung up the phone and looked over the totals. Despite John's re-
assurances, I was really worried. I was running third, but eight of
the nine towns reporting in were from northern Windsor County,
where I was running behind Herb Ogden—well behind. Lee Davis
could expect a big vote in the southern part of the county, especially
in the populous Springfield area. Neither Lee's home town of Springfield nor my home town of Norwich had reported. Springfield had a
population of 10,063, with 5,670 registered voters. Norwich had a
population of 1,966, with 1,020 registered voters.

My only hope was to get a good vote in Norwich—a very good vote—
while not running too far behind Lee in Springfield. I thought about
the Norwich vote. Less than 200 Norwich people had voted in the
1970 primary, but this was above the county average, which was 15
percent of the checklist in a primary. I was hoping to get a 30 percent
turnout from Norwich, which would give me about 300 votes. However, this was a long shot. Dartmouth wasn't in session yet. I knew
that a lot of faculty members who lived in Norwich were away on
vacations or attending professional meetings, so I wasn't at all sure of
my home-town vote. If that broke down, I was in trouble.

I walked back into the living room to announce that I was still
running third with nine towns in—behind John Alden and Herb
Ogden. Another big cheer. This time Donny jumped up and said,
"Ladies and gentlemen, I would like you to meet my father, Senator
Frank Smallwood of Windsor County." Everybody cheered again.

We waited through another agonizing, unending hour before we
got any further results. What we could manage to hear from the
Springfield radio was virtually useless anyway, because it was reporting
on towns that we had already heard about via John Alden's grapevine
telephone system. Then, just before eleven, the phone rang again.

I grabbed it and blurted, "Hi, John! Any more results?"

"John who?" the caller responded. "Is this you, Frank?"

"Yes," I replied sheepishly, not quite sure who was on the other end of the line.

"This is Maurice Aldrich," the caller identified himself in a slow casual twang. "I'm calling from the Norwich Town Hall."

"Hi, Maurice. How are you."

"I'm fine, Frank. Just fine. We've finished counting the ballots down here. It took a long time because the turnout was very heavy for a primary election."

"I really appreciate your call, Maurice. Do you have the final results?"

"Oh, yes, that's why I called. I wanted to let you know that you did real well here in Norwich, Frank. Your home town came through for you. You should be mighty proud of yourself. You did very well."

There was a pause in the conversation. Maurice was an old-time Vermonter. I didn't want to push him too fast, but I could hardly stand the suspense. I waited for a few seconds, maybe five, and finally said, "Gee, that's great, Maurice. Do you have any final figures?"

"You mean the actual votes, Frank? Oh yes, we have all the final votes. That's why it took us so long. We had a very heavy turnout, so we checked the votes twice. You certainly did very well."

Another long pause.

"Maurice, would it be possible for you to tell me how many votes I got?"

"You mean the actual totals, Frank?"

"Yes, Maurice, the actual totals."

"Let's see, they're here somewhere." There was another interminable wait as I could hear Maurice shuffling through his papers.

"Ah, here it is," he said at last. "You did very well. You came in first in Norwich. Now let's see. You got 422 votes. Yes, that's right, 422 votes."

"Are you serious, Maurice?" I gasped. "Are you sure that's the correct total?"

"Oh yes, Frank. That's why it took so long. We had to check everything twice. That's interesting. We checked all the ballots twice because we had more than twice as many to check as we did in the 1970 primary."

"Maurice, that's great. Really great. Do you have any results on the other Senate candidates?"

"Yes, you led the ticket. Now let's see. These are the others. Senator Alden came in second with 336 votes. Mr. Ogden came in third with 252 votes. Representative Davis came in fourth with 86 votes. Former Senator Arnold came in fifth with 60 votes. The other candidates each got less than 50 votes."

"That's great, Maurice," I repeated once again. "Many thanks. I really appreciate your call."

I added up the tally sheet: Alden 2,652 votes; Ogden 1,887 votes; Smallwood 1,740 votes; Arnold 901 votes; Davis 771 votes.

I felt a little more secure. I was running much closer to Herb Ogden now. It was possible I could push ahead of him in the southern towns. Of even more importance, I was running almost a thousand votes ahead of Lee Davis. He was going to have to carry Springfield with a very heavy margin to make up that kind of deficit. It was still possible for him to do it with a combined sweep of Springfield, Weathersfield, Chester, and Ludlow, but this was becoming more doubtful.

I told the group about the Norwich results, and everyone was elated.

"Gosh, that's almost half the checklist," John Fieldsteel whistled. "A great turnout."

One of the guests went to the refrigerator and pulled out a bottle of champagne he had brought to the party.

"Let's all drink a toast to our next Vermont senator."

Everybody drank the champagne except me. I declined in favor of a cup of coffee, not being a champagne-drinker, and was kidded for being superstitious. A couple of guests apparently felt secure about my place on the ticket, however, and said that it had been a delightful evening, but they had to leave. The others joined the exodus. John Fieldsteel indicated he would stay a while longer. My departing friends congratulated me on their way out. I thanked them all for their help.

Susan phoned from the University of Vermont, and when we told her that it looked like I had won a nomination, she was very pleased. "You worked hard, Dad. You deserve it."

We headed Sandy and the boys in the direction of their bedrooms before Senator Bill Doyle called from Montpelier and expressed delight that I would be serving in the legislature with him. I phoned John Alden to report the Norwich results. He was excited, not only for me but with his own total. He checked his back figures, which indicated he had come in first in the 1970 Norwich primary with only 196 votes. Today he got 336 votes, and came in second.

"You really got the town to turn out, Frank. That's really phenomenal for a primary election. Congratulations. It looks like you will be one of the next state senators from Windsor County."

Ann, John Fieldsteel and I chatted casually in the living room, before picking up glasses and trays and stacking them in the kitchen. Finally, Ann asked if I would mind if she went to bed. I gave her a big kiss before I sent her on her way.

"Thanks, very much, honey, for all your help," I whispered in her ear. "I know you really don't like this political business, but you've been a good sport about it all the way."

Ann smiled and blew a series of kisses in my direction as she backed down the hall into the bedroom.

John Fieldsteel and I were alone again, just as we had been on our first and last all-day field trips to Rochester and Stockbridge.

"I wish the hell we could get the Springfield vote," John complained. At 11:40 the phone rang again.

"Hello, Frank. This is Lee Davis. Congratulations. I'm very glad you made it."

"What happened, Lee?" I asked him. "Do you have the Springfield results?"

"Yes. I carried Springfield. I received 970 votes and John Alden was right behind me with 966. You did very well. You came in third with 562 votes.

"It was funny, Frank," Lee continued. "Earlier in the evening, when I was getting all the returns from the southern towns, I was running neck and neck with John Alden for first place. Then, later in the evening the results started coming in from the northern towns. I just couldn't handle the totals you fellows piled up in places like Woodstock, Hartford and Norwich."

"I'm sorry, Lee. I really appreciate your call. I'm sorry we both couldn't have won."

"Well, Frank, that's politics. Never apologize if you win an election. We both ran hard, but I couldn't do as well in the northern towns as you did down here. But you worked for it. You deserve it."

"Thanks very much, Lee. I'll come down to see you this week. Please give my best to Mrs. Davis."

"She sends her best to you. Goodbye, and good luck in the November election."

I couldn't believe it was all over. I sat at the kitchen counter with John, and said quite simply, "John, we won."

He smiled. "You won. It was a lot of fun. I enjoyed every minute of it."

After John left, I went back into the kitchen and poured a glass of milk. It was just before midnight when the phone rang again.

"Is this Frank Smallwood?" the operator inquired. "You have a long-distance call from Mrs. Carolyn Schade of Moorestown, New Jersey."

My sister, Carol. How good of her to call, I thought—but what if I had lost!

"Hello, Frank, this is Carol. Did you win the election?"

"Yes, I just got the final results. It looks like I'm in."

"Oh, good for you. I'm sorry, but I've got some bad news. The nurse just called from Florida. Dad died tonight, just a few minutes ago.

It took awhile for the news to sink in. My father had been terribly sick for over three years, but I still had difficulty comprehending the finality of his death. I tried to express my feelings to Carol who was pretty broken up. At the end we discussed travel plans to Florida and arrangements for the funeral.

After I hung up the phone, I sat silently at the kitchen counter for quite a while before walking into the bedroom to wake up Ann.

"Carol just called. Dad died tonight in Florida."

Ann jumped up like a shot. "I'm sorry," she murmured softly. "He was a wonderful person."

We chatted quietly for a few minutes. Then she said, "This has been an incredible day for you, and you've got a long trip ahead of you tomorrow. Do you think you can get some sleep?"

"I'll try." I went back to the kitchen to finish my glass of milk. It was shortly after midnight when I dropped into bed, but it was hours before I finally fell asleep.

5

★ ★ ★ ★

What Makes Sammy Run?

Men and women are drawn into politics by
a combination of motives: power, glory,
zeal for contention or success, duty, obli-
vion, hate, hero worship, curiosity, and
enjoyment of the work.

Stimson Bullitt
To Be a Politician

FOLLOWING my father's funeral, I remained in Florida for a few days
to be with my mother who, like Dad, was seventy-nine years old. Mom
had been very upset with my decision to run for the Vermont Senate,
explaining that it was not in keeping with family tradition: I was the
first one ever to become a politician. Then she corrected herself, re-
calling an obscure branch on the family tree in the form of a great-
uncle who served as mayor of Hackensack, New Jersey, around the
turn of the century. She concluded, however, that my great-uncle's
earlier fling in the rough-and-tumble of Hackensack politics didn't
constitute a sufficiently noble precedent to justify my entry into the
political arena.

As she continued to talk, my mother clarified the real focus of her
anxiety. As far as she was concerned, I was still, and always, the
youngest member in a family of four children. She was afraid of
politics. More specifically, she was afraid I would get hurt in politics.
She zeroed in on the shenanigans at the Democratic headquarters in
Washington to indicate where she feared I would end up if I didn't
watch my step:

"Be careful, Frank, politics is a dangerous business," she warned
solemnly. "Why just look at what has happened at the Watergate.
Your father and I have always been good Republicans, but I can't

imagine how a Republican could ever get involved in such a thing. Please be careful. Politics is a very, very dangerous business."

"For Lord sakes, Mother," I protested, "I'm not going to have anything to do with Watergate. Vermont isn't Washington. As a matter of fact, I don't even know if there is a Democratic Party headquarters in Vermont; and if I do find out, I'm certainly not going to try to bug the place. I'm only a part-time participant, an amateur, trying to supplement my teaching at Dartmouth with some practical experience in the state legislature. It's all that simple."

The more I thought about it, however, the more I wondered if the allure of the political arena was quite that simple. I reflected on the summer's primary campaign, still a mass of confused impressions with only the hazy frame of reference of commitment, excitement, and hard work. I had to admit that once I became immersed in the campaign, it had taken on an exhilarating, stimulating, almost contagious quality that I couldn't really mesh with my protestations of academic detachment. I had pushed myself very hard, often to the edge of exhaustion. Was there some hidden dynamic within the political process that had taken on a momentum of its own? The more I thought about the campaign, the more I wondered. The entire affair had been marked by a sharp sense of excitement and intensity that was unique in my experience.

Then my mother was expressing her concerns again, this time to a point where I became increasingly dismayed.

"Oh, Frank," she sighed wistfully, "I hope you're doing the right thing. I wonder what your father would think about all of this. He always wanted the best for you. He was so proud when you became a college professor. I wonder what he would think about his youngest child becoming a politician."

Good grief, I thought, I'm the all-American boy, a cinch to make it to the White House with this kind of overwhelming family support. My wife isn't interested in politics; the children accepted my decision quite reluctantly; and now my poor mother is pouring out her woes. I felt we would do better by changing the subject.

"I'm sure Dad would understand, Mom. He always taught all four of us to make our own decisions. I'm glad Bill, Mimi, and Carol were able to make the trip down to Florida. It was a beautiful service. Very moving."

"Yes, it was beautiful," my mother replied almost abstractedly. "I hope you will remember the eulogy. It was the same passage that was used when your father and I were confirmed together at the Union Avenue Church in Paterson, New Jersey, 'way back on March 24, 1905. I asked the minister to use the same lesson for your father's service."

I had mixed feelings about the significance of the lesson my mother had chosen. It was from First Corinthians, chapter fifteen, verse ten: "By the grace of God, I am what I am."

After I returned to Norwich, John Fieldsteel and I went over the final returns from the primary election in considerable detail. I had ended up with 3,061 votes.

"Whew! Pretty sharp planning for a political science professor," John kidded me. "We couldn't have come much closer to our 3,000-vote target, even if we had rigged the election."

Actually, although my final vote tally was very close to our projections, it hadn't come about the way we had planned. The final totals for the top four candidates were John Alden 5,015, Herb Ogden 3,115, Frank Smallwood 3,061, and Lee Davis 2,782.

John Alden's showing was extremely impressive across the board. He came in first in nineteen of the twenty-four Windsor County towns, and second in the five remaining towns. Lee Davis, on the other hand, carried a number of southern towns, including Springfield; however, he was mauled in the northern part of the county, running sixth or seventh in many areas.

Herb Ogden and I both made exactly the same kind of showing. I came in first in only one town—Norwich—and Herb didn't come in first in any. Still, we consistently ran second, third, or fourth throughout most of the county, so we didn't get badly hurt anywhere.

I finally figured out the problem Lee Davis had faced: namely, his apparent asset had proven to be a liability. He was the only candidate from the southern part of the county. Six of us were from the northern towns. Lee did very well in his home territory, but he couldn't make

any inroads at all in the north, where the six of us were splitting up
the vote. Through no fault of his own, he was screened out of all the
northern towns.

"Boy, that Norwich vote was crucial," John declared. "You were
only 279 votes ahead of Lee Davis throughout the entire county, but
you led him by 336 votes in Norwich alone."

John was right. The big turnout in Norwich had been the key to
the election for me. Close to half the town's checklist had voted, which
was an extremely high turnout for a primary election. I decided that,
in the final analysis, political campaigning really boils down to four
basic considerations. First, plain brutal physical stamina. Second, public exposure that succeeds in getting a candidate's name, face, and
reputation imbedded in the mind of enough voters. Third, a willing-
ness on the part of these voters to go to the polls. And last, lots of help
and support from lots of volunteer workers.

It was this final commitment that really made the difference, all
those volunteers who worked so hard, with John Fieldsteel being at the
head of the group. John was now planning a fall trip to Europe, before
picking up a job during the winter and spring months to help cover
his expenses at law school.

Remembering our first conversation when he had come into my
office in June, all dusty and shaky from the jackhammer, I now wanted
to give him something for his hard work. He protested at first, but
finally agreed to accept five hundred dollars, which he felt would be
helpful in buying all those law books he would eventually need.

In October we received a postcard message from London: "Hi Everybody. $500 equals 208 pounds and 30 new pence. Having wonderful
time. Wish you were here. Thanks for everything. Best to all. John F."

¶WITH THE PRIMARY over, John Alden told me to stop worrying.
Nevertheless, there still was a general election scheduled for November
7, and the Democrats did nominate three candidates for the Vermont
Senate.

The first to announce was Fred Niland, a young lawyer from nearby
White River Junction. He was followed by Nick Jacobson, a Norwich

neighbor of mine, who was a writer and retired farmer. The third Democrat was a former representative to the Vermont House, Alan Chalmers from Weston at the southwest corner of the county. John Alden turned out to be right. There wasn't anything to worry about, since all three Democrats took the view that their major role was to offer the voters a choice by appearing on the ballot, and none of them campaigned very hard.

Actually, most of the fall consisted of "meet the voters" meetings organized by local civic groups—get-togethers that almost always turned out to be meet-the-other-candidates meetings, since the general public didn't seem to be terribly interested in the upcoming general election. As a result, groups of candidates, ignoring their party differences, tended to huddle together at the various meetings throughout the county, exchanging jokes and stories in an effort to shore up their morale.

The most depressing meeting of all—a statewide candidates' open house—took place on a Sunday afternoon in the gymnasium of the Woodstock high school. The problem was pretty basic: the meeting conflicted with the final game of the World Series. With the choice between baseball and politicians for entertainment, we came in a poor second.

A total of twenty-seven candidates, and approximately the same number of voters, showed up during the course of the afternoon. There were three candidates for Governor, numerous nominees for Lieutenant Governor, Attorney General, Secretary of State, Auditor of Accounts, and State Treasurer; and six candidates for the state Senate, plus local aspirants for seats in the House. In view of the large candidate turnout and the small size of the audience, the organizers of the meeting mercifully agreed to limit the program to brief remarks from only those who were running for statewide office.

I happened to sit next to Thomas Salmon, the Democratic nominee for Governor, who was running a very hard race. During a particularly boring and long-winded oration, I asked him in frustration how he could stand this type of verbal onslaught day after day.

"Welcome to politics, Frank," he smiled. "You'll find that it sort of grows on you with the passage of time."

I often thought about Tom Salmon's comment. I wasn't at all sure that politics was really growing on me during the fall campaign—especially when I went out into the field to listen to all those speeches and to meet all those invisible, nonexistent people.

In addition to attending the candidates' meetings, I also participated in a series of county caravans where key statewide aspirants would come down to Windsor County to circle through the various towns during the course of a day.

Herb Ogden would have none of this, indicating, in a widely publicized "letter to the editor," that October was the peak month for cider, which kept him tied up at his Hartland cider- and gristmill. John Alden and I made a number of the caravans, although John was usually able to peel off by midday because of the demands of his insurance business. I was on sabbatical leave, though, with no ready-made excuse, so I'd stick around to the bitter end. Actually, the caravans weren't too bad. For one thing, Vermont's scenery was spectacular in October, as the reds, oranges, and yellows of the hardwoods flamed on the hillsides amidst the softer dark green of the conifers. Also, the caravans gave me a good opportunity to talk with a lot of different candidates, plus the party faithful, those toilers in the vineyards who organized the trips and greeted us at the different towns along the way.

¶It was these excursions that led me to speculate on the various political types I encountered during the campaign. The more I thought about it, the more I realized that we really don't know very much about political motivation, although it is a key ingredient—probably *the* key ingredient—in the entire political process. What kind of psychological drive induces people to participate in politics?

I reflected on the candidates I had already met. Since there is very little in the way of money or other tangible rewards offered in Vermont politics, most of them were motivated by personal considerations. They were a mixed lot. Some were idealists, pushed by a personal vision of a better society they hoped to create. Others were more partisan, committed to work toward the realization of a structured party ideology. Others were caught up in the fun and drama, stimulated by the roar of the crowd (if they could find a crowd). Still others were public-service compulsives, driven by a sense of duty, by an inner belief that they had a personal obligation to play a public role in the democratic process. The most interesting people of all were the power-seekers, a species I suspect is as prevalent in Winnebago, Wisconsin, and Walla Walla, Washington, as in Windsor County, Vermont.

The power-seekers take to politics like ducks to water. They are political by nature, tending to identify their own personal ambitions so closely with the political process that their ego involvement becomes synonymous with politics as way of life.

To me, the most astonishing group of power-seekers was the professional candidates, a small band of hearty individuals who seemed to develop some kind of internal fixation over the very act of running for office as an end in itself, without too much idea of what they hoped to accomplish if successful. They were caught up in a frenetic orgy of activity that took on a meaning of its own: "the fun is in the chase." Many of them truly seemed to get stronger as the campaign wore on, fed by public exposure, or some other energizing force, that nourished them as they were using themselves up in their political exertions.

I really couldn't understand this. Politics can be fun, but it can also be a tough, grueling, bone-tiring business. It wasn't the conflict and controversy that wore me down, it was the massive public apathy and indifference. You can work your butt off, but an awfully large segment of the public doesn't seem to give a damn. It takes a tough hide, and a great deal of ego drive, to adjust to a situation like that.

The power-seekers were a fascinating breed. Political scientist Harold Lasswell tried to put his finger on them in his *Power and Personality,* but I'm not sure he succeeded. He advanced the controversial and hardly flattering thesis that the political personality seeks power as "a means of compensation against deprivation. Power is expected to overcome low estimates of the self, by changing either the traits of the self, or the environment in which it functions." To Lasswell, the pure power-seeker constitutes the ultimate manifestation of "homo politicus," the most driven of all political types, who is "characterized by an intense and ungratified craving for deference."

Could this be the key? Were the power-seekers really a bunch of psychological misfits who were getting some kind of strange inner kicks out of the act of political involvement? No, I didn't think this fit too well. I met too many people who were involved because they really cared, or really enjoyed the process. They hoped to make a contribution, and they chose politics as their means of expression in an effort to do so.

The question of political motivation remained an enigma to me. During flights of introspection, I thought back to that conversation with my mother in Florida. Is there some hidden dynamic within the political process that takes on a momentum of its own? What makes Sammy run? I really don't know. Probably a thousand different things. Maybe my real dilemma during the fall campaign was that I had too much time on my hands. By nature I'm all work-ethic—a nagging trait I inherited from my father, a successful, self-made businessman. In retrospect, the general election was a low-key anticlimax to the much more intensive primary race. The Republican candidates were in a strange state of limbo, almost home free—but not quite, because nothing is ever certain until election day. As a result, I felt I had to hover around and go through the motions, but without really exerting myself. This proved to be a restless, somewhat frustrating experience, so I spent a lot of time studying up on issues and drafting legislation I hoped to sponsor if elected.

It's one thing to seek power, and quite another to use it wisely.

As soon as the first results started to come in on election night, I knew John Alden had been right. It was no contest.

With one exception, the Republicans swept all the major races. These were the top Windsor County vote-getters:

John Alden, Vermont Senate	13,463
Richard Mallary, U.S. House	13,073
Frank Smallwood, Vermont Senate	12,936
Herbert Ogden, Vermont Senate	12,880
Richard Nixon, U.S. President	12,420

The Democratic candidates for the state Senate ran far behind, with between 5,600 and 5,700 votes each. The only Democratic winner was

Tom Salmon, who carried Windsor County by 1,000 votes over Fred Hackett, the Republican nominee, on the way to a surprising upset victory which swept him into the Governor's chair.

I was very pleased and thankful it was all over.

"How about that!" I exclaimed to Ann and the children. "I got five hundred more votes than Richard Nixon on my very first try for elective office."

The kids seemed impressed, but Ann was a little more realistic. "Knock it off, Mr. Big," she said. "We hereby reserve judgment on your dazzling political abilities until we have a chance to see what you're able to accomplish in Montpelier during the next two years."

PART II

□ ☒ □ □

The Legislature

6

★ ★ ★ ★

The Senate Chamber

The Senate . . . is just like living in a
small town.
                    Donald R. Matthews
                    "The Folkways of the Senate"
                    in *Readings on Congress,*
                    R. E. Wolfinger, ed.

I ARRIVED in the Vermont State House in Montpelier for my first
official day of legislative duty a little before nine o'clock Wednesday
morning, January 3, 1973. I was lugging a huge canvas shoulder bag
that was loaded with a *Vermont Legislative Directory and State
Manual,* a copy of the *1972 Information Please Almanac,* a pile of
state budget reports, an annotated edition of the Vermont Constitution, and sundry other documents I had brought up from home the
preceding night.

Ann had accompanied me on the trip from Norwich and was at the
bus terminal waiting for Susan, who was coming down from the
University of Vermont to watch the opening ceremonies, officially
scheduled to begin at ten o'clock.

There was a sense of excitement in the air as small clusters of
visitors were beginning to gather within the august confines of the
Senate Chamber, a room of extraordinary elegance, style, charm,
warmth, and quiet dignity that grows out of a subtle blending of
intimate size, graceful design, and soft tasteful colors. Its semicircle of
thirty brown walnut desks is arranged in double rows, divided evenly
down the middle by a spacious central aisle covered with light green
carpeting that blends into darker green velvet draperies and soft yellow walls. The room is crowned by a white domed ceiling, supported
by four Corinthian columns. The arrangement of the columns com-
plements the semicircular pattern of the desks, which face an elevated

dais at the east end of the room that is occupied by the Lieutenant
Governor, who serves ex officio as President of the Senate. A few
plain decorations add to the sense of history: a United States flag,
a Vermont State flag, and four oil portraits in the front corners of the
room. The small visitors' section, located behind the senators' desks,
was already becoming crowded, as was a narrow visitors' balcony that
overlooks the entrance to the room.

The purpose of my early arrival was not to greet visitors, but to
find out which desk I was supposed to occupy for the next two years.
I knew the Windsor County delegation was assigned to Seats 13, 14
and 15, the three back desks in the northeast corner of the room. John
Alden had indicated he wanted to keep Number 13 from the previous
session, but I didn't know where to unload my shoulder bag (which
was growing heavier by the minute) because I was unsure whether
I should sit at Desk 14 or 15. I discussed the situation with Robert
Gibson, the secretary of the Senate. He was sympathetic when he saw
me staggering under my bulging bag, but couldn't offer any advice on
specific desk assignments. After milling around for a while, I deposited
the bag on the floor near the dais, and went downstairs to check on my
desk assignment with Lieutenant Governor John Burgess.

The Lieutenant Governor's office was jammed with an assortment of
well-wishers, reporters, and a TV camera crew preparing to record his
observations on the forthcoming legislative session. I finally managed
to nudge my way through the crowd to reach his side. "Pardon me,
Jack," I said, "but could you please tell me which Senate desk I am
supposed to use?"

He looked completely nonplussed. "Desk? Which desk? I'm really
not sure, Frank. They're assigned by counties. You sit with the Windsor County group—with John Alden and Herb Ogden. I'm sorry, but
I'm getting ready for a press conference. Why don't you check with
John Alden? I'm sure he can help you."

Back upstairs to find John Alden, but there was Senator Herbert
Ogden instead comfortably ensconced at Desk 15. "Hi, Frank, I've
been looking for you. Nobody around here seems to know which desks
we should use."

"So I've discovered. I think it's our choice. Do you want to flip a
coin?"

"No, I've already deposited some of my material in Fifteen. Would you mind taking Fourteen?"

"Not at all. The sooner I can stash away the stuff in this damn bag the better off I'll be."

Herb left the room, and I began to hum a cheerful tune as I unloaded my paraphernalia. Just as I was about finished, a young man came over and introduced himself as a reporter from a local newspaper. I explained that I was a new senator from Windsor County, and asked if I could be helpful.

"Yes, I know; you're Senator Smallwood," the reporter replied in a casual tone. Then he looked at me quizzically before continuing, "Would you mind if I asked you a question?"

I perked up immediately, eager to respond. This was pretty heady stuff. My first news conference. The Senate hadn't even officially started, but the press had smoked me out already. I gazed back at the reporter cautiously. Now don't blow it, Frank. Just keep cool. True, there are no TV cameras, but maybe you can analyze the forthcoming session just as Jack Burgess is doing in his big office downstairs. I collected my thoughts, adjusted my tie, and smiled. "O.K., fire away."

The reporter hesitated, obviously framing his question, then he addressed me in a matter-of-fact tone. "Senator Smallwood, would you mind telling me where you bought your canvas shoulder bag?"

My shoulder bag! I could hardly believe it. The question was so totally unexpected that it almost knocked me over.

"My canvas shoulder bag. You can't be serious," I said, my mind racing. "You don't really want a canvas shoulder bag?"

"Oh, yes. Oh, yes," the reporter nodded. "It would be very useful. You see, I often carry around cameras and a tape recorder. I'd love to have a big shoulder bag like that for myself."

Good Lord, I thought, he *is* serious. Completely at sea, I began to respond aimlessly: "Let's see. You want a canvas shoulder bag. Very good. Where did I buy mine? To tell the truth, I can't remember. I think I got it from the man who assigns seats in the Senate, but he isn't here today. I'm sorry about that, but I've looked all over the place, and I haven't been able to locate him anywhere."

The reporter looked as dumfounded as Jack Burgess had looked when I'd asked him my seat number.

"The man who assigns seats in the Senate—who is he? Does he sell shoulder bags? How can he assign seats in the Senate if he's not even here today? It's the opening day of the session."

"Good point," I said, beginning to recover. "You're right. I'm wrong. It couldn't be the man who assigns seats in the Senate. Let's think this through. Where did I buy my shoulder bag? Ah yes, now I remember. The Plaka, Athens, Greece. That's right. It cost seventy-five drachmas. Two dollars and fifty cents even."

"Gee— Athens, Greece: that's pretty far away. Too bad. It's a great big bag. Oh well," he shrugged, "I guess you can't win 'em all."

The young reporter retreated toward the center aisle, shaking his head sadly. He obviously had some real doubts about the new senator from Windsor County. I returned to my unpacking chores, opening the lid of Senate Desk 14. Inside the desk, written on the wood, were two signatures; in blue ink, *Olin Gay, 1957 session,* and in red ink, *Margaret Hammond, 1966–1972.* After eight months of effort, I was back again with Olin and Margaret, seated at the old Senate desk they had both once occupied in an area which later became known as "the DMZ"—demilitarized zone—of Windsor County between John Alden and Herb Ogden.

By ten o'clock the Senate Chamber was jammed with visitors attending the opening ceremonies of the General Assembly of the State of Vermont, Fifty-second Biennial Legislative Session, 1973–74. Then at 10:15 A.M., only fifteen minutes behind schedule, Lieutenant Governor Burgess banged down his gavel to mark the official opening of the Senate. The small galleries were packed. I looked up and smiled at Ann and Susan, who had arrived and were sitting in the balcony. Despite the psychological deflation that had followed my first official press conference, I couldn't help thinking that this was a unique, momentous, historical occasion.

Our first ceremonial act, taking the oath of office, was very simple. We all stood, raised our right hands, and in unison solemnly swore that we would be "true and faithful to the State of Vermont," and that we would not, "directly or indirectly, do any act or thing injurious to the Constitution or Government thereof, so help us God."

Following the oath we began our first official business, the election of Senate officers.

Edward Janeway was unanimously chosen for a third term as President Pro Tempore. Senator Janeway, a seventy-one-year-old gentleman of courtly grace who owned a dairy farm in Windham County down in the southeastern part of the state, had served in the Senate since 1959, and also was Vermont's Republican National Committeeman from 1952 to 1972. His election as President Pro Tem was more than honorific. Although his formal duties were relatively light (he filled in as presiding officer in the absence of the Lieutenant Governor), he was automatically designated to serve as the Republican majority leader in the Senate by virtue of his election to this post. John Boylan, another veteran, was chosen to join Ed Janeway and Lieutenant Governor Burgess to form the powerful three-member Committee on Committees, the group responsible for designating all committee chairmen and members. Senator Boylan, at sixty-five years old an incredibly hard-working legislator, was a retired railroad storekeeper from Essex County in the northeastern corner of Vermont.

The remainder of the opening day's session was undramatic. We approved the appointment of Senate staff before ending with a fairly lengthy debate over what type of special committee we should set up to investigate a seating challenge in Chittenden County. Thereafter, it was impossible to move ahead on any major business until the committees were organized, so we all marked time as we waited to learn our fate from the Committee on Committees.

¶DURING the two-day hiatus which marked our wait for committee assignments, I began to feel my way around the State House. It quickly became apparent that the legislative arena I was entering was characterized by a considerably different set of dynamics from those of the campaign I had conducted during the summer and fall.

A political campaign is dominated by a specific series of events, sharply focused on the pursuit of a single well-defined objective (elective office), which results in either clear-cut victory (Gee, I'm a hero!) or depressing defeat (Oops, I'm a has-been).

Once an election is over, however, and the victorious heroes move
into the legislature, the story-line becomes considerably more mud-
dled. For the individual participant, the legislative process becomes a
baffling series of divergent experiences without any apparent logical
sequence at all. It often seems to be disjointed and unrelated because
it is characterized by a bargaining process that consists of a never-
ending mix of uncertainty, adjustments, and compromise.

Since I had taught some courses in legislative behavior at Dartmouth, I thought I was at least partly prepared to deal with some
of the complexities I was destined to face in Montpelier. Little did I
realize how much I had to learn as I groped to discover some under-
lying patterns that would provide a coherent understanding of the
new world that lay before me. It was only after considerable effort
that I managed to uncover four central frames of reference that helped
guide me through the legislative arena. Such guidelines are presented
here as hindsight in the hope that they will help the uninitiated to
unravel the seeming confusion I faced after I eventually managed to
find my seat in Vermont's elegant Senate Chamber.

1. Calendar and Agenda

A key factor that influenced legislative business was the chronological
span of the session, which obliged us to work within the confines of a
specific opening date and somewhat more amorphous adjournment
date. Harking back to an earlier agricultural heritage, Vermont's state
legislature meets annually during the winter months for a twelve- to
fourteen-week period. The opening date is clearcut: the first week in
January. The adjournment can range from late March to late April—or
beyond—depending on the press of business.

This framework is important because it helps to determine the
legislative agenda throughout the winter months. The great majority
of bills pour in during the first few weeks of each session. I realized this
with a vengeance during my second working day in the Senate when
we were deluged with no less than forty new bills that had been prepared between the election and the opening of the 1973 session. It was
like somebody dumping a wastebasket over our heads. Not that the
bills were all bad, but they dealt with such a wide variety of subjects.

The first bill, S. *1*, covered planning for unorganized towns and gores, and before we reached S. *40* (state assistance to mass transportation), we had been introduced to trading-stamp redemptions, property-tax notifications, licensing television technicians, land-use planning and taxation, proposed modifications in the teachers' retirement system, procedures governing collection of traffic fines, prohibitions on plastic milk containers, tourist-sign regulations, and health inspections for employees working in food establishments. It is important to realize that very few of these bills dealt with the creation of new statutory law from scratch. Instead, the overwhelming majority involved incremental amendments to existing state laws which were already codified in *Vermont Statutes Annotated,* the thirty-three green-bound volumes that constituted our legislative bible. Each of these volumes covered one or more titles that dealt with a general subject. Title 24 of *Vermont Statutes Annotated,* for example, encompassed municipal government and local town concerns. Therefore our first bill, which dealt with planning procedures for unorganized towns and gores, was presented as S. *1:* AN ACT TO AMEND 24 V.S.A. ss1408, 4303 (2), 4322, 4403, 4410 (d) AND TO ADD 24 V.S.A. ss4404 (h) AND 1410 RELATING TO MUNICIPAL PLANNING.

It's pretty obvious that the average citizen-legislator doesn't dream up amendments like that during a sleepless night. Hence arises the interesting question: Where do bills come from and how are they written?

Many of the bills were originated by individual legislators who had identified needs or problems they wanted to do something about. At this point they took their ideas to the Legislative Council, which in Vermont consisted of a four-man staff of technical assistants who drafted bills for members of the General Assembly. The staff worked the idea into bill form before presenting it to the legislator for review. Once the legislator was satisfied with the draft bill, he approved it for printing, and it was then introduced into its appropriate chamber depending on whether the originator was a senator or a member of the House.

In addition to formulating their own ideas for bills, lawmakers received suggestions from constituents, their home towns, interest groups, the executive-branch agencies, or other sources who wanted legislators to introduce bills on their behalf. If such requests were honored, the same procedure was followed in drafting the bill, although the individual legislator had the option of indicating that the bill was introduced "by request" if he cared to exercise this right when he first presented the bill on the floor.

During the first few weeks of the session, so many bills came flooding into both houses of the legislature that the draftsmen on the Legislative Council were working overtime to keep up with the demand. Interestingly enough, however, once this initial spate of bills had been introduced and shunted off to appropriate committees for study, the floor aspects of the legislative process quieted down completely. Instead of sticking to a tight schedule to organize our work, during the first couple of months we tended to diddle around on the floor quite a bit, accomplishing relatively little. Then in early March, just when the sap started to run in the maples, the logjam began to break. The final weeks of the session were tumultuous, with bills flying back and forth between the Senate and House so quickly that we hardly had time to read them, much less comprehend what was going on. In part this haphazardness appeared to be due to simple human procrastination. I've rarely met a group anywhere that actually tends to expedite its business before a final deadline approaches.

In addition, though, there was also a tactical and strategic dimension to the logjam phenomenon. As the adjournment deadline approached, different committee chairmen in both houses liked to hold up action on major bills so they could "trade" these against other bills with which they were more personally involved. The natural result was a great deal of procrastination and delay during the first couple of months of a session, at least as far as floor action was concerned. Paradoxically, therefore, rather than adding an element of discipline to the legislative process, the chronological limits of the schedule tended to increase the uncertainty and confusion of policy-making.

2. Leadership and Committees

A second major factor that provided glue to the legislative process consisted of the leadership structure, which embraced floor leaders as well as committee chairmen. The criteria determining this leadership hierarchy were healthy old age, experience, and Republican Party affiliation. Since Republicans dominated both houses, all the key floor leaders were from the GOP: Lieutenant Governor Burgess, Ed Janeway and John Boylan in the Senate, Speaker of the House Walter Kennedy, and the Majority leader and whips in the House. The Republicans' majority in the Senate was so overwhelming (23 to 7) that they gobbled up twelve of the thirteen committee chairmanships in addition to the key floor positions.

Age and seniority were crucially important in determining committee chairmanships. Although the average age of all thirty senators was only (sic) fifty-seven, the committee chairmen averaged a ripe old sixty-four years of wisdom. Only six Senators were under fifty, with four (including yours truly) in their forties and two in their thirties. In addition to being one of the youngsters in the Senate at the age of forty-five, I enjoyed the dubious distinction of being the most geographically remote "transplanted native." Fifteen of the thirty senators had been born in Vermont, and twenty-three in New England. Seven of us were not bona fide New Englanders: six were originally from New York State, and I, the most distant resident alien of all, was born in the faraway reaches of northern New Jersey.

There have been numerous debates in political literature about the virtues, vices, and basic rationale behind legislative leadership structures, especially the role of seniority in the leadership process. I think seniority grows out of what Anthony Lewis Dexter describes in "The Job of the Congressman" as the legislative "social system." According to Dexter, the social system within any legislative body really amounts to "a complex web of interdependence as a result of the fact that each member must work through others to get what he wants." This is true "because any bill compounds many issues, and action on any one bill affects action on other bills too." The result is individual bargaining, where members line up support for a particular bill by trading off support for another bill.

In addition, actions can be taken on the basis of personal considerations—such as friendship or respect for another legislator's opinion—especially when things begin to pile up at the end of a session and it's simply impossible to study every bill in detail. At this point the role of leadership becomes pivotal. Because there are thirty members of the Senate and one hundred and fifty representatives in the Vermont House, it would be impossible for a group of this size to accomplish anything by individual bargaining without strong leadership direction. Unless the constant bargaining were managed and focused, the whole shooting match could fly apart, either because of internal conflicts or external pressures. Somebody had to hold the system together, and provide it with the internal cohesion necessary to transcend the often frenetic intensity of individual bargaining. The most senior legislators were entrusted with this responsibility precisely because they had had the most experience in dealing with the system. As a result, I didn't find the seniority system objectionable. We were fortunate, however, in having good leaders in the Vermont Senate, and I realize that seniority can be something else again if it produces incompetent leadership. We were very lucky in this respect.

The elaborate committee structure of the Senate grew out of the necessity to provide specialized scrutiny to the mass of different bills which flooded into the legislature. During the 1973–74 session we had thirteen standing committees in the Senate: Agriculture, Appropriations, Education, Finance, General and Military, Government Operations, Health and Welfare, Highway Traffic, Highways and Bridges, Institutions, Judiciary, Natural Resources, and Rules. The three most powerful committees were Appropriations (which had to review any bill involving the expenditure of state funds), Finance (which dealt with all revenue bills), and Judiciary (which could request just about any bill dealing with an important legal issue—or in effect, any bill at all, since we were dealing with the creation of statutory law). Rules was a prestigious committee; but not super-powerful, because it confined its work to recommending a general set of complicated rules that governed the entire two-year session. Usually this committee did not attempt to intervene in regulating the procedure for handling individual bills.

I had asked to be placed on the Education Committee because of my academic background, and on Government Operations because I had taught courses in local government at Dartmouth. Instead, I was

assigned to the Natural Resources and the Health and Welfare committees. It turned out that there were already two college professors on
Education—my old friend Bill Doyle of Johnson State College and
Graham Newell of Lyndon State College—and the leadership determined that this was a large enough bloc of academe to impose on any
one body. Hence I was assigned to Natural Resources as my morning
committee, and Health and Welfare as my afternoon committee.

These assignments turned out to be a very lucky break, because both
committees dealt with highly important substantive legislation. Natural Resources handled all the big environmental and planning bills,
and Health and Welfare was involved with a mass of human-services
legislation. They were two of the most interesting, enjoyable and
overworked committees in the Senate.

3. Rules and Procedures

A third point of cohesion in legislative deliberations was an elaborate
system of very strict rules, ninety-three in all in the Vermont Senate,
which governed every technicality from committee organization to
floor amendments. Unfortunately the rules tended to drive me nuts;
I could never master all their intricacies—a fact that certainly put
me at a disadvantage since rules can be vital in determining the
outcome of a specific issue.

Very briefly, in terms of basic floor rules, any bill had to go through
three separate readings before being passed. It's a rough obstacle-
course, and reminded me of the tortuous upriver runs of spawning
fish. Many of the seven hundred fifty bills introduced during the
1973–74 legislative sessions didn't really make it into the river at all,
even to the first fish ladders. Instead, there were carcasses strewn all
over the place as bills were clawed to death by committees, lobbyists,
inept floor presentations, leadership trade-offs, and the like.

At least the journey upstream started out gently enough. The "first
reading" of new bills was always perfunctory: they were merely cited
on the floor by number, and by name of sponsor, before quickly being
shunted off to the appropriate committee for detailed study. It was at
this point that the trip became more turbulent. Many bills were

simply swallowed up within the various committees, never to be dis-
gorged again into the bright light of the legislative day.

If a committee eventually did decide to vote out a bill—to present it
for formal consideration—the bill would appear on the Notice Calendar for "second reading" under The Orders of the Day. This was the
crucial floor hurdle where major debate took place. Every committee
assigned to a specific committee member each bill it "voted out," and
this reporter was responsible for guiding the bill through the rocks
and shoals of second-reading floor debate. It was up to the reporter to
explain the bill's contents, to answer questions from other senators,
and to defend the bill against any and all assaults from a potentially
hostile environment. Second reading could be a shoo-in, with no debate to speak of, or could involve long and heated discussion. Brief
or lengthy, the debates were always concluded by a formal vote, which
would either kill the bill, or stall it, or send it on its happy way to
"third reading."

Once past the rigors of second reading, a bill went through an iden-
tical, though less demanding, third reading the following legislative
day, when its safe passage was usually automatic—unless, of course,
it was a particularly controversial measure. After a successful third
reading the bill left the Senate, going either to the Governor for
signature into law (if it had originated in the House, and not been
amended in the Senate), or over to the House to do further battle with
more fish ladders (if it had originated in the Senate, or been amended
in the Senate).

It was a tough uphill fight all the way; deliberately so, because the
creation of statutory law is a weighty business. Each step represented
a checkpoint where the legislature could evaluate what it was attempting to accomplish, before deciding whether to move ahead. And
because there were so many checkpoints, a negative bias was built into
legislative deliberations: it was a lot easier to kill a bill than to get it
passed. This fact can grant a questionable advantage to the forces of
the status quo, but it also reflects the cumulative experience built into
the Anglo-American political process over the course of many cen-
turies. James Madison summarized the problem quite concisely in
"Federalist Paper 51":

If men were angels, no government would be necessary . . . In framing a government which is to be administered by men over men, the great difficulty lies in this: you must first enable the government to control the governed; and in the next place oblige it to control itself.

The elaborate system of legislative rules was an internal-control mechanism designed to ensure that, if a bill finally became law, its enactment did not take place in a casual or haphazard fashion. In many respects, therefore, the spawning-fish analogy is pretty accurate. Although some junk bills occasionally managed to get through, it basically was a survival-of-the-fittest process of legislative selection. As a result, any issue could be subjected to the most intense and minute scrutiny under the light of the rules which governed legislative deliberations.

4. Social Norms

The last, and very important, ingredient that held the legislature together was the internal set of informal social norms that guided members' behavior. This is a tricky subject, because any legislative body is a partial reflection of the larger society it is elected to represent. Yet despite this fact, a legislature, once convened, also is inclined to become a miniature world unto itself. It is characterized by certain internal patterns of behavior that have a socializing influence on most of its members. Occasionally an individual legislator would wander off to declare war on the system through independent appeals to the press and other news media, but, by and large, such wayward action was rare. Most legislators leaned instinctively towards working as a team, developing some basic sense of legislative loyalty in the process.

In describing the United States Senate, political scientist Donald Matthews observed a number of "folkways"—standards of proper behavior—which also were very evident in the Vermont Senate. These folkways encompassed such considerations as courtesy (don't try to make your opponent look too bad) ; apprenticeship (don't speak too often, too soon) ; commitment (respect for hard work over grandstanding) ; specialization (concentration on key areas of committee expertise); reciprocity (helping each other achieve common objectives) ; and institutional patriotism (a loyalty to the traditions of the Senate, and acceptance of its elaborate system of rules) .

After observing the Vermont legislature in action, I would suggest that the process goes beyond Matthews's folkways. In terms of internal communication, for example, the legislature operated in a very interesting fashion. The role of rumor was quite important, and the role of perceptions was tremendously important. After weeks, or months, or even years of inaction, a "feeling" would suddenly develop that the time was ripe for a particular bill to pass. This feeling was fed into the grapevine of the legislative rumor-mill. Whereupon the bill would begin to build up momentum, which developed into a self-generating force as the gates were opened to let it through relatively unmolested. Conversely, some other bills would remain mired down by a belief that "they don't have a chance." It was extremely difficult, if not impossible, to make any progress at all on such bills: any built-in thrust they might have possessed was inactivated by this type of negative reaction.

In sum, the legislature, despite its links with the public, tended to become something of a closed world that generated its own sense of internal dynamics or inertia, depending on its own perceptions of an issue at hand. In this respect, the Vermont Senate was "just like living in a small town."

This, then, was the arena which the academic neophyte-senator from Norwich, Vermont, prepared to enter following his smashing election victory in November 1972. It's time to pick up the thread of his story, which begins to become more fragmented and disjointed as he settles into his job at the State Capitol in Montpelier. . . .

CHAPTER

7

★ ★ ★ ★

Initiation Rites

In the beginning was the Word . . .
John I : 1

As a FRESHMAN, I followed the prevailing norms of the Senate and managed to remain relatively silent during the first month of floor deliberations. It wasn't until Friday, February 2, that I first spoke at length on the floor of the Senate. I was reporting a bill, *S.59*, for the Health and Welfare Committee. The measure was designed to liberalize the Sunday hours of sale for beer and wine. I almost blew it because I thought I was home free after second reading, and I dropped my guard completely in a burst of overexuberant self-confidence before third reading took place.

Under Vermont regulations, grocery stores were permitted to sell wines and beer from six A.M. to ten P.M. on Mondays through Saturdays. However, the old Sunday "blue laws" prohibited the sale of "malt and vinous beverages" before twelve noon on Sundays, presumably in order to avoid any potential temptation during the time of church services.

Since I felt this was a pretty silly prohibition, I had no difficulty supporting S. *59*, which permitted grocery stores to begin the sale of beer and wine at eight o'clock Sunday morning. Although I would probably be in the Norwich Episcopal church listening to one of Charlie Miller's sermons, I couldn't see any point in restricting others from buying a six-pack at Dan & Whit's General Store if they wanted to do so. In effect, I didn't want to impose my morality on others through the old busybody blue laws.

Well, it was hardly a momentous matter of state, but I suspected it would be controversial on the floor when the Health and Welfare Committee split, 4 to 2, before deciding to report the bill favorably. It was the type of issue which cut completely across party lines to embrace two quite divergent lifestyles: the traditionalists who were opposed to changes in the old way of doing things, and the more moderate innovators who were willing to relax some of the more restrictive statutes they felt were outdated.

I reported the bill for second reading on Friday morning, and was amazed and delighted when it passed on a simple voice vote. There was considerable moralizing, pro and con, during a fairly lively floor debate, but the bill eventually passed and was placed on the Notice Calendar for third reading the following Tuesday.

Apparently, though, some senators had second thoughts during the weekend recess, because a heated floor debate busted out all over again when the bill came up for third reading on Tuesday morning. Although in retrospect I can hardly believe it, I wasn't even on the floor at the time. Instead, I was downstairs in the Natural Resources Committee room, casually chewing the fat with some reporters about a proposed recycling bill. And all hell broke loose.

Boom! The Senate doorkeeper burst into the room and signaled to me. "Frank, upstairs quick! Your bill is in trouble!"

I was momentarily puzzled. My bill? What bill? Oh yes, S. 59—but that was Senator Orzel's bill; he was the sponsor. Then it hit me full force: *I* was the reporter. It was my bill to love and to cherish 'til death us did part, at least as far as its fate was concerned on the floor of the Senate.

I rushed upstairs two at a time and gasped into the Chamber just in time to hear Senator Gerald Morse, a retired poultry farmer from Caledonia County, intone: "Mr. President, after discussing this bill with many of my constituents over the weekend, I am convinced that this legislation is not in the best interests of the citizens of Caledonia County, nor do I feel it is beneficial to the people of Vermont. Therefore, I request a roll-call when the vote is taken on this matter."

Dammit! A roll-call vote. Obviously intended to separate the men from the boys.

There are three ways the Senate can vote on any issue: a simple voice vote, when anyone can hide behind the anonymity of a mass oral expression of Yeas or Nays; a division, when the senators stand to be counted, but no official record is kept of individual votes; and that most deadly device of all, a roll-call, which can be requested by any senator at any time on any issue. When this last option is used, an official record is kept of each senator's vote, and the next day said record is printed in the Senate *Journal* for all posterity to see forever and ever, amen.

Because of their enduring quality, roll-call votes can be exciting and dramatic. Their obvious tactical significance lies in the fact that they are designed to make any hesitant members crystallize their wavering views into a single Yea or Nay response.

As an academic, I was always fascinated by a roll-call. No matter how complex the issue, no matter how much you know, or often don't know, the ultimate choice always boils down to a simple affirmation or rejection of the issue at hand. A roll-call can be very rough. It's the moment of truth. There is no place to hide, no luxury of equivocation or vacillation. Every perplexity, ambiguity and uncertainty must be frozen into one of two words: Yes, or No. I often wondered if Plato really expected his philosopher-kings to respond to every single roll-call vote.

Fortunately I didn't have any intellectual doubts about this particular issue. As soon as Gerald Morse sat down, all eyes turned to me. As the reporter of the bill I felt obligated to make some response. I had already tried to explore every conceivable nook and cranny of the measure during the previous Friday's debate, so I decided to give my argument a light touch. Rising to my feet, I explained that this modest bill was merely designed to eliminate a burdensome inconvenience on both the general public and the grocers, particularly the small grocers—"Mom and Pop" stores, the little guys—who dutifully opened their doors on Sunday mornings to sell newspapers, but were prohibited by law from dispensing even a can of beer to a fine young Vermont family who wanted to enjoy a picnic in the sun. Quite frankly, I doubted if my idyllic picture of a family outing in the sun would change any floor votes (especially since it was a freezing February day outside) ; and my doubts were confirmed immediately when

Senator Fred Westphal, the conservative kingpin of Lamoille County, greeted my remarks with a loud guffaw of disbelief.

My spiel completed, there was nothing more to be said. The battle lines were drawn with Fred Westphal's guffaw. The issue was clear cut. The sovereign State of Vermont was about to decide whether its citizenry could purchase beer and wine in grocery stores on Sunday mornings.

Jack Burgess instructed the Senate secretary to call the roll to determine whether the bill should have its third reading.

"Senator Alden."

"Yes."

"Senator Bedford."

"Yes."

"Senator Bloomer."

"No."

"Senator Boylan."

"No."

"Senator Brannon."

"No."

(Whew! This was going to be close. I was twenty-fourth in the alphabetical order of a roll-call, and on many occasions issues already had been decided by the time I had a chance to vote. But this was going to be tough: 5 votes recorded, and the bill was already on the short end of a 3-to-2 count.)

"Senator Buckley."

"Yes."

"Senator Cooley."

"Yes."

"Senator Crowley."

"Yes."

"Senator Daniels."

"Yes."

(All right already. All four of these fellows were members of the younger generation; the fifty-and-under gang. My fears were obviously premature. This was going to be a breeze after all.)

The secretary continued to read the roll in a steady, metronomic tone:

"Senator Doyle."

"No."

(Ouch! What's happened to my old pal Bill?)

"Senator Gannett."

"Yes."

"Senator Gibb."

"Yes."

"Senator Harwood."

"No."

"Senator Janeway."

"Yes."

"Senator Jones."

"Absent."

(I looked at the back of the old envelope where I was keeping a crisscross tally. Fifteen votes counted; half the Senate: 9 in favor, 5 opposed, 1 absent. Very good. Ho, ho, ho, Henry Higgins. My very first bill and all is well. Power corrupts and absolute power corrupts absolutely.)

It was at this point that the erosion began to take place.

"Senator Morse."

"No."

"Senator Newell."

"No."

"Senator Niquette."

"Yes."

"Senator O'Brien."

"No."

"Senator Ogden."

"No."

(I looked down again at my tally: what's going on?—10 Yeas, 9 Nays, 1 absent. An all-too-apparent drift was well under way. Something's wrong. Maybe I wasn't home free after all. Why the hell hadn't I been on the floor during the debate that preceded third reading?)

"Senator Orzel."

"Yes."

"Senator Partridge."

"No."

"Senator Purdy."

"No."

(Good God, it's really getting tight! All tied up—11 to 11 with only 7 of us left to vote, including Fred Westphal, who has already laughed his opposition loud and clear. The very first bill I report on the floor and I'm going to blow it. What a way to go—my fledgling legislative career awash in a tumultuous sea of beer suds and vinous beverages. Why didn't I try to line up votes ahead of time? How could I have been stupid enough to miss the third-reading floor debate? Why did I make that silly comment about the family picnic in the sun? I must have lost five votes right there, since nobody wanted to hear a fancypants Harvard Ph.D. make light of Vermont's hallowed blue laws. What a disastrous way to report a bill. Where was I going to get 15 votes?)

"Senator Shea."

"Yes."

(Number 12)

"Senator Smallwood."

"Yes."

(Number 13)

"Senator Donald Smith."

"Yes."

(Whew! Number 14, only one to go. Good old Fred Smith will put it over the top. The only Republican from Chittenden County, an enlightened, innovative, progressive banker. Way to go, Fred! The fate of humanity is about to be placed in your capable hands.)

"Senator Frederick Smith."

"No."

(What! I could hardly believe it. The God of Mammon must be dead as a doornail if the president of Burlington Savings Bank can't even support a timid extension of the free enterprise system on Sunday mornings. Now it's all up to Fred Westphal, plus the two remaining Democrats—Esther Sorrell and Richard Soule. Since Senator Westphal is obviously against this one, I hope at least one of the Democrats is a beer-drinker; after all, it's the party of the working man.)

"Senator Sorrell."

"Yes."

(I gazed up at the Senate balcony. Enter G. Handel with large choral assembly: *Hal-leluja; Hal-lelujah; Hallelujah-Hallelujah; Hal-le-lu-jah!* I looked admiringly at Esther Sorrell during the height of the oratorio. A woman of real integrity. The precious fifteenth vote. Home free at last. I sighed in relief as the choral anthem faded from the balcony.)

"Senator Soule."

"Yes."

(Good for Dick, too! Another statesman. One vote to spare.)

"Senator Westphal."

"No!"

(Very loud and clear, as predicted.)

The Senate secretary handed the checklist up to the dais, and Jack Burgess scanned it before nodding over the podium to me.

"Listen to the results of your vote. Those voting Yea: 16. Those voting Nay: 13. The bill has been read for the third time. The clerk will now proceed with The Orders of the Day."

The bill made it, but I never forgot the lesson: Don't take anything for granted on the floor of the Senate.

Despite my near disastrous initial encounter with the anti-Sunday-morning-beer league, I grew to love reporting bills, mainly because this particular facet of the legislative process had all the dramatic intensity of teaching. Each bill I reported represented a unique and exciting challenge as I attempted to strip it down to its basics with three criteria in mind: brevity, clarity, and precision. I really worked very hard at reporting bills, checking relevant statutory references, reviewing committee testimony, and, before floor debate, actually interrogating myself for hours on every conceivable question I could imagine would be asked.

In due time my efforts paid off. Except for one hopeless case where I agreed to serve knowingly as a sacrificial lamb for the Natural Resources Committee, I never lost a bill I reported on the floor. By the second year of the session, members of the House would come over to ask me if I would report their bills in the Senate. I always tried to do so if the bill was in one of my committees—but only after initially asking one haunted question: "O.K., I'll try to report your bill, but first tell me, do you drink beer on Sunday mornings?"

"Good Lord, no," was always the reply. "What's Sunday-morning beer got to do with reporting bills?"

"Everything," I would answer. "That, my friend, is precisely the issue which taught me never to take anything for granted when reporting a bill on the floor of the Senate."

¶THE FLOOR reports on different bills produced triumphs and tragedies, pathos and humor. Individual senators used quite different styles in presenting bills for second reading, and nowhere were the contrasting styles more apparent than in the reports of Senator Gannett of Windham County and Senator O'Brien of Chittenden County.

Robert Gannett, a fifty-five-year-old Republican from Brattleboro, down by the Massachusetts border, was a lawyer (Harvard 1942) who had a meticulous eye for detail coupled with an uncanny ability to unravel the most complicated bills so they would be understandable to the rest of us. He had served in the Vermont House for four terms in the 1950's and then retired from the political arena until 1972, when he was elected to the state Senate. His reporting style was deceptively simple. Speaking always in a quiet, thoughtful voice, he always knew what he was speaking about. I enjoyed his reports so much that I reached an informal gentlemen's agreement with him that I would interrogate him at least once on any bill he reported to see if I could trip him up. Most of his bills came out of the Finance Committee, and he knew so much more about tax law than I did, that it was impossible for me to catch him on anything at all. However, my chance finally came in early March, when, for the General and Military Committee he reported out *S. 13,* which called for state licensing of radio and television repairmen.

(Incidentally, the assignment of bills to committee was never entirely clear to me. They were made by Lieutenant Governor Burgess with the advice of Robert Gibson, the Senate secretary. Most bill assignments were reasonably clear cut, but some of the more marginal ones mystified me. Virtually all licensing bills went to the Health and Welfare Committee, but this particular one had ended up in General and Military.)

At any rate, when *S. 13* was called up for second reading, Bob Gannett rose to his feet to explain the background of the bill in an informed, but hardly exhaustive, fashion. It was pretty obvious that he didn't think licensing TV repairmen was the major problem facing the State of Vermont, and I moved in to see if for once I could back him into a corner.

As soon as he finished his report I rose to ask the chair for permission to interrogate the Senator from Windham County, and my request was quickly granted.

"Senator, I have been extremely interested in your exposé of licensing television repairmen. However, it seems to me that you ignored a major consideration in your report: namely, why do we need this bill at all?"

Gannett smiled and inclined his head courteously in my direction. "Well, Senator," he replied in his calm, unperturbed voice, "we received a considerable amount of testimony from television repairmen throughout the state on this bill, and it is my understanding that a television set can be very dangerous if it is not treated with utmost care. Indeed, we were told that a person could be electrocuted trying to take apart a color television set if he didn't know what he was doing."

"Electrocuted! Bob, did you say electrocuted? How much voltage does a color television carry?"

"Well, I'm not sure of the precise amounts involved, but if the Senator from Windsor County cares to take off the back of his set and place his hand inside, I'm sure he could find out the answer."

Senator Westphal let out a huge laugh before turning around and whispering to me out of the corner of his mouth, "You professors are all crazy. Sit down for God's sakes, before you make a complete jackass out of yourself."

I smiled back at Bob Gannett, and tipped my hand in a gesture of surrender. I obviously wasn't going to trip him up on this one. And indeed I experienced no real success in ever really catching him off guard during two years of interrogatory thrusts. He was simply too damn good as a floor reporter.

There was, however, an interesting sidelight to this particular exchange, and it came after we had adjourned for the morning. Senate President Jack Burgess came over to me after the session, put his arms around my shoulder, and said, "Frank, I was interested in your interrogation this morning, but I picked up something that was rather disturbing and I thought I ought to talk with you about it."

His comment threw me for a loss, and I was completely nonplussed. "Fine, Jack; fire away. What was the problem?"

Jack paused and then looked me in the eye. "Frank, during the formal floor discussion you referred to Senator Gannett as 'Bob.' I'm sorry, but I'm afraid we never use first names during formal floor discussions in the Senate."

I was really stunned. "Gee, I'm sorry, Jack. It must have been a slip-up that emerged during the heat of our fiery interchange. I'll certainly try to do better in the future."

"That's fine, Frank. Nothing too important. Don't get worried. You're doing a very good job. I simply wanted you to know that we never use first names during formal floor deliberations." Jack nodded firmly before walking out of the Senate Chamber.

It wasn't too much later that Jack Burgess got his own comeuppance in a floor debate, and the instigator was none other than seventy-five-year-old Jack O'Brien, the small, wiry, unpredictable Democratic Minority leader.

Because Senator O'Brien lived in populous South Burlington, an environment that offered little opportunity to hunt or fish, a perverse tradition had grown up that he should report all the fish-and-game bills for the Natural Resources Committee. On the particular occasion when he was reporting a bill that established a limited season for wild turkeys in southern Vermont, he concluded with an unexpected burst of enthusiasm:

"To tell the truth, I'm in favor of this bill, although I've never even seen one of these wild turkeys." His voice rose to a crescendo. "They live in southern Vermont, down around the Pawlet area, where they are some kind of a national state bird. But I'm in favor of this bill. Yes, indeed, I strongly favor this bill, even though I've never seen one of these turkeys because they don't fly around very much in the South Burlington area; nope, they don't fly around in the South Burlington area at all."

As soon as he sat down, Jack Burgess made a good-natured crack from the dais. "If the senior Senator from Chittenden County really wishes to see a wild turkey, he can do so tomorrow morning when he is shaving."

There was a momentary silence before the Senate erupted into laughter. But Jack O'Brien ended with the last word. He jumped quickly to his feet, waved his finger at the chair with a mischievous smile and declared, "Mr. President. The rooster is calling the kettle black. *I* don't drink at all!"

The Lieutenant Governor retreated by announcing a five-minute recess to restore order and decorum to the Senate Chamber. The Senate could always use a brief recess after Jack O'Brien had finished reporting a fish-and-game bill.

Not all floor discussions were in light vein, and some led to long interrogations and formal speeches.

I hardly ever delivered formal speeches, although once in a great while, if I felt particularly strongly about an issue, I would make a statement which I prepared ahead of time and distributed in written form. In such rare cases I followed the same procedure I used in reporting bills, trying to keep my comments brief and to the point.

The first written speech I delivered was in late February when I supported the ratification of the Equal Rights Amendment to the United States Constitution, an issue which passed the Senate by a 19-to-8 vote after some very impassioned debate. I also issued some written statements on a Senate reapportionment bill which Bill Doyle had slaved over, and in favor of a "right-to-know" (public access to government meetings) bill sponsored by John Alden.

The most time I ever spent preparing a written floor speech was in opposition to the restoration of the death penalty in Vermont. I felt very strongly about this, so I studied the *Furman v. Georgia* case and

other precedents for ammunition to convince my colleagues that such
a measure would be an unwise and undesirable step backwards. Despite my plea, the Senate passed the death penalty 18 to 12. However,
it was only one section of an omnibus criminal-code revision bill that
was killed in a later vote, so the death penalty did not become law
during Vermont's 1973–74 legislative sessions.

Even though I failed, I felt pretty good about this particular speech
because three different senators came up to me and said my remarks
had convinced them to vote against the death penalty. This sort of
thing was very rare; I was never convinced that many votes were actually changed during floor debate. Senator Esther Sorrell, my good
Democratic friend from Burlington, also requested that my written
remarks be placed in the Senate *Journal,* the official record of the
Senate proceedings, an honor I much appreciated.

On the whole, however, written speeches were not delivered very
often on the floor. Rather, we used spontaneous comments to spar with
each other in an effort to present our points of view. Sometimes the
interrogations got a little rough. Senator Garry Buckley of Bennington
County, the chairman of Judiciary, could be very intimidating when
he boomed out his questions, but the decorum of the Senate was such
that none of us ever got too violent during debates.

This floor restraint was as much a part of the "social system" of
the Senate as the leadership structure and other more formal rules.
Over time, we came to know each others' strengths and weaknesses
pretty well. Some senators were wizards with parliamentary procedures; such an expert was the veteran legislator Graham Newell, the
Lyndon State College professor from Caledonia County. Others were
tremendously hard committee workers, typified by Senator John
Boylan, who slaved over the Appropriations' bills mornings, noons
and nights. Still others helped to keep the floor proceedings moving—
particularly President Pro Tem Ed Janeway, who commanded tremendous respect from both the Republicans and Democrats, and Jack
Burgess, who used his quick humor to cool off overheated debates. In
addition, the various committees came to rely on key members to
report particularly tough bills. Bob Gannett, as I have indicated;
Democrat Dick Soule of Franklin County, who did yeoman's service

on education bills; and another Democrat, Bob Brannon, a farmer from Franklin County, who reported out many bills for the Agriculture Committee in his deep bass voice, to name only a few.

Interestingly enough, there seemed to be a variation on one of Parkinson's Laws which governed the length of floor debates: namely, the more complicated the bill, the shorter the debate, and the less complicated a bill, the longer the debate. If a complex bill was well presented, we would usually avoid much detailed questioning. But take a smaller issue, like the Sunday-morning sale of beer and wine, and we could really be off to the races.

One time Herb Ogden reported a bill that exempted bees—that's right, bees—from the business-inventory tax. Everyone was so flabbergasted by bees being covered under the inventory tax that the entire Senate began to buzz around. It was pretty wild. People wanted to know how many beekeepers there were in Vermont, and how it was possible to assess a bee for tax purposes. Herb Ogden had a lot of fun with this one, especially at the end of the debate when Garry Buckley rose to his feet to inquire, "Tell me, Senator, precisely what does a beekeeper in Vermont actually do?"

After a momentary pause, Herb replied quietly, "Well, occasionally he gets stung."

Without any further questions, the Senate voted unanimously to exempt bees from the business-inventory tax.

The daily sessions in the Senate Chamber could be lengthy or abbreviated depending on the size of the calendar. During January and February we held fairly short floor meetings because much of the major legislation, which originated in the House, was still working its way over to the Senate. As the winter months wore on, however, the load grew heavier. By late March and early April we were meeting in the evening in an effort to keep up with the frantic rush before adjournment.

In order to be really effective on the floor, it was necessary to know the procedures and rules inside-out (a subject I was never able to master fully); to do your homework, and speak out with clarity and precision (one of my stronger points); to respect the decorum and traditions inherent in the Senate's "social system" (I was O.K. here) ; and, above all, to be decisive in the face of complexity and uncertainty (which was often tough for me). The floor of the Senate was no place for hesitation or indecision. Very often you had to tough it out, even when you weren't sure in your own mind, since, in the end, every floor deliberation eventually boiled down to a simple yes-or-no decision (no "maybes" were allowed).

The formal sessions in the Senate Chamber were the most visible part of our operations, with the press in attendance and the galleries often filled when we were considering some major item—not bees or Sunday beer sales, but big environmental issues or "law-and-order" bills. The most majestic floor sessions of all were the joint meetings, which were held in the House Chamber to hear Governor Salmon deliver his budget message; or to honor a special dignitary like United States Senator George Aiken, who spoke to both houses shortly after he announced his retirement upon completion of more than forty years of public service.

Despite the excitement and dramatics, however, the floor sessions were actually the culmination of a long, arduous process. An issue never even reached the floor unless the groundwork had already been laid by means of a complex web of previous interactions: committee meetings, public hearings, hallway conversations, party caucuses, discussions at breakfast, lunch and dinner with other legislators.

These interactions constituted the heart of the legislative process. The formal doings on the Senate floor were the frosting on the cake; elegant and refined, sweet or bitter depending on your point of view, they were the finishing touch. You had to look beneath this surface to understand the real work that went into the making of the laws of the state.

8

Natural Resources:
The Search for the Public Interest

The Senate always gets the bill after the
House . . . We're the court of last resort.
Quoted by Richard F. Fenno, Jr.
Congressmen in Committees

EVERY LEGISLATIVE MORNING at 8:30 sharp, the six members of the
Senate Natural Resources Committee gathered together in Room 8
on the first floor of the State House to rub the sleep out of their eyes.
We tried to complete the day's agenda before the 9:30 floor sessions,
but we usually had to re-assemble later in the morning to hear additional witnesses, and wrap up unfinished business.

Arthur Jones, the senior senator from Orleans-Essex counties, served
as committee chairman. Arthur, a fifty-nine-year-old Republican, was
from the tiny town of Morgan on Lake Seymour in northern Vermont
up near the Canadian border. An electrical engineer with a degree
from Princeon, he had been a colonel in the Second World War,
serving on the First Army Headquarters staff under General Omar
Bradley, where he played a key role planning the field communications
system for the invasion of Normandy, before participating in the
sweep across France. He often reminisced with me about his uniquely
intense wartime experiences, which were still sharply etched in his
memory almost a quarter of a century later. After the war Arthur
worked in the communications industry, eventually ending up as a
vice president of a large industrial conglomerate in New York City,
before migrating north to Lake Seymour where he had gone to summer camp as a youngster. He was a very fine committee chairman

who knew his way around, having served in the Senate since 1967. Also, he asked me to handle a lot of key committee bills, which was work I really appreciated because I was only a rookie senator in my freshman year.

In addition to Arthur and me, there were three other Republicans on the committee, plus one Democrat. The Republicans were Ed Janeway, the courtly Senate President Pro Tempore, who served as our committee vice chairman; Arthur Gibb, a sixty-four-year-old former banker and investment counsel who was an Angus cattle breeder from Weybridge; and Fred Smith, the fifty-seven-year-old president of the Burlington Savings Bank, a fellow Republican freshman like me, and a close friend despite the fact that he had almost cast the crucial floor vote against the first bill I had reported, on the Sunday sale of beer and wine.

The sole Democrat on the committee was the seventy-five-year-old Senate Minority leader, Jack O'Brien, our resident fish-and-game expert from the city of South Burlington. A mercurial Irishman with wispy white hair and a lively twinkle in his eyes, he was a curmudgeon, a real character who had been educated in the hard knocks school of life. Since the rest of us had attended Princeton, Yale, Harvard or Dartmouth, he used to complain that the Natural Resources Committee consisted of "five Ivy Leaguers, plus me." After I sided with him on a couple of bills, he modified his description of the committee to encompass "four rich guys, plus Frank and me."

Jack, a very down-to-earth and opinionated individualist who complained constantly about "environmental nuts" and "bureaucrats on executive welfare," helped the rest of us keep our feet on the ground rather than getting carried too far aloft on idyllic flights of ecological fancy. A fiery practical pol, he would continuously rant and rail, "This is a lousy bill; who in God's name ever thought this one up? The people of South Burlington will never buy this kooky idea; etc., etc." I had a terrible time trying to get him to support a statewide recycling bill because he adamantly insisted, "I'm very sorry, Frank, but the answer is No because I won't vote for any bill that tries to tell the people of South Burlington how they're going to separate their garbage."

At Art Jones's request, I served as clerk of the committee, a job that turned out to be pretty time-consuming. I had to keep minutes of our meetings, plus file all our bills and Resolutions. Although we could call on the staff of the Legislative Council, it consisted only of a secretarial pool, plus four legislative draftsmen who were responsible for serving all one hundred eighty members of the House and Senate; the Senate had a Secretary and Assistant Secretary, plus a three-member office pool and two doorkeepers. Since it was impossible for them to cover everything, the committee clerks had to pick up a lot of the slack.

Many of our key bills originated in the House, which meant we had to wait out the early part of the session. Then, just before final adjournment, the House would pull the plug. Boom! We would be deluged with bills, and crowds of lobbyists who would pour into our little committee room to push for some special amendment or revision they favored. The lobbying often became very intense, because we ranged across a staggering assortment of legislation during the 1973–74 sessions: bans on phosphates, nonbiodegradable plastic jugs, and nonreturnable bottles and cans; regulations of outdoor signs and advertising; licensing of snowmobiles and motorboats; state land-acquisition planning; fish-and-game bills; regulation of automobile junkyards; state soil surveys; local zoning-enabling acts; shoreland and flood-plain zoning; regulation of surface mining of copper; oil spills on Lake Champlain; mobile-home parks, designation of Class "A" waters; nuclear power-plant siting; termination of camp leases at Groton State Park; control of porcupine population in state forests; emergency energy powers for the Governor; the state Land Capability and Development Plan, and the state Land-Use Plan, to name some of the bills that crowded our agenda.

Believe it or not, we even considered a bill to permit barber poles to turn in Vermont. It was an act of legislative oversight, an attempt to control the bureaucracy. Art Jones and I sponsored it after we were astonished to discover that a state agency had issued a regulation that prohibited any barber poles from turning under an earlier law designed to eliminate gaudy flashing signs; you know, blinking neon lights and that sort of thing. The earlier law was a scenic protection measure, but the bureaucracy had gone berserk, and used it to pro-

hibit barber poles from turning. That wasn't the intention of the
legislature at all, so Art and I put in a new bill to get the barber poles
moving again throughout the state.

When we met to discuss the issue early one morning, four representatives of the state regulatory agency showed up to argue against our bill
on the grounds that it would set a dangerous precedent. It turned
out to be a rather incredible get-together. Jack O'Brien wandered into
the committee a little late. After looking somewhat skeptically at our
four agency visitors, he turned to me and asked abruptly: "Hi, Frank.
Who are these guys?"

"Good morning, Jack," I replied. "They are representatives of the
agency that regulates signs in Vermont."

"Regulates signs. I didn't know we regulated signs. What bill are
we talking about this morning?"

Jack seemed a little testy. I was afraid he might fly off the handle
unless we treated him with care, so I looked over at Art Jones, who
picked up the conversation.

"It's *S. 168*, Jack," Arthur replied casually, knocking the ash from
his thin cigar into an empty wastebasket by the table. "It's a bill Frank
and I sponsored to permit barber poles to turn in Vermont."

"Barber poles? You must be kidding. Stop pulling my leg. Who are
these guys anyway?"

There was an embarrassing silence as the chairman of the agency
delegation covered his mouth with his hand and produced an abbreviated cough. I was fighting to keep a straight face, not quite sure
whether I should laugh or cry. Ed Janeway, Art Gibb and Fred Smith
looked at each other cautiously, obviously fearful that Jack might ex-
plode completely if we dug into this matter more deeply. Finally, the
chairman of the delegation looked at Jack and said, "You see, Senator,
we're really very worried about setting a most dangerous precedent
here."

Jack didn't wait to hear the complete explanation. He simply
circled around in his tracks and wandered back out of the room without even sitting down.

"Barber poles," I could hear him mutter as he reached the door.
"My God, what will they think of next?"

Later that morning, after the floor session, Jack came over to my desk in the Senate Chamber.

"Frank, I want you to level with me." He looked me straight in the eye. "Those four guys this morning, were they really trying to run the barber poles in Vermont?"

"It's even worse than that, Jack," I told him. "They won't let them turn. They say it's a dangerous precedent."

He shook his head. "How many barber poles do you think we have in Vermont?"

"Well, I'm not sure. Maybe a couple of dozen."

"There you have it! You see what I mean? Four bureaucrats trying to run two dozen barber poles. What's that come out to? Let's see. Six barber poles apiece. That's it! Each one of those guys regulates six barber poles. I told you they don't do nothing. They're all on executive welfare. Bureaucrats on executive welfare. Plain and simple. Good Lord, I wish we could get them under control. Hey, wait a minute"—his eyes lit up—"why don't we try that thing, that word you use in the committee all the time, to control the executive welfare?"

"Word, Jack?" I said. "I don't remember any word about executive welfare. You're the guy who thinks up these terms, not me."

"No, no, no," he came back at me, "you said the professors have a word for it. I remember now. It sounded like some kind of clothes: overcoats, or overalls, or overshoes. Something like that."

I was really baffled by this latest twist in Jack's thinking. What was he talking about—overcoats? overalls? overshoes? Then a light flashed on. "Oh, yes, now I remember. You must be referring to oversight—legislative oversight. I said we need to exercise more legislative oversight over the bureaucracy."

"That's it. Oversight. Don't that mean controlling the executive welfare?"

"Well, maybe, in a way." I hesitated before deciding to continue. "You see, Jack, the legislature plays a number of different roles. One is policy formulation, you know, passing laws. We do that all the time. Another function is policy and program control. This involves legislative oversight and review of agency programs to determine who's

doing what, and how well are they carrying out the policies we enacted into law. I don't think we do enough of this around here."

"By God, I agree with you. I think you're right," he said, pounding
my desk. "But to tell the truth, I'm afraid it won't work because we're
outgunned. There's too many of them and too few of us. How can
180 legislators keep up with 9,000 state employees? We're really outgunned. Also, we're only part-time. Once we go home in April, all
hell breaks loose around here. That's how you end up with four guys
running six barber poles apiece." He paused and shrugged. "Oh,
forget it. What's the use? It would never work. Come on, let's get
some lunch."

All the way out of the room he kept mumbling, "Six barber poles
apiece. Legislative oversight. No, I'm afraid it would never work."

He turned out to be right. The agency representatives kept promis-
ing to deliver additional information on the barber pole situation, but
it didn't materialize, and the entire issue was finally dropped in the
last minute confusion surrounding adjournment. Jack was dead on
target. Barber poles; legislative oversight. My God, what will they
think of next?

¶ THE TWO biggest issues the Natural Resources Committee handled
in the 1973–74 sessions were the Capability and Development Plan
and the so-called "bottle ban." The plan was mandated by Act 250,
Vermont's pioneering environmental law which had been passed in
1970. This act set up a regulatory permit system to control the quality
of large-scale developments in Vermont, particularly vacation-home
developments and condominiums. When the act was passed, it called
for a plan that would set forth guidelines and criteria which described the capability of Vermont land to absorb future development.
This, in turn, was to serve as the basis for a subsequent State Land-Use
Plan and Map which would specify where development could, and
could not, take place.

During the 1973 session there was a major battle over the capability
plan in the House, where it was subjected to so many confusing floor
amendments that it was pretty well hacked up by the time it reached

us. As a result, Art Jones asked Art Gibb and me to see if we could try to work the plan back into shape. The problem was to find a workable balance between those groups who wanted very strict criteria to control future development, and those who were opposed to any state planning at all and wanted very loose criteria. Since both groups were very large and vocal, it was an enormous job trying to reconcile these differing viewpoints. Art Gibb and I slaved like dogs, driving to Montpelier early to work all through Mondays, before the regular Tuesday morning sessions. We were joined by Jonathan Brownell, a Montpelier lawyer. The three of us made a pretty good team. Art had been chairman of the special committee that had originally drafted Vermont's Act 250, so he knew the legislative history of the state planning effort inside-out. I was chairman of the planning and regional studies program at Dartmouth (on sabbatical leave, fortunately) so I offered a more academic outlook. Jonathan provided the legal expertise necessary to translate our ideas into the language of statutory law.

We reworked the House version of the plan all during the month of March, finally compromising on a formula where the state would severely limit development in a series of critical areas (*e.g.*, high elevations, fragile ecological locales, primary agricultural soils, headwaters), but flexibility was provided to enable local and regional planning commissions to permit reasonable development in the noncritical areas of the state. By the beginning of April we had the plan ready for review by other concerned Senate committees. The revised plan passed the Senate just before our mid-April adjournment. Since our amendments were accepted by the House, it constituted one of the major legislative achievements of the 1973 session.

The battle erupted all over again when the legislature considered the final requirement under Act 250, the state Land-Use Plan and Map, during the 1974 session. This time the plan went down the drain. The responsible state agencies made a decision to present a series of detailed county maps which weren't available until halfway through the legislative session. Instead of mapping just the critical areas we had designated under the Capability Plan, the proposed maps attempted to set up "population density criteria" for every single acre of land in the state. As soon as people saw some of their own land in a restricted-growth zone, they decided they didn't like the State Land-Use Plan at all. During my service in the Senate, I met a lot of people who favored planning (in theory), but who suddenly opposed the idea once they discovered that their house was in the middle of a zone of restricted development. When the proposed land-use maps were finally made public, there was flak all over the place. The House decided not to act on the land-use plan during the 1974 session, so it never got to the Senate. It was a wise decision, since we wouldn't have had enough time to review it carefully. The State Land-Use Plan and Map will have to be considered again as part of a future legislative agenda.

While the Capability and Development Plan had rough going, the "bottle ban" legislation was a real nightmare; without doubt it was the most emotionally volatile and snarled-up public policy issue I ever encountered, or ever want to encounter. It was also an issue which brought the really big lobbyists to Montpelier, the national representatives of the can and bottling industry, plus spokesmen for the United States Brewers Association and the like. But let me first back up and explain the reason for all this turmoil.

At the outset, it is important to understand that the "bottle ban" was not a ban on bottles at all. Instead, it was a container-deposit law that required a mandatory five-cent or ten-cent deposit charge on all soft drink and beer bottles and cans sold in Vermont stores, and applied to returnables and nonreturnables alike.

It was designed to achieve two purposes. First, by getting people to bring all their bottles and cans back to the grocery stores (to collect their deposits), it attempted to reduce roadside litter. The potential lure of collecting a deposit redemption on used bottles and cans was designed to keep people from tossing them out of their car windows, thus eliminating blight alongside the roads. Second, the law was designed to encourage the re-use of bottles. Although it didn't accomplish this directly (since many of the bottles were not made for re-use), it was hoped that the deposit system would put pressure on the bottling industry to move toward re-usables, rather than going through the inconvenience of picking up all their nonreturnable bottles and cans from the grocers simply to haul them off to the local dump.

The impetus for the legislation had come from Vermont's "Green-up Day," a statewide clean-up effort that had been launched in the late 1960's when groups of volunteers went out and picked up debris along the roadsides during the first weekend in May, after the winter snows had receded. Actually, however, the issue had originally arisen in the 1950's, when the Vermont Farm Bureau had pushed through a real ban on nonreturnable bottles (which had lasted for two years) because of the farmers' concern over their cows eating broken glass in pastures along the Vermont roadsides.

At the tail end of the 1972 session (which was before my time), the legislature had enacted a new container-deposit law, to go into effect fifteen months later, on July 1, 1973. Hence the 1973 winter session was subjected to prolonged and fiery debates over whether this new law should be repealed, amended, or left alone before it actually went into effect on July first. The Senate and House Natural Resources committees were the eye of this particular hurricane because we had jurisdiction over the issue.

The forces that lined up on both sides were numerous, ponderous, powerful, and intractable. It was like being encamped between two huge massed armies. Those in favor of the law were the environmentalists, the Farm Bureau, a variety of citizen public-interest groups, and most of the press, especially the Rutland *Herald,* which adopted a crusading zeal on this one. The big guns on the other side were a variety of powerful economic interests including the Vermont Retail Grocers' Association and various spokesmen for the bottle and can industry, plus organized labor. The grocers were worried that the extra deposit charges would lead to a loss of sales, and the bottling industry and the labor unions were concerned about the potential loss of jobs if the state moved towards re-usable bottles. It was a classic "economics versus environment" struggle which took on national implications since Oregon had already passed its own version of a "bottle-ban" law one year earlier. Although Vermont was a small state, with less than 1 percent of the national beer and soft-drink market, the large economic interests didn't want this particular virus to spread east from Oregon and infect New England. The reason was simple: It might influence adjacent states, such as New York and Massachusetts, to adopt bottle-ban legislation of their own. The bottling industry and labor interests felt that this could lead to economic catastrophe. As a result, we became a test case; the East Coast guinea pig. The big lobbyists moved up to sleepy little Montpelier from all over the country to stamp out this infection before it spread any further.

I was basically in favor of the objectives of the legislation (*e.g.*, cleaner roadsides, re-usable bottles). However, I had to deal with a very tough "representation" problem on this one. Since I was elected from a county that snuggled up against New Hampshire, I was concerned about the potential loss of sales that might take place in Vermont grocery stores along the Connecticut River border. In terms of public policy, Vermont and New Hampshire are two remarkably different states, like day and night. Whereas Vermont ranks close to the top in state and local taxation per capita, New Hampshire is the only state without a broad-based sales or income tax. In effect, Vermont is a very progressive state which attempts to attack almost every conceivable public-policy issue. New Hampshire is a very conservative state which does little, or nothing, about any public-policy issues.

This difference was important because Vermont already had a 3 percent sales tax, plus a business-inventory tax, which placed our border retailers at a real competitive disadvantage with their New Hampshire counterparts. Now we were about to add a substantial deposit charge to the price of soft drinks and beer, which constituted up to 40 percent of the sales volume of the small grocery stores. I was worried that we might simply drive this business across the border.

Also, the proposed law, which had been spliced together during the last minute rush of the 1972 session, was very poorly written. It didn't provide for any bottle collection centers or recycling capability. It merely encouraged the public to dump all their empty bottles and cans back into Vermont grocery stores, where they would have to be stacked and sorted before the bottlers collected them. Hence, the grocers became garbage men, and many of the smaller stores argued that they didn't have the space or manpower to handle all the empty bottles and cans that would be returned.

The reason for all this detail is to indicate that the job of a legislative representative in a democratic society is damned difficult. Many public policy issues are muddy, with no clear-cut black or white, right or wrong, answers. I had taught a lot of my classes at Dartmouth about different theories of representation—you know, Edmund Burke's classical 18th-century "statesman" model versus the more modern "constituency" theories. Well, believe me, all that was pretty academic. How do you weigh the value of clean roadsides against the plea of a small grocer who tells you he is going to be driven out of business if this law goes into effect? What is *the* "public interest" in such a situation? Like the Capability and Development Plan, it was probably somewhere in the middle. But, how and where do you find the middle ground? Such was our dilemma.

It was really a messy can of worms which became all the more hopeless because of the intransigent posture of the opposing armies. Before long both sides turned into "true believers," fanatical in their conviction that their cause was holy and just. The environmental-public interest–Farm Bureau–Rutland *Herald* coalition adopted an increasingly more adamant "clean up the litter" stance, while the grocer-labor-industry coalition countered with an increasingly more adamant "economic disaster" stance. As a result, the middle ground eroded completely. Although compromise is the essence of the democratic process, we had no room to maneuver. The controversy mounted in intensity to a point where the House and Senate Natural Resources committees were buried under a growing mound of broken glass and crushed cans.

If all this sounds complex and confusing, it *was* complex and confusing. We tried every tactic to reach some acceptable compromise solution, without success. At the request of the Senate committee, I wrote a comprehensive statewide recycling bill which attempted to deal with the entire issue of solid waste disposal—glass, paper, metals, the works. This passed the Senate, but the House was afraid to touch it for fear that it might open the door to repeal of the less comprehensive 1972 container-deposit law. In a similar vein, Representative Sam Lloyd of the House Natural Resources Committee proposed a "certifiable bottle" amendment designed to make the container-deposit law more workable, but the Senate rejected the amendment for fear that it, too, would lead to repeal of the 1972 law.

Over time, the issue became unmanageable. Whenever the Senate Natural Resources Committee attempted to discuss the situation, little Room 8 filled with so many lobbyists and newspaper reporters that we could hardly fit around the table. After the entire affair had solidified into a sticky, solid, immovable mass, the Senate committee finally voted not to recommend any new changes in the 1972 legislation, which meant that the previously enacted law would go into effect, untouched, on July 1. In short, after months of intensive lobbying and confusing debate, we decided to do absolutely nothing.

The outcome was about as predicted. Once the law was implemented, the Vermont roadsides seemed to be cleaner, but some border grocers lost a sizable percentage of their soft-drink and beer business to New Hampshire and other surrounding states.

It was a frustrating experience, and one which taught me a great deal about the political process. If an issue becomes too polarized, it's all over. The most politically expedient solution may not be the most rational long-range solution. Because of overintense lobbying, many policy issues are subjected to incremental, interim, short-range settlements, with little chance of comprehensive solutions. At least that was the case with Vermont's bottle-ban law that really didn't ban anything at all. Perhaps, future legislatures will be able to wave some magic wand that will calm down the opposing forces long enough to formulate a more workable system. I hope so, but after two years in the pit, I suspect the bottle issue will lead to more prolonged and bitter controversies in future legislative sessions.

¶During the course of our deliberations, Art Jones tried to keep the Natural Resources Committee on track by encouraging us to work together on particularly complicated bills. Art Gibb and I collaborated on the Capability and Development Plan; Fred Smith helped me on a shoreland zoning bill; I helped Fred with a flood-plain zoning bill; and so it went. Ed Janeway had a more difficult time following the committee's deliberations because, as Majority leader of the Senate, he was constantly being called out of our meetings to handle one crisis after another.

Through some strange alchemy, I spent more and more time with Jack O'Brien despite our almost totally divergent backgrounds. We were a pretty unlikely combination. I was forty-five, an Ivy League college professor, and a freshman Republican Senator with virtually no practical political experience. Jack, thirty years older than I, and the Democratic Senate floor leader with six previous terms under his belt, possessed a wealth of political know-how. He was really pretty remarkable, an intriguing mixture of opinionated outbursts that were ameliorated by a quick wit, a captivating Irish flair as a story-teller, and a tremendous zest for life.

Above all, Jack was a scrappy little fighter who had literally fought a dozen professional bouts as a featherweight in Massachusetts before migrating up to Vermont in 1921. He told me his old fighting weight had been 126 pounds, but he was now up to 133 pounds, which was still barely enough to fill out his five-foot, six-inch frame. Whatever his size, he certainly didn't let anything, or anyone, stand in the way of his political opinions. Whenever he would wander into the Senate and find me sitting alone reading or writing at my desk, he would stroll over and plop into an empty seat next to me to describe a little more of his life history and political philosophy.

After he moved up to Vermont and settled in the Burlington area he became active in local Democratic politics, and engaged in a variety of other activities before he finally ran for the state Senate in 1959. Among other things, he had been a sports promoter—mostly boxing and wrestling—but he had also sponsored the first night baseball game ever held in Vermont.

As Jack unfolded the multiple facets of his diversified career, I learned about his friends and enemies, as well as his pride and prejudices. Jack's pride was the "glory days of the Senate" in 1959, '61 and '63. "Just look at the men we had in those days, Frank." And he would reel off the names almost reverently: "Ace Bloomer from Rutland; Russ Niquette and me from Chittenden; Jim Oakes; Judge

Clark from Bennington. John Boylan was here then, and so was Ed Janeway."

He shook his head with a sigh. "Those were great men, Frank. You don't get them up here any more. Today a good man can't afford to come to the Senate for a lousy one hundred fifty bucks a week. You've got to pick some old fellow like me who's got nothing else to do.

"So most of the people who come up here nowadays are social-minded. Not me; but most of the rest. They want to give all the tax-payers' money away to the welfare. But I will say this. In all the years I've been here, I've never seen anyone being a crook. It's not like Washington. They may be crazy here, but they're not crooks. No, I don't think you can beat it anywhere in the country."

Jack's prejudices grew out of various signs he interpreted as symbolizing the breakdown of society, a subject he usually lumped together into a nonstop outburst against a variety of evils. Although the Democratic Minority leader of the Senate, he was the most utterly conservative political figure I have ever encountered, and very proud of the fact. He was constantly complaining about environmental nuts, legal aid, drug pushers, welfare, and above all, government bureaucrats.

"You know, Frank, the simple fact is that many of those people out there in government can't make a living. That's a fact. They go into politics, and some of them reach the heights without no work record of any kind at all. They never worked nowhere. Look at the Kennedys. Where did they ever do a day's work? I voted for John Kennedy against Nixon because I never had no use for Nixon, but I didn't vote for McGovern. No sirree. Not McGovern. It's the first time I never voted for nobody for President.

"To tell the truth, I can't understand how the bureaucrats can confuse a man of your intelligence. All you've got to do is just vote No. It's very simple. I don't have problems; I just say I'm going to vote No, and that's the end of it. My mind is made up. I'm not going to listen to those lousy bureaucrats sell me a bill of goods. Seventy percent of them couldn't make twenty-five dollars a week, and they're trying to tell me how to vote bacause they pull down fat government salaries. Executive welfare, that's it. Executive welfare, pure and simple."

I never knew quite what to expect when Jack O'Brien would wander over to share a few of his political insights with me. At one point we got into a pretty violent fight when I refused to support a bill he sponsored which covered mandatory sentences for assaults on police officers. Even though the bill passed the Senate by an 18-to-10 vote, I figured I was in for a real tongue-lashing the next morning when, as I was sitting alone writing some letters, Jack sauntered into the Senate Chamber and dropped into the seat next to me.

Such, however, was not to be the case. "Say, Frank, did I ever tell you about the time I had my heart attack?" He uttered the totally unexpected question with a twinkle in his eyes. "That's right. It was in January of 1967. My heart stopped for thirty-eight seconds," he began to gesture excitedly. "Honest to Pete. Thirty-eight seconds. It's the God's truth. It was a miracle. Nobody can figure it out. They give lectures about me in medical schools all over the country, even at Dartmouth." His small frame puffed up considerably. "Did I ever tell you what happened when I had my heart attack?"

I put down my pen and prepared to hear the latest episode in the ongoing saga of Senator John J. O'Brien. "No, Jack," I replied as I folded my hands behind my head and leaned back in my seat, "tell me what happened when you had your heart attack back in 1967."

In the Senate Natural Resources Committee we worked together, argued together, laughed together, and strained mightily to stay on top of the enormous amount of proposed legislation that was dumped into our laps.

Above all, we faced some very tough decisions in our perpetual search for "the public interest." How do you weigh cleaner roadsides against the livelihood of small border grocers? What's a reasonable balance between state planning controls and the rights of private property? Could it really be a dangerous precedent to permit barber poles to turn in Vermont?

These conflicting clashes of interest posed very real problems for me. But Jack O'Brien, with his mind made up, was much more comfortable amid all this uncertainty. On rare occasions, however, even he experienced difficulties with some of the issues we faced.

Very late in the 1974 session we received a last-minute bill from the House that would have prevented the Agency of Environmental Conservation from issuing any regulations that prohibited the burning of wood in Vermont. It was part of an anti-environmental "backlash" that grew out of the energy crisis and a downturn in the state's economy. At this point, many legislators were becoming fed up with environmental controls, and they were ready to throw all existing rules and regulations out the window.

We met with a representative of the state Environmental Conservation Agency, who explained that they had no problem permitting the burning of relatively small quantities of wood to heat homes, evaporate maple sap in sugarhouses, and the like. However, they felt they had to regulate the larger industrial operations, such as furniture factories, which used sizable quantities of scrap wood as fuel for their boilers. In such cases, stack emissions could violate federal air-pollution standards. If we removed all state regulations, the feds would move in, and impose their own standards on us.

So even the burning of wood constituted another sticky problem. We didn't want overkill at the state level, but we certainly didn't want the feds to muscle in and impose their own regulations on us. We were groping before we finally decided to see if the agency representative could come up with a formula that would differentiate between the larger industrial operations and normal home use, so we could pass a law that would regulate the big guys while exempting the small home operators from any state controls. He indicated he would work on it over the weekend, and I suggested he consider using British Thermal Units, or some such criterion, as a base for defining the larger industrial use.

At the time, I could see that Jack O'Brien was quite impressed. He looked over at me admiringly and raised his eyebrows. After the meeting, he came up to me. "Hey, Frank, those British units; they sound pretty good. Tell me, what are they anyway?"

"BTU's are units of measurement, Jack," I explained. "The quantity of heat necessary to raise the temperature of one pound of water by one degree Fahrenheit."

He whistled. "Gee, that's pretty good; that really sounds pretty good to me."

The following Tuesday the agency representative came back with an incredibly wordy proposal which would require a state permit to burn wood as fuel in all boilers of more than 40 horsepower, with the horsepower rating to be computed by dividing by 10 the square feet of boiler heating-surface area.

We were flabbergasted. Jack O'Brien was obviously the most crestfallen of the group, and blurted out, "I don't like this at all. What's the matter with the British units that Frank wants? Where did they go?"

The agency representative had barely started to explain the problem before Jack interrupted him. "I'm sorry, but I think we should use the British units. You know, I'm an Irishman, but if the British came up with something that's O.K. with Frank, then it's O.K. with me."

Jack looked over at me and smiled; I smiled back; the agency representative shook his head despondently. The Natural Resources Committee was in the middle of another great public-policy debate over burning wood in Vermont.

We really worked hard, wrestling with everything from A to Z—air pollution to zoning—always trying to uncover that illusive public interest that was buried somewhere down deep inside.

We even spent some time on legislative overalls—— I mean overcoats—— No, no, no, I mean oversight; that's it, on legislative oversight, in an effort to control the bureaucracy. We were a very remarkable group.

9

★ ★ ★ ★

Health and Welfare:
The World of Technical Expertise

> You know, we always have trouble with
> those professor types during committee
> sessions.
>
> Congressman John Rooney,
> quoted by Donald Riegle
> O Congress

THE BRIGHT February afternoon sun was streaming through the front window as I walked into Room 17 to meet with the Senate Health and Welfare Committee. I dropped down into a chair next to Senator Madeline Harwood at the upper end of our oval committee table where the sun warmed my back. I was the last of the six committee members to arrive. Looking up, I saw three middle-aged men, sitting in a row of grey metal chairs which backed up against the opposite wall of the room. They were gazing at me with their arms folded across their chests. Senator Harwood also looked at me with a mixed expression of chagrin and relief.

"Well, we're finally all here," she stated with a cheerful smile. "Today we are meeting with the funeral directors on *Senate Bill 117.*"

The funeral directors. I repeated the phrase to myself silently to make sure I had heard her correctly. I looked at the three men in their immaculate dark suits. They continued to gaze back at me with uniformly expressionless stares. So that's who these fellows were; funeral directors. I opened my thick red Senate bill book, and thumbed through the pages until I found S. *117.* Unfortunately, it was there, right in front of my eyes. S. *117.* AMENDS THE LICENSING REQUIREMENT OF FUNERAL DIRECTORS BY PROVIDING FOR THE LICENSING OF ANY PERSON INVOLVED IN THE PRACTICE OF FUNERAL SERVICE (BY REQUEST) .

Good grief, I thought, another licensing bill! Worse yet, another bill involving death. During the previous month we had struggled with bills involving the reporting of fetal deaths, and the payment of burial expenses for indigent welfare recipients. I wondered what had happened to the health and welfare of the living—all those 460,000 breathing, laughing, lovable souls out there in Vermont. Well, there was obviously nothing we were going to be able to do for them on this particularly sunny afternoon. We were meeting with the funeral directors to discuss S. *117*. I braced myself for yet another charge into the valley of death.

The Senate Health and Welfare Committee met virtually every afternoon at one-thirty in Room 17 on the first floor of the State House.

Madeline Harwood, an attractive fifty-eight-year-old senator from the lovely little town of Manchester down in Bennington County, served as chairman of the committee. Madeline was a registered nurse who had been active in Republican Party politics for many years; she had served as chairman of the state platform committee among other leadership positions before her election to the Senate in 1969. Although Madeline's political views were generally more conservative than mine, we got along very well. I admired and respected her tremendous capacity for hard work. She was an extremely conscientious legislator, often laboring late into the night to keep up with her correspondence and stay on top of the mountain of bills which poured into the Health and Welfare Committee.

In addition to Madeline and myself, there were four other members of the committee: two Democrats and two Republicans. Our vice chairman was Russell Niquette, a sixty-five-year-old Democratic veteran from Chittenden County, who had served off and on in the legislature since 'way back in 1935. Russ, a lawyer from the City of Winooski outside Burlington, had run as the Democratic candidate for Governor in 1960. Jack O'Brien had served as his campaign manager, and Russ had amassed more votes than any Democrat up to that time, although he lost the election. He was a handsome man with thinning streaks of white hair which, in his earlier days, had won him the sobriquet of "the Silver Fox." He was very sharp in the committee, possessing an uncanny ability to pick apart a bill with a great deal of finesse and a masterful eye for detail.

A second committee lawyer was Robert Bloomer, a fifty-one-year-old Republican from Rutland, who served as clerk of the committee. Bob's father, Asa—known as "Ace"—Bloomer, had literally run the Senate in the 1950's. After his father died, Bob succeeded him in the Senate, serving for three years before taking a break and then returning to the legislature in 1972.

Dorothy Shea, a warm, matronly seventy-year-old from Montpelier was the other Republican on the committee. Dot was one of the most popular of all the legislators, a cheerful person with a great deal of common sense and a real way with people. She had been in the Senate since 1966, and also served as chairman of the General and Military Committee.

William Daniels, a forty-six-year-old professor of history at the University of Vermont, was the second Democrat on the committee. Since Bill and I were both college professors and both freshman senators, we spent a lot of time together, discussing committee business. On numerous occasions after the committee had finished slogging through a particularly tough bill, Madeline Harwood would beam enthusiastically and exclaim that she chaired the best committee in the legislature: "two women, two lawyers, and [pause] two college professors." It was a nice gesture, but I always looked over a little sheepishly at Bill Daniels. The truth of the matter was that both of us had a tendency to get carried away on flights of academic oratory during committee meetings, and we often tied up the group in knots as we engaged in lengthy displays of verbal erudition. On the whole, however, Madeline was right. Health and Welfare was a strong committee, just like Natural Resources. This was lucky because we inhabited a world of technical expertise that made some of the bills we attempted to consider barely comprehensible, to say the least.

¶MOST OF the Health and Welfare bills involved the exercise of state "police powers," that ambiguous and glorious euphemism which Chief Justice Marshall first coined in the *Barron v. Baltimore* case back in

1833. Although the courts have never been very precise in defining a state's police powers, these have generally been regarded as the sovereign state authority to regulate the "health, safety, morals and welfare" —or at least that's what I always told my students. They are a very broad set of powers, which serve as the basis for a great mass of state legislation, on everything ranging from the inspection of milk, to the regulation of hours of liquor sales, to licensing funeral directors.

Not all the state police-power bills came to the Health and Welfare Committee, but a lot were steered in our direction. As a result, we considered an astonishing range of legislation during the 1973–74 sessions, including a nurse practices act; inspections of restaurant and food establishments; fees charged at state hospitals; involuntary commitments to mental institutions; payment schedules to the state unemployment insurance fund; reorganization of the Human Services Board; state administration of federal welfare programs; Sunday hours of sale of beer and wine (remember that one?) ; reorganization of child development services; regulation of nursing homes and old-age custodial facilities; infant coverage under family health insurance programs; substitution of generic drugs for brand-name drugs; certification of medical students; dental care for children; marketing of products produced by the blind; social rehabilitation services; state general-assistance programs; death benefits for dependents of law-enforcement officers; sale of liquor on state college campuses; ambulance services; comprehensive health planning; reporting of fetal deaths; and, last but certainly not least, professional licensing bills.

The realm of professional licensing bills was a new one to me, a real eye-opener in terms of the delegation of public power to private groups. The basic rationale behind licensing bills was to protect the public (health, safety and welfare) by ensuring that the various professions policed themselves in a manner sufficient to provide quality services. The licensing system started out modestly enough more than a century ago in the health professions, when doctors, nurses and other medical specialists were required to pass exams or present educational credentials before being permitted to practice in the state. In other words, the initial aim was to protect the public by eliminating unqualified "quack" practitioners.

That was the original aim, but over the years the licensing system had blossomed magnificently. With the advent of the public-interest advocacy movement in the mid-1960's, literally everybody and anybody was anxious to jump on the licensing bandwagon, ostensibly to protect the public against consumer fraud. As a result, the legislature was deluged with licensing bills of all sizes, sorts and shapes. During the 1973–74 sessions we considered licensing bills involving optometrists, opticians, radiological technologists, psychologists, hearing-aid specialists, television repairman, welders, well-drillers, septic-tank installers, automobile mechanics, bartenders, private detectives, and, of course, funeral directors.

I was utterly fascinated with this veritable Niagara of potential licensees until I finally began to appreciate the political dynamics at work here. In essence, when a state licenses a profession, it delegates very strong regulatory powers to the professionals themselves to police their own activities. Virtually every licensing bill established a professionally dominated licensing board which was authorized to examine future applicants and grant subsequent licenses if these applicants were professionally qualified and of "good moral character." Since the term "good moral character" was never defined, the state was really delegating authority to a group of private boards which could establish a potential monopoly in any given field. The boards had a stranglehold on their professions since they could control future competition by limiting the number of applicants who could practice in the state. Indeed, some of the bills established almost medieval guild systems whereby candidates were required to serve as apprentices for fairly lengthy periods of time before they were even permitted to be examined to determine whether or not they possessed good moral character.

It was an intriguing wrinkle in the free-enterprise economic system, and one which is widely used in all the states. A Dartmouth student of mine, Paul Lukeman, became quite interested in this neglected area of public policy, and he wrote a crackerjack senior honors thesis on the subject of state licensing practices. I hope that more political scientists, as well as more public-interest research groups, will look at the wonderful world of state licensing.

At any rate, the Senate Health and Welfare Committee certainly grappled tenaciously enough with the subject during many a long afternoon meeting. A glance into a projected triple play by the optometrists will suffice to indicate the complex strategy of the game.

The triple-play option was possible only because there are three different groups involved in the field of eye care: ophthalmologists, optometrists, and opticians. Actually, "triple play" may be somewhat of a misnomer because the three groups were basically arguing against each other, rather than co-ordinating their energies to defeat a common foe. In the corny phraseology of one newspaper reporter, they didn't see "eye to eye" on the subject of licensing. This led to a prolonged and agonizing conflict which used up the better part of both the 1973 and 1974 legislative sessions.

In order to understand the contest, it is necessary to identify the three groups of players.

Group I is the ophthalmologists. They are at the top of the heap— licensed physicians (M.D.'s) who specialize in the care of the eyes, including surgery, pathology, refraction, the whole works.

Group II is the optometrists. They are in the middle. Not medical doctors, they're trained to correct visual abnormalities, but not to treat diseases of the eye or use medications. Their main activity is to examine eyes and prescribe glasses.

Group III is the opticians. They are dispensers similar to pharmacists. They fill lense prescriptions and fit and sell glasses, but do not prescribe lenses or examine eyes.

The bill under consideration, S. 105, drafted by the optometrists, and submitted to the committee by request, revised the criteria and procedures used to license optometrists in Vermont. The first problem was that the revised criteria would have permitted only licensed optometrists (Group II) to sell glasses, thus knocking the opticians (Group III) out of business completely. The committee picked up this restriction pretty quickly, and after the optometrists explained that the provision had been included due to a drafting error during the preparation of the bill, we deleted it to protect the future livelihood of the opticians. So much for the vertical relationships downward between the optometrists and the opticians.

The real problem involved the hierarchical relationship upward between the optometrists (Group II) and the ophthalmologists (Group I). The proposed bill specified that a licensed optometrist could examine the eye "by any means or methods." A number of committee members were confused by this rather amorphous phrase. Dotty Shea summarized our concern very crisply when she observed, "This bothers me. Quite frankly, I don't know what 'by any means' means." Since Madeline Harwood was getting expressions of concern from the ophthalmologists who warned her to be careful with the bill, we decided to hold a public hearing to receive expert testimony on the subject.

Two weeks later, after due notice, the hearing took place. So many optometrists, ophthalmologists and opticians showed up that we had to move to a bigger room to accommodate the crowd. Following the formal presentation by the first witness, I asked if he could clarify the phrase "examination by any means or methods."

At this point a small, energetic-looking man jumped up in the back of the room to indicate he wanted to testify on precisely this part of the bill. Madeline Harwood asked him to come forward. He sat down on a chair directly in front of the committee members, and introduced himself as Arthur Geltzer, M.D., president of the Rhode Island Ophthalmological Society. He explained that he had flown up to Montpelier at the request of the Vermont ophthalmologists to testify. Rhode Island had already adopted a bill similar to the one we were considering, and he felt it would be very undesirable for Vermont to pass this particular bill. Madeline thanked him for making the trip, and he began his testimony in slow, careful, measured tones.

"The purpose of this particular phrase, 'examination by any means or methods,' is to permit optometrists to use drugs in the treatment of the eye." Dr. Geltzer paused briefly, apparently to collect his thoughts before continuing. "In my opinion, this would be very dangerous, because optometrists are not trained physicians. It just so happens that the eye has an extremely high concentration of blood vessels because it is one of the most sensitive and complex organs in the human body, extraordinarily complex. As a result of its high concentration of vessels, the absorption of drugs on the surface of the eye is very rapid —roughly equivalent to the intravenous injection of a drug directly into the bloodstream."

I glanced sideways at Dot Shea, who was sitting next to me. She was beginning to quiver nervously.

Dr. Geltzer continued with his testimony. "Now, in the professional care of the eye, a qualified ophthalmologist who has been trained as a doctor may use three different kinds of drugs. The first are corneal anesthetics, which include such drugs as cocaine."

I looked at Dot Shea again. "Cocaine, Good Lord, they use cocaine on the eyes," I heard her mutter.

Dr. Geltzer, who was now speaking in a quicker, crisper tone of voice, continued his testimony: "The second type of drugs are known as mydriatics. They dilate the pupils of the eye, and unless they are administered very carefully, they could, in certain cases, result in heart attacks."

"Heart attacks!" Dotty Shea was markedly nervous now. "Oh, Good Lord, Frank," she whispered to me, "I'm terribly glad we insisted on a public hearing before we voted on this bill."

"Finally, there is a third group of drugs." Dr. Geltzer paused thoughtfully. I couldn't imagine what was coming next, but I was beginning to worry that Dot Shea might faint dead away on the spot if things got any worse. "This third group of drugs is classified as miotics, and they can be lethal if improperly used, since they are related to nerve gas."

"Nerve gas!" I thought Dot was going to fall off her chair. "Oh, my goodness, Frank," she whispered, even more excited than before, "I don't like this bill at all."

Dr. Geltzer's testimony constituted the death blow for S. _105_. Although the optometrists fought back valiantly, attempting to work out a compromise definition of the phrase "examination by any means or methods," the committee didn't really have much heart for S. _105_ after the good doctor had finished his oration. Dot Shea summed it up very well: "I'm in my seventies now, Frank, and I've been fortunate enough to live a good full life. I don't want to wake up some morning and find out that someone went blind because I voted for a bill like this. Why. I never heard anything like it! Cocaine, heart attacks, nerve gas; I never heard anything like it. I can't support this bill if the professionals don't even agree on whether it's safe. I'm sorry for the optometrists, but I can't vote for this bill."

In her usual practical, down-to-earth manner, Dotty Shea had summarized the challenge, and the dilemma, that faced the Health and Welfare Committee. None of us, other than Madeline Harwood, had any formal medical training at all. It's all very well to use amateur "citizen" legislators in a democratic society, but some of the terrain out there can become pretty swampy: what were we supposed to do when the "experts" disagreed among themselves?

Another beautiful case in point was S. *150*, which once again tied the committee in knots for the better part of a legislative session.

This measure was sponsored by Senator Bill Daniels. Its purpose was to allow the substitution of less expensive (generic) drugs for more expensive (brand-name) drugs, provided they were chemically, biologically, and clinically equivalent. The basic thrust behind the bill was to reduce the skyrocketing costs of medical care—particularly for the elderly on fixed incomes, who were using sizable amounts of prescribed drugs for medicinal purposes. The bill directed the State Department of Health to develop a formulary (an authorized listing of equivalent drugs) which pharmacists could use in substituting less expensive generic equivalents unless specifically prohibited from doing so by the physician who prescribed the drug.

The system had already been tried in Massachusetts and some other states. I was interested in the bill because, as a member of the Governor's Commission on Medical Care, I had learned that Vermonters spent $10 million each year on prescription drugs. I figured that if we could reduce this amount by even a modest 10 percent, the result would be a saving of $1 million each year.

But the issue was very complicated and very controversial. The first question was whether the state could really prepare a decent formulary at all. We were given a copy of the Massachusetts formulary, and, quite frankly, it was a complete mystery to me. For example (given here with the brand-name drug in quotation marks, followed by its generic equivalent) : "Acidulin OTC" is glutamic acid hydrochloride; "Cardilate" is erythrityl tetranitrate NF; "Wyamine" is mephenter-mine sulfate USP; "Zactane" is ethoheptazine citrate NF; "Zephiran Chloride OTC" is benzalkonium chloride USP.

I shook my head in utter bewilderment. Maybe I should have been a professor of chemistry. It was explained to us that many large hospitals use formularies, but only under controlled conditions that were not the same as for the open marketplace.

There was also a second major issue: namely, was there any such thing as a "clinically equivalent drug?" We held a public hearing on this question—and found that the experts were in violent disagreement. Representatives of the big drug companies showed us a movie where various doctors and pharmacologists in spotless white uniforms argued that, even if a drug were chemically and biologically equivalent, it might not be *clinically* equivalent because different patients react in different ways to exactly the same drug (that is, every human being is unique) . Other doctors testified, however, that this was not a problem. In effect, the different groups lined up on completely opposite sides of the aisle. The State Department of Health, and some of the doctors and druggists who testified, favored the bill. The drug companies, plus other doctors and druggists, argued that the system was not fail-safe, and they strongly opposed the bill.

It was small wonder that the committee split right down the middle. Three members—Madeline Harwood, Bob Bloomer and Dot Shea—were strongly opposed. The other three of us—Bill Daniels, Russ Niquette and I—felt the bill should be reported on the floor for consideration by the full Senate. To make a long story short, we spent so much time arguing over the bill that we didn't even get around to voting it out of committee (3 to 3, without recommendation) until the very last week of the session. As a result, it never made it to the floor because of lack of time.

Maybe it was for the best, but I really don't know. It was typical of the kind of questions we wrestled with in the Health and Welfare Committee.

As if the substantive issues weren't difficult enough, we also had to contend with one further problem that complicated things immeasurably. This was the incredible acronymic jargon that had sprung up over the years around the fields of health and welfare.

It was really quite an ordeal; like learning an exotic foreign language without any vowels. The basic health programs, just to give you a taste of what we were up against, were dominated by CHP, RMP, EMS, PSRO, and EHSDS (Comprehensive Health Programs; Regional Medical Programs; Emergency Medical Services; Professional Standards Review Organizations, and Experimental Health Services and Delivery Systems). Many of these programs were carried out under *Sections 314a* and *314b*, plus *Title XVIII* and *Title XIX*, with co-ordination provided by HEW and CHICV (Department of Health, Education and Welfare, and Co-operative Health Information Center of Vermont).

Things were no better in the welfare field, where we wrestled with such morsels as AABD, ANFC, SSI and the like (Aid for the Aged, Blind and Disabled; Aid for Needy Families with Children; Supplemental Security Income). When Tom Davis, the Secretary of Human Services, and Paul Philbrook, the Social Welfare Commissioner, would visit the committee, we had a tough time communicating since the whole health-and-welfare field was so snarled up with indecipherable terminology that we had difficulty understanding one another.

It just so happened that Senator Bill Daniels, an authority on Russian history at the University of Vermont, is a very accomplished linguist. In addition to speaking Russian, he has a widespread grasp of other European and eastern European languages. One day I challenged Bill to see if we could conduct a health-and-welfare discussion that would be completely incomprehensible to the other members of the committee. We agreed to open our conversation at the beginning of the next afternoon's meeting. Once we were all duly assembled, I began the proceedings:

"Bill, how do you read the new SSI program?" I asked in a fairly loud voice.

"I don't know," he replied, "I'm uncertain how it will interface with AABD."

"Why AABD?" I countered. "What about ANFC?"

Although we had barely begun to warm up, the other members of the committee were already displaying looks of mystified alarm. I snapped my finger, which was a prearranged signal to shift into the field of health alphabetese. Bill picked up the tempo.

"I'm afraid AABD really is the crux of the problem, Frank. However, ANFC will be O.K. if CHICV can finalize the statistical correlations needed to determine whether RMP or CHP should cover recipient costs and needs."

The committee had taken the bait by now. Dot Shea put her hand over her mouth, and gazed at Madeline Harwood with a confused expression, while Russ Niquette leaned forward with a puzzled frown on his face. Only Bob Bloomer seemed to be skeptical as he looked at me with a questioning glance.

"Why CHICV?" I protested. "What about the PSRO's?"

"It's a *Section 214a* matter, not *214b*," Bill replied curtly. "You should know better than that."

At this point Bob Bloomer abruptly blew the whistle. "O.K., learned professors," he interrupted. "Let's bring it out into the open. Could you please tell the rest of us what the hell you're talking about?"

I looked over at Bill Daniels, who had already dropped his head in a fit of coughing. "Gee, I'm sorry. I guess Bill and I got a little carried away with ourselves. We were just elaborating on a thesis that was advanced at a recent meeting of the HEW regional co-ordinating subcommittee on medical delivery systems for northern New England."

Madeline Harwood burst into laughter. Russ Niquette and Dot Shea also realized we were putting them on, and both sighed with relief.

"I must say this is quite an experience," Dot chuckled. "I've been in the legislature for over twelve years, and this is the first time I ever served on a committee with two college professors."

"You can say that again," Russ Niquette nodded. "I've been in the legislature for over twenty years, and it's a first for me, too."

"We were only trying to make a point," I declared. "To be realistic about it, this committee is trapped in a frightfully messed-up bureaucratic morass. It's astonishing. America is the most technologically advanced nation in the world. We can send men to the moon, but we can't deliver basic services—basic health and social services. All we seem to be able to do is create incomprehensible administrative agencies which provide employment opportunities for the middle class, and use up all the money that's supposed to go to the sick and needy."

"I agree, Frank," Madeline Harwood said, "but the state is caught in the middle. The federal government draws up the guidelines, and we're left trying to supply matching funds for programs over which we have no control. It's a mess, but I don't know what we can do about it in Montpelier. The problems are created in Washington, and we're left holding the bag."

"Well, it's a lousy way to run a railroad," I replied. "Some day I hope we're going to learn how to deliver services, to set up effective delivery systems, so that we can get all this marvelous technology out to the people where it will do some good. Let me give you one more statistic. Do you realize that only 10 cents of every federal health dollar goes to support medical services for young children? I know medical costs are astronomical, and all of us older folk need help, but anyone who has his head screwed on right should realize that money spent on preventive medicine for the young will produce very real long-range benefits for years to come. Yet we only spend 10 cents out of every federal health dollar in this area."

"That's a good point, Frank," Russ Niquette said. "I'm not a political scientist, but I've been around this legislature for a long time." Then he pointed his finger at me for emphasis. "I just want to ask you one question. Who represents the young children in the political process? Every other group in society can create their own lobby if they want, to represent their own interests, but young children don't even have the right to vote."

"Good Lord, Russ, that's a very powerful and penetrating observation," I told him. "You've got the makings of a great political scientist. It's too bad you're wasting your talents in the law."

Russ laughed, and Madeline brought us back to the cold reality of the Health and Welfare Committee. "This has been an interesting seminar," she said, "but we face a very crowded agenda. I'm afraid we've got to get some of these bills out of committee, so I suggest we suspend class for the next couple of hours and get back to work."

Madeline was right. Life goes on. First I thought of Robert Frost, Vermont's poet laureate: "The woods are lovely dark and deep/But I have promises to keep/And miles to go before I sleep." Then, a comment Representative John Rooney had made about the Congressional committee system jumped into my mind. "You know," Rooney said, "we always have trouble with those professor types in committee sessions." He shook his head. "Professor types," he mumbled again, and went on his way.

I let out a sigh of frustration as the committee went back to work. Only later did I realize that the afternoon's discussion on the political underrepresentation of children must have triggered an interest on my part that subsequently led me to sponsor a bill to strengthen the state's child-abuse reporting law.

Believe it or not, the group we ran into once again on that particular afternoon was our old friends the funeral directors. They came back at three o'clock for another of their interminable visits to discuss S. *117*, "amendments to the licensing requirements for the practice of funeral services."

It was really an incredible bill. The educational requirements alone were mind-boggling. They provided that any person of "good moral character" should be entitled to an examination "after graduating from a school of funeral service accredited or approved by the American Board of Funeral Service Education in a course of instruction of not less than two academic years." Following this, the applicant was required to serve "a traineeship, of 12 months of full-time employment . . . [and] . . . during the traineeship, the trainee shall embalm at least 25 bodies and assist in 25 funerals."

Both Bill Daniels and I inquired whether a University of Vermont or a Dartmouth graduate could qualify, but the funeral directors told us that neither institution met the standards, since they had not been accredited by the American Board of Funeral Service Education. "I'm sorry, gentlemen," one of the funeral directors explained. "They are both very fine schools, but the funeral business is a very technical field. Why, embalming fluids alone could contain arsenic, zinc, mercury, copper, lead, silver, antimony, chloral, or cyanogen. Liberal arts graduates simply aren't prepared to handle these kinds of responsibilities."

Well, after weeks of such interchanges, I was so sick and tired of the bill that I would have voted for just about anything simply to get it out of the committee. As a result, I hardly paid attention even when the funeral directors requested one final simple amendment before we voted to report the bill out onto the floor for second reading. The amendment provided that no *body* (not "nobody") could be released for cremation less than forty-eight hours after the time of death.

"It's a safety precaution," they explained. "Let's assume for example, that someone died during an airplane flight into Burlington. If the body were cremated immediately, there would be no chance even to investigate the possibility of foul play. You know, poison and things like that. The new forty-eight-hour provision will make sure that the body is around long enough to check into this sort of thing."

It seemed O.K. to me, and I shrugged my agreement along with the rest of the committee members, hoping to get the damn bill out of committee. We finally approved the bill unanimously, and Bill Daniels agreed to report it for second reading.

And Bill got slaughtered in his floor report. I thought it was going to be easy sailing when his opening remarks drew appreciative groans from senators all over the room: "I am pleased to report S. *117*, the licensing of funeral services. This bill has been buried in the Health and Welfare Committee for so long that many of you may think it is a dead issue. Let me assure you, though, that it raises a number of grave questions."

However, when Bill had outlined the major provisions of S. *117* Senator Graham Newell got up and began to question him about the forty-eight hour amendment that had been added at the last minute. Graham explained that the funeral directors had been after this provision for years, and charged that it was designed to strengthen their hold on the burial business. After a lengthy, and confusing, debate the Senate voted to recommit the entire bill to the Health and Welfare Committee for further study (help!) —which actually turned out to be a polite way to kill it for the session.

Bill Daniels took the floor massacre pretty well. It was obviously no fun being hacked to shreds on a funeral bill, but he adopted a stoical attitude, and I tried to bolster his ego.

"You know, Bill, we deal with an awful lot of complicated issues on the Health and Welfare Committee. Most of the time we're right on top of them, but I guess it's only human that occasionally we're going to blow a couple."

"Yeah, you're right. But why did I have to end up as the floor reporter? And why such an uproar over a funeral bill? In the light of all the other complexities we deal with, I never suspected we would run into such a buzz saw over a funeral bill."

"Come on, Bill, cheer up. We've got other things to worry about. Say, I wanted to talk with you about one of them, as a matter of fact. I'm very concerned about the confusing organizational morass that characterizes health-planning in Vermont. We've got so many different agencies working in this area that I'm not sure there is any comprehensive planning at all. Let's go down to the cafeteria, and talk about it over a cup of coffee." I headed him down the hall. "I really think we should try to do something."

As we walked into the cafeteria Bill said, "Let's see if we can put together a coalition—the Daniels-Smallwood-Democratic-Republican-Freshman-Senator coalition—to help restore our battered political image by reforming Vermont's health-planning system."

"That's the spirit," I told him, and we settled down to discuss the situation. The Senate Health and Welfare Committee was back in business.

CHAPTER
10
★ ★ ★ ★
Friends and Neighbors

> I woke up this morning feeling that things
> were moving too fast; the pace of life was
> just too frantic . . . It was hard to get out
> of bed, dress and head toward the office.
>> Donald Riegle
>> O Congress

MONTPELIER, Vermont's capital, lies exactly sixty miles north of my
home town of Norwich. During the worst of winter, the drive on
Interstate 89 can be awesome, a miserable conspiracy of snow, sleet,
ice, slush, and freezing rain. All this is forgotten, however, on the crisp,
clear days.

On a clear day you can see forever, all the way from Norwich to
Montpelier. The view becomes increasingly more dramatic halfway
through the trip, beginning with the long climb from Bethel to
Randolph. The last twenty miles are sky high, with the Northfield
and Green Mountain ranges providing sweeping vistas across the
western half of the state. The drive culminates with a long descent into
the Winooski River valley where Camel's Hump, Vermont's most
scenic peak of all, juts up sharply to the west to dominate the Green
Mountains. Moments later the golden dome of the State House marks
Montpelier, nestling in a plain against the backdrop of still another
mountain chain, the Worcester Range.

The 1970 census-takers counted 8,609 permanent residents in
Montpelier. This may seem pretty small for a city, but it's a healthy
agglomeration by Vermont standards, since only one-third of the state's
population lives in urban areas. There are only nine Vermont communities which call themselves cities, ranging from Vergennes (the

smallest in the United States) with 2,242 people, to Burlington on
Lake Champlain with a whopping 38,633.

To get back to Montpelier, it's strictly a two-industry community:
the home office of the National Life Insurance Company, and the home
base of the state government bureaucracy. To be completely truthful
about it, the capital's cultural and social life is not overly diverse or
dynamic. There is only one movie theater plus a few pretty good
restaurants and two major hostelries: the Tavern Motor Inn and
the Brown Derby Motel. Some Holiday Inn people wanted to put up
a building near the State House, but the legislature didn't like the idea
so they turned the area into a capitol complex which blocked construction by reserving the land for public buildings. Lacking outside
distractions, Montpelier is a politically incestuous place, where legislators spend most of their time talking to other legislators. Much of
this chatter takes place at one of the two local hotels.

Members of the legislature scattered all over the surrounding area
for their lodging. Approximately half the thirty senators commuted to
their own homes near by or rented houses in the Montpelier area; another seven resided at the Brown Derby on the southern outskirts of
the city; and nine, including myself, lodged at the Tavern, a square
red-brick structure just a hop and a skip (or a slip, in the icy winter)
across the street from the State House. I stayed there out of a sense
of loyalty, since an old Norwich friend owned the place. It had the
usual lounge, dining room and coffee shop, plus a minuscule swimming pool and a sauna, which allowed me to get some exercise and
relaxation after working in the State House all day.

This was my home away from home during each legislative week
(Tuesday through Friday) for two long winters. Much of my social life
revolved around the comings and goings of numerous friends and
neighbors who passed through the portals of this inn, which dubbed
itself "Vermont's meeting place at the Capital."

My daily routine began at seven o'clock in the morning when an
alarm radio jolted me awake with the local weather report, followed by
international and national news (usually bad) plus "Highlights of

Late State Happenings" (alternately good or bad depending on the legislative session the day before) .

During my first winter in Montpelier I generally ate breakfast alone, a deliberate strategy that enabled me to bury my nose in the Rutland *Herald* and the Burlington *Free Press,* reading up on our previous day's legislative exploits. This was a universal practice, as most of the coffee shop's legislative clientele was engaged in this same search for political recognition in the morning newspapers. The only major exception involved a boisterous group of House Democrats who whooped it up every morning in an almost continuous din of jokes and laughter. It reminded me of the perceptive distinction captured by political scientist Clinton Rossiter in his book *Parties and Politics in America:*

> One cannot spend much time in the clubhouses and convention halls in which the parties do their political business without becoming aware of certain vague but substantial differences in character or, as I prefer, style. A gathering of Democrats is more sweaty, disorderly, offhand and rowdy than a gathering of Republicans . . . A gathering of Republicans is more respectable, sober, purposeful, and businesslike than a gathering of Democrats . . . The Reublicans look like Rotarians at the speakers' table, the Democrats like Rotarians at table 16, back near the entrance to the kitchen . . . At table 16, things are more relaxed and less self-conscious. Arguments are aired with abandon and settled (or forgotten) with a shrug. Dress is more casual, salutes are more boisterous, jokes are more earthy. They are leaders, but at the moment they are just the boys at table 16.

I obtained a firsthand education in the accuracy of this observation during the second winter of my stay in Montpelier when the Democrats quite unexpectedly asked me to join them at their Table 16 in the front corner of the coffee shop.

The invitation came early one evening as I was sitting in the lobby reading still another newspaper. Representative Frank Esposito, a Democratic labor leader from Rutland, joined me on the sofa, and, after exchanging a few pleasantries, he popped the question: "Senator, my colleagues in the House have asked me to inquire whether you would like to join us each morning at the HDBC."

"That's very nice of you, Frank," I replied, "but exactly what is the 'H-D-B-C'?"

He seemed surprised at my ignorance. "It's the House Democratic Breakfast Club. Actually, it's not a club at all. We just sit around together and have breakfast in the front corner of the coffee shop. And it's not all Democrats either. There are House Republicans like Bob Graf, Al Peake and Joe Caracciola. But it's mostly Democrats—me, Danny DeBonis, John Mulligan, Kermit Smith, John Murphy. Some times Flossie Robillard sits in, and Tom Candon, the House Minority leader. It's mostly Democrats, but only House members. You'd be the first Senator. Quite frankly, we'd like to have you join us to exchange intelligence. You know, so we could each find out what's going on in the other body."

Exchange intelligence: it sounded like intriguing intrigue. Well, why not? It could be interesting, and I was tired of the morning newspaper routine.

"O.K., Frank," I replied. "I'd like to join you."

"Fine, Senator. We'll see you tomorrow morning at seven-thirty."

My association with the breakfast club really perked up my mornings. It was a joking, laughing, complaining, bragging group, in a constant turmoil of nonstop conversation. On my first day I sat down at a table next to John Francis Murphy, who subsequently became my almost constant breakfast partner. Murphy, one of the five House Democrats from Windsor County, was something special. He worked as a machinist in the General Electric plant in Ludlow, taking off the winter months to serve in the legislature. Although only five feet two inches tall, he managed to pack over two hundred pounds into his solid, square frame. He had a great sense of humor, and his quick and alert mind had landed him a position on the important House Ways and Means Committee. Also, although he hardly looked the part of a classical statesman, he was a vivid speechmaker on the floor of the House, with a real flair for the dramatic phrase. Just the previous week he had made a speech supporting a drug bill which had been recorded and quoted extensively on the local radio's "Late State Happenings." I remember listening to him say, "I'm for civil rights, but the drug problem is getting serious in the State of Vermont. This is one area where we need to place the long arm of the law firmly on the shoulder of the pusher."

"Murphy," I told him after we had nodded our morning greetings, "I heard your speech on the radio about the long arm of the law on the shoulder of the pusher. I thought that was a pretty dramatic phrase. Do you make speeches like that very often?"

Frank Esposito cut in from the next table before Murphy had a chance to reply. "Senator, I want you to know that Murphy is one of the most persuasive speakers we have in the House. You should have heard him a couple of weeks ago when your party, the Republicans, were trying to scuttle a bill. Toward the end of the debate, he got up and said, 'I oppose these tactics; I simply can't support DLWK on the floor of this House any longer.' Then after a brief pause, he repeated himself, 'That's right: D-L-W-K—Delay, Linger, Wait and Kill.' It was terrific. You could have heard a pin drop. The bill was still killed anyway, but it was really something."

Murphy, who had been beaming throughout Frank's narration, joined the discussion. "I appreciate your comment, Smallwood. I work very hard on my speeches, but to tell the truth, I never had a college education like you. I went to Black River Academy and then I went to work. I'm a machinist, but I work very hard on my speeches."

"Hey," Frank Esposito interrupted again, "that's an idea. Senator, you're a college professor. Why don't you help Murphy with his floor speeches? He's very good, but you could really help him."

Murphy nodded. "That's not a bad idea, Smallwood. I'm planning to give a speech today against the poll tax, but it's going to be a real squeaker on third reading in the House."

I thought about the situation. I agreed that the poll tax was undesirable. Actually, it wasn't really a "poll" tax at all in the sense that it deprived anyone of the right to vote, which would have been unconstitutional under the Twenty-fourth Amendment to the United States Constitution. Rather, it was a head tax, a local levy that towns set for each resident adult, usually at $8 or $10 per person; and as such it was a regressive tax that did not relate to ability to pay. On the other hand, many small-town legislators felt the tax, authorized under state law, should remain to help support local needs. The issue had split the House along small town–big town lines, rather than by party affiliation. On second reading the previous day, 33 Democrats and 42 Republicans had voted in favor of repealing the tax, and 26 Democrats and 45 Republicans were opposed to repeal.

"Yup, it's going to be a real squeaker," Murphy repeated. "On second reading yesterday morning we barely voted to repeal the thing, 75 to 71. Then, in the afternoon, the state Supreme Court overruled a lower court decision that had said it was unconstitutional to suspend a person's driver's license for failure to pay the tax. Some timing! Yesterday morning we were finally getting around to repealing the poll tax after many years of effort. Then, the very same afternoon, the Court indicates it's O.K. to collect the tax. The decision is bound to hurt us. I don't think the preliminary House vote will ever hold up on third reading this morning in light of the Court's decision."

"I think you're right about this one, Murphy," I replied. "It's not a good tax, but I'm afraid some of the House members will renege on their vote, with the Supreme Court's decision as their alibi. You know, if it's that close, they may hide behind the shadow of the Court."

"Hey, that's not bad," Murphy said. " 'Hide behind the shadow of the Supreme Court.' That's not bad at all."

I was somewhat startled. Good grief, he's a fast worker, I thought— he's already starting to compose his floor speech.

"Yeah, that's not bad," Frank Esposito picked it up. "Hey, Mulligan, the Senator is helping Murphy write a speech against the poll tax," he yelled over to the next table. "He says that the House can't hide behind the shadow of the Supreme Court. What do you think of that?"

John Mulligan raised his eyebrows. "That's pretty good," he nodded before taking another sip of coffee.

Pretty soon everybody was in the act trying to help me help Murphy compose his floor speech against the poll tax. We kept modifying the House-Court relationship until we finally reached a consensus on the language: "Some of you may want to change your votes in light of yesterday afternoon's judicial decision, but there's not enough room for the House members to hide under the long, black robes of the State Supreme Court."

"That's good," said Murphy with a note of finality. "That's what I'm going to say in my speech on the floor."

Later that morning I couldn't resist sneaking out of the Senate to take in some of the House debate. John Murphy was finally recognized by the chair, and he rose to his feet. After exhorting his colleagues not to change their votes, he ended his remarks with an emotional appeal: "If you feel strongly and want to march forward, vote to repeal the poll tax. But if you feel weak and someone has to hold you up, walk in the shadow of the Supreme Court."

The speech was unsuccessful. A number of House members changed over from the previous day, and the repeal bill was killed on third reading by a 5-vote margin.

The next morning we held a post-mortem at the breakfast club. I sympathized with Murphy, who was pretty gloomy, but I couldn't resist asking why he had spoken about the shadow of the Court, rather than about hiding under the Court's long, black robes.

"Holy smokes!" he banged his head with his hand. "That's right, Smallwood. I got so excited, I forgot all about that. Holy smokes, I talked about the *shadow* of the Court instead of the robes."

"It's too bad, Murph." Frank Esposito shook his head sadly. "It's really too bad. I've been in the House since 1966, and this is the closest we've ever come to getting the poll tax repealed. Well, that's the breaks of the game. The unexpected twists and turns of politics: you talked about shadows instead of robes. It's really too bad. But we came close. And we appreciate your help, Senator. Let us know if there's anything we can do for you in the House."

As Frank Esposito predicted, as the days went by we did manage to exchange a lot of useful information about House-Senate activities during our breakfast hour. Three members of the HDBC were on the House Natural Resources Committee, so we kept each other posted on the status of bills in this area. Mostly, however, we were joking and rehashing each other's exploits in a noisy and often combative fashion. We reached our highest decibel count one Friday morning when Murphy hit his fifty-second birthday. The previous night the group had held a party for him at a local night spot where Murphy had unsuccessfully tried to cut a birthday cake that Flossie Robillard had made out of sponge rubber. Now the festivities were continuing into the morning breakfast hour.

"Come on, gang, let's sing Happy Birthday to Murphy." Frank Esposito jumped up and waved his arms. We all struggled through an off-key rendition, which was followed by a sedate round of polite applause from the other coffee shop patrons.

Murphy responded with a gigantic smile, a sure sign that he was already beginning to click into high gear for another day's legislative activity. "Hey, Smallwood," he said to me, "are you going to the Windsor County Farm Bureau meeting in Woodstock tonight?"

"Yes, Murph, I'll be there. I couldn't bear to miss it."

"O.K., but you better be on the ball. I'm driving over with Henry Hicks from Weathersfield. We're going to raise hell, telling all those people that the Senate is sitting on its duff, not getting out any bills."

"Drop dead, Murphy," I replied. "We're sitting on our duff all right—waiting for the House to send us a bill or two so we can get to work."

"Listen to that, will you," John Mulligan jumped into the fray. "It's not even eight o'clock in the morning, and the high-and-mighty Senator is already starting to pontificate."

We roared off into a wild free-for-all over the relative merits of the House and the Senate. Since I was outgunned about nine to one, the result was a foregone conclusion, but I put up a good scrap before we called it a breakfast. We had some pretty crazy times on the HDBC. John Murphy was tremendous, and when Frank Esposito and the others joined the chaos, it was really bedlam.

Clinton Rossiter was correct. The members of the House Democratic Breakfast Club had a unique style all their own.

Since I was tied up all morning in the Natural Resources Committee and on the floor of the Senate, my social schedule didn't pick up again until the noontime break.

I guess it is obvious by now that most meals were utilitarian, providing both sustenance and an opportunity to exchange political information. This is probably bad for the digestion, but the simple fact of the matter is that a lot of legislative activity takes place over drinks and meals.

Whenever possible, I liked to eat with senators who were not on one of my two committees, in order to find out the status of various bills they were considering.

I also ate lunch with different groups of House members.

The first group were some of the power-brokers: Speaker Walter Kennedy; Peter Guiliani and Emory Hebard, chairmen of the Ways and Means and Appropriations committees, respectively; Dick Snelling, a former Republican candidate for Governor, and the like.

The second were the Windsor County House members. We kept each other particularly well informed on bills which had a direct impact on any towns within the county.

Third were the sixteen women among the 150 House members, and a lot of them were interested in bills that landed in the Senate Health and Welfare Committee, so they would often come to me for information.

Finally, there was a sizable number of young legislators in the House, ten under the age of thirty, and I spent quite a bit of time with them. The influx of young House members into the 1973 legislature was an encouraging development. Ken Parker, a Democratic neighbor from White River Junction, had been the youngest member of the previous House, when he was the only legislator under twenty-five years of age. In the 1972 election, however, eight representatives younger than Ken were elected to the House, so Ken became the grand old man of the youth coalition.

Of all the House members, my real favorite was Judy Rosenstreich, a twenty-eight-year-old Republican from Waterbury Center, near the ski resort of Stowe. In the summer of 1973, Judy and I made a trip together to Florida to attend the Eagleton Institute's National Conference on State Legislatures. Judy had been chosen as the freshman representative from the House and I was selected from the Senate, so we decided to fly down together from Boston to West Palm Beach.

All during the flight we compared notes on why we had run for the legislature, and what we were trying to accomplish. She was such a solid legislator that I'll be surprised if a great many more Ver-

monters don't become familiar with her name in the not too distant
future.

¶AFTER LUNCH I met with the Senate Health and Welfare Committee,
usually until about four in the afternoon. During my first year in
Montpelier I had some free time before dinner after the committee
adjourned. The second year was different, though, because I stupidly
let myself get tied up virtually every afternoon before the dinner hour.

On Tuesdays I met in the late afternoon with either the Governor's
Commission on Higher Education (Tom Salmon had asked me to
chair this), or with the Governor's Commission on Medical Care (another special committee I was serving on). Wednesday afternoons I
taught a seminar on state politics. Since my sabbatical leave had ex-
pired at the end of the 1973 academic year, I was back teaching at
Dartmouth again, and during winter term I met with students in
Hanover on Mondays and Fridays, and in Montpelier for a late
Wednesday afternoon seminar. Senator Bill Doyle was also teaching a
group of students from Johnson State College, so we conducted the
seminar together from four to five-thirty. The seminars consisted
mainly of discussions with key state leaders: Governor Salmon, Lieutenant Governor Burgess, House Speaker Walter Kennedy, and the
like, plus lobbyists and members of the press corps. It was a great
opportunity for the students to gain firsthand knowledge of the
political process, but by the time we were finished I was pretty ex-
hausted.

Late Thursday afternoons were usually devoted to Republican
Party caucuses. Although we held a 23-to-7 majority in the Senate, we
had difficulty trying to hammer out a cohesive legislative program.
In the first place we disagreed with the House (although it was also
Republican by a 91-to-59 margin) over many priorities, and we
weren't very successful in getting together with the House leadership
on many common concerns. In addition, although we were all Republicans, we disagreed among ourselves about a sizable number of
bills.

Perhaps this was a reflection of the historic Vermont Yankee inde-

pendent tradition, but we all tended to go off in our own directions
to a point where I couldn't see much philosophical difference between many members of the two major political parties. Professor
Duane Lockard had picked up this trait fifteen years earlier in his
study *New England State Politics* when he had observed, "Vermont
is a land of political paradox. It is conservative, but it has a liberal
strain. It has a one-party system, but it lacks many of the common
attributes of one-partyism. Early in its history Vermont was liberal,
even radical, in belief and action; later it abruptly turned to marked
conservatism and in this century it has by fits and starts been both
conservative and liberal in its public policies."

Lockard's observation held up quite well in the 1973–74 legislative
session. By this point, however, Vermont was no longer a one-party
state. The Democrats had come on strong in more recent elections,
and there was now even a third party, the Liberty Union, the most
radical group of all, which hadn't won any elections but was beginning to build up support at the grass-roots level.

Within the two major parties there was no clear-cut pattern of
political ideology at all. Jack O'Brien, the Democratic Minority
leader, was the most conservative member of the Senate, while John
Alden, the youngest Republican, was one of the most liberal. At first,
I sided with John on a lot of bills, and we often voted against our
third Windsor County colleague, Herb Ogden, who was more conservative. Later in the second session, however, I began to agree with
Herb on a number of issues, especially those involving budgetary expenditures since I felt Vermont was getting into a very precarious position in its financial commitments.

During the period 1966 to 1974, the state combined General and
Highway funds had climbed from $68 million a year to $190 million.
At the same time, the debt had also soared to a point where each Vermonter owed an average of $600 in net long-term state debt, com-
pared to a national average of only $217 per capita. Three-quarters of
our General Fund expenditures went to education and human services
programs—both were worthwhile but very costly—while the Highway
Fund chewed up another big chunk of money. Since Vermont had
only 460,000 people, we were being taxed black and blue to carry this

load. In addition to a 3 percent sales tax and all sorts of splinter taxes, we had a brutal state income tax which was piggy-backed on top of the federal tax at a 28 percent rate. In other words, we paid our federal income tax, and then added 28 percent on top of this in the form of a state income tax. Our over-all per capita rankings among the fifty states were very heavy: *fourth* in per capita total state expenditures, *fifth* in net long-term state debt, *fifth* in total per capita highway expenditures, *sixth* in total per capita welfare expenditures; and last, but not least, *first* in state and local tax burden in relation to personal income.

The more I looked at this situation the more I became concerned that we were trying to take on too many commitments for a small state. We simply didn't have the resources to be all things to all people. Paradoxically, one of our major financial problems resulted from the fact that Vermont received a sizable bundle of federal grants. This meant, however, that we became locked in to matching-fund programs, and we were also overwhelmed by a tangle of federal regulations that made it impossible for us to breathe in many areas. The worst of all was in human services, where we had virtually no control over welfare or any other programs.

Another difficult area was environmental controls, where the feds mandated a series of water-quality standards; which meant we had to revise our own state water-quality program, already one of the most progressive in the nation. Jack O'Brien and I rebelled on the Natural Resources Committee, and refused to vote out a new bill incorporating the federal standards, but it passed anyway since it contained a hook: if we refused to accept the federal regulations, we lost our federal grants—which we couldn't afford to lose, because we didn't have sufficient revenues to cover our own programs. The states are really caught in the middle. About the only flexible federal funds we received came from revenue-sharing, and these were minuscule in terms of our needs.

The more I thought about federal-state relations, the more I concluded that we had been naive to get sucked into such a dependency relationship. However, what was done was done. We were now dealing with existing realities, and it was very uncomfortable to realize that we were relatively powerless to withstand the Washington juggernaut.

I think the area of federal-state coercion represented the single most frustrating aspect of my entire legislative experience in Montpelier. I'm not so sure that you should never look a gift horse in the mouth.

¶AFTER the fast pace of the legislative day, dinner was a welcome relief. Some evenings I was so bushed that I'd simply have a quiet meal in the coffee shop, then yawn my way back to my hotel room, read a few bills on the next day's Notice Calendar, and drop off to sleep rather early.

If I had more pep I would go out to dinner with one or two legislative colleagues, either in Montpelier or to one of the nearby ski resorts, such as Stowe, where the restaurants were pretty good. Occasionally, I was lucky enough to be invited out for a home-cooked meal, either by a local Senate couple, like Bill and Olene Doyle, or by Senate couples who were renting houses in the Montpelier area, like Ed and Elinor Janeway, Fred and Marjorie Smith, or Ward and Molly Bedford. The two who really looked after me above the call of duty were Bob and Aldie Gannett. Bob and I became very close in the Senate, so he invited me over to dinner quite often. Because Aldie's mother, Mrs. Richard Derby, the younger daughter of President Theodore Roosevelt, lived in the Windsor County town of Cavendish during the summer months, Aldie always referred to me rather proudly as "Mother's senator."

In addition to the dinner circuit, there were a couple of other diversions to occupy the evening hours.

Public hearings on pending legislation were scheduled for most Tuesday and Thursday evenings, and these could be interesting and exciting, especially if a proposed bill was controversial. I attended a lot of hearings, and learned a great deal in the process.

The biggest social event of the week was "farm night" scheduled in the House Chamber every Wednesday evening when the legislature was in session. Organized by Representative Tony Buraczynski, these affairs consisted of entertainment provided by groups drawn from all corners of Vermont. There were high school band concerts, Stratton Mountain yodelers, Robert Frost poetry readings, singing groups from the Burlington area, and a host of other attractions. It was hardly sophisticated big-city entertainment, but we had a lot of fun. After the formal programs we adjourned to the State House cafeteria for a round of square dancing, with some good callers and fiddlers, followed by a group sing around a piano accompaniment by Representative Kenalene Collins of Readsboro.

If nothing else was taking place, I would often conclude my day with a swim and a sauna at my hotel. Quite a bit of legislative business was conducted in the swimming pool. Since it was only about thirty-five feet long, there was no place to hide if another aquanautic legislator wanted to discuss the affairs of state during an evening swim.

One night I was treading water in the deep end when Representative Esther Cohen began to paddle vigorously in my direction. Esther, short and stout and sixty-two years old, was a Democrat from Burlington who served on the House Health and Welfare Committee. We were old friends, having worked together on a number of education study committees when I was a member of the State Colleges Board of Trustees. On this particular evening, I could see fire in her eyes which contrasted sharply with her white bathing cap as she navigated in a beeline towards me.

"Frank," she gasped as she reached my side, "our committee is completely overrun with licensing bills. Everybody in Vermont wants to get licensed for one thing or another—septic-tank installers, hearing-aid specialists, well-drillers, the list is endless. We've got to do something to get some order into this licensing situation. It's a scandal."

"I agree with you completely, Esther," I told her as I continued to tread water to keep from sinking. "It's the same thing in the Senate. We're talking with everybody from bartenders to funeral directors. I don't know what to do about it. Do you have any ideas?"

"What would you think of setting up a statewide licensing board?" she asked, even though she was huffing and puffing for breath. "A licensing board could monitor the whole system, and hear appeals if applicants felt they were not being treated fairly."

"That's not a bad idea," I started to reply just as I noticed some fun-loving Republican lawmakers jumping in our direction in a high cannonball trajectory. "Watch out, Esther!" I yelled. But it was too late—*boom, crash, splat!* The pool exploded, with water erupting around us in every direction. Esther bounced up like a cork before descending rapidly right in front of my eyes.

Somehow I managed to stay afloat, and when the first one's head emerged I really let him have it. "Dammit, why can't you watch out where you do your crazy cannonballs," I shouted at him as I grabbed for Esther, who was beginning to resurface from the bottom. She emerged with a gasp, and I could see real fire in her eyes now as she looked in the culprit's direction.

"Oh, you Republicans!" she sputtered at him. "It's disgraceful. I don't know how you expect us to get anything done in this legislature if you carry on like that."

After coughing for a few more moments, she looked back in my direction and said, "Where were we before we were so rudely interrupted? Oh yes, a state licensing board. Think about it, and let me know how you feel."

That was the end of our conversation, but that night turned out to be a double-barreled legislative session, because I was in for still another public-policy discussion when I arrived at the sauna downstairs. It was occupied by Gerald Morse, the senator who had demanded the roll-call vote on the first bill I had reported, the one on Sunday-morning sale of wine and beer. Gerald, a massive man, was sweating profusely as I entered the sauna. He had a towel wrapped around his middle, and he was leaning back dreamily on the upper bench as I closed the door.

"Ah, Frank, I'm glad I have a chance to talk with you," he greeted me as I arranged myself on the lower bench. "I'm concerned about a bill which is stuck in the Senate Natural Resources Committee. I submitted it on the first day of the session, and nothing has happened in over a month. It's S. 45, permitting the state to sell land titles to people who have built camps on state-owned land in Groton Pond. There are about twenty-six camps in all, every one of them owned by a Vermonter. Now the state wants to terminate the land leases, and the residents will have to burn down their camps. It doesn't seem fair. The state should allow the people a chance to buy the land before they throw them off."

"Good Lord, Gerald, I don't remember the bill at all," I replied. "I'll look it up tomorrow morning, and let you know where we stand on it."

"Thanks a lot." He leaned back against the upper bench to soak up more of the dry, crackly heat. "Anything you can do will be appreciated."

Well, to make a long story short, the Natural Resources Committee held eleven separate meetings on his bill before the Senate finally voted to pass it. The House went along, so I thought the affair was ended happily until we discovered that the Groton Pond sale was one of only two bills which Governor Salmon vetoed. The Governor was willing to work out some long-term lease arrangement, but felt it would be a bad precedent for the state to sell the land outright. During the adjourned 1974 session, the Senate overrode his veto, but the House refused to go along, so a long-term lease arrangement was finally consummated.

The entire controversy took the better part of a year. I wasn't convinced it was worth the effort, but there was no place you could hide in the legislature. You weren't even safe in a sauna bath.

The continuous stream of contacts and confrontations which took place all during the day constituted an integral part of the legislative process. Information was exchanged, new ideas were aired, compromises were ironed out during a stream of chatter morning, noon and night. Political interaction was a nonstop endeavor. Breakfast, lunch, dinner, swimming, saunas—it didn't make any difference what you were doing, all conversation invariably drifted around to politics, politics, and still more politics.

Yet this was only half the communications network. The other half involved constituency contacts with the general public, and the special-interest groups who spoke for selected segments of this public. Even when we left Montpelier for weekend adjournments, we were still engaged in the unending business of political communication.

There were a lot of restless, demanding people back there in the home towns who wanted to know what we were doing, and why we were doing it. Liaison with this public sector was another crucial ingredient in the legislative process.

PART III

The Public

11

Vox Populi

> If Abraham Lincoln was alive today, he
> would turn over in his grave.
> Grocer, testifying on the Vermont
> "Bottle Ban" Law

THE KEY LINES of communication between me and the public ran in two directions, incoming and outgoing. The incoming switchboard lit up whenever constituents made an effort to reach me, at all hours of the day or night, by means of public hearings, telephone calls, letters, conversations in the local store—you name it, they used it.

What was really at work here was a public desire for ongoing participation in the political process. Sure, we had been elected to represent their interests, but many people wanted to be very certain that they expressed these interests to us directly so that we wouldn't go veering off on unknown tangents. Consequently, people communicated with their legislators on a wide variety of issues, especially if they felt they had real or imagined grievances they wanted to call to our attention. Let's look at the major ways people took it upon themselves to make their views and concerns known to us.

1. Public Hearings

During both my winters in Montpelier I was astonished at the large number of people who showed up for public hearings. Admittedly, some hearings were small if they dealt with fairly narrow issues, although spokesmen and lobbyists who were concerned about that particular problem were always at hand. But the more visible, emotional issues really drew big crowds, who poured into the State House to argue about bills involving morals and/or sex (such as the Equal Rights Amendment and the regulation of marijuana), or about economic concerns (such as the "bottle ban" legislation or land-use regulations). When these matters came up, public hearings were scheduled for the evening hours in the House Chamber to accommodate the hundreds of people who would flood into Montpelier from all over the state.

I went to my first big hearing with Jack O'Brien during the opening month of the 1973 legislature. It concerned the ratification of the Equal Rights Amendment to the United States Constitution. When the issue originally came up during the first weeks of the session, it didn't seem to be controversial since it breezed through the House in no time flat. Then it got bogged down in the Senate, allowing enough time for the opposition to get itself organized. The amendment was under the jurisdiction of the Judiciary Committee, where Chairman Garry Buckley was so deluged with phone calls that he felt obligated to hold a public hearing to let the people ventilate their views, pro and con.

Jack O'Brien and I arrived in the House Chamber early, about seven-fifteen, and took seats in the row just across from the witness table. It soon became evident that this was destined to be a major event, as all the seats in the House filled up quickly and the crowd began to overflow into the balcony.

"It looks like this is going to be a big one," Jack remarked casually as he surveyed the room with his arms folded across his chest. "You know, Frank, it may surprise you, but I'm going to support this amendment. Now don't get me wrong. I'm not for the women-libbers, but I promised my daughter I'd support this. She's a schoolteacher in Burlington who feels very strongly that she should have the same equal rights along with the rest of us."

"I'm with you all the way," I told him. "I committed myself to support the amendment last summer during the primary campaign. The question came up every time I met with a League of Women Voters' group. You know, I'm surprised at the size of this crowd. I didn't think this was a very controversial matter. I just assumed that,

in the year 1973, everybody would want to support an Equal Rights
Amendment to the United States Constitution."

"Oh, no. Oh, no. Just you wait and see," Jack replied warily. "This
is very controversial. Just you wait and see."

So many people signed up to testify at the hearing that the Judiciary
Committee had to adopt special ground rules. They decided to limit
statements to five minutes apiece, and to alternate the testimony, the
first ten witnesses speaking in favor of the amendment, with the next
ten speaking against it, until everybody had a chance to testify. Bill
Daniels, the clerk of the committee, wandered over and told us that
more than fifty people had already signed up. Even by limiting statements to five minutes apiece, the hearing would run until well after
midnight. Jack O'Brien was right. This was obviously very controversial.

The first ten witnesses to testify in favor of the amendment were all
women, all extremely articulate, all professionals (lawyers, doctors,
etc.) or chairpersons of key civic groups throughout the state. Most of
them wore smartly tailored suits, a form of apparel that increasingly
dismayed Jack O'Brien.

"Good God, Frank," he moaned as the eighth witness walked down
the aisle, "here comes another one wearing pants. What the hell is
the matter with these women anyway? Don't none of them know
enough to wear dresses?"

"It's the new style, Jack," I reassured him; "they're very up to date.
And I'm quite impressed with their testimony. All these women are
extremely articulate."

"Articulate, hell. They don't even know how to wear a dress. Fred
Westphal told me I'd made a mistake on this one. You know Fred's a
real conservative from Lamoille County. The women up there don't
wear pants. I should never have promised my daughter I'd vote for
this amendment. Good Lord, what a display."

I didn't pay much attention to Jack's rumblings until the original
ten supporters of the amendment had finished. As soon as the first
opposition witness stepped forward, I couldn't help but be startled
by the contrast. She looked about the same age as the previous group,

in her late twenties or early thirties, but her appearance was completely different. She wore a starched white blouse with ruffles down the front, a black woolen skirt, and plain black shoes. She was also carrying a book in her hand. I couldn't make out what it was until she reached the witness table, where she opened it right in front of me. It was the Bible. She placed her hand on top of one of the pages, and made what seemed to be a short, silent prayer before she began to speak.

Unlike the earlier more confident witnesses, she spoke in a nervous, halting voice; and her hands were trembling. The heart of her message was simple: God had created woman from Adam's rib, so the Equal Rights Amendment was not only dangerous and undesirable, but it violated the Scriptures.

I was utterly overwhelmed, not only by the woman's appearance and testimony, but by my own reaction to it. Although I couldn't really follow much of her statement, I was tremendously impressed by her courage. She was testifying in a strange setting before a very big audience, probably the biggest she had ever spoken to in her life. Despite her fear and trembling, she spoke out with a real display of conviction. She seemed to be drawing on some inner source of strength, undoubtedly the Bible in her hands, to get through the ordeal. Then, just as she was finishing her testimony, and spoke about Adam's rib, a titter of laughter erupted in various parts of the audience.

Garry Buckley reacted instantly. Banging down his gavel, he announced in an angry voice that no disruptions of any kind would be tolerated during the hearing. Jack O'Brien was even more angry.

"Dammit, just listen to that!" he exclaimed. "Just listen to that. Here this fine lady comes down from Lamoille County, and she's greeted with laughter when she quotes from Scripture. This is an outrage. I'm not going to put up with it. I'm not going to sit here all night and take this kind of treatment. Fred Westphal was right. I never should have promised my daughter to support the equal rights." He rose from his seat and stomped out of the House Chamber.

I stayed for a long, long time, however, despite the fact that the testimony became monotonous and the witnesses repetitious: tailored suits versus starched white blouses; articulate statistics on employment discrimination versus quotes from the Bible. It was two totally dif-

ferent worlds, two fundamentally different lifestyles—urban versus
rural America. The women in their tailored suits came from the
larger population centers: Burlington, Rutland, the Barre-Montpelier
area. The women in their white blouses came from the smaller towns
to the north: Jeffersonville, Danville, Burke, Wheelock, Brownington.
I stayed because it opened up a whole new Vermont for me in the
form of the women who came down from Lamoille County and the
small towns in the Northeast Kingdom. This was a Vermont with
which I had had no previous contact.

It was a humbling experience. I still supported the Equal Rights
Amendment, but I realized it was difficult to take anything for granted
in politics. There's no such thing as a noncontroversial issue. A lot of
people out there held opinions diametrically opposed to my own, and
I hadn't even been aware of their concerns. As a legislative representative, at least I owed them the responsibility to listen to their views,
even if I disagreed with them.

I decided then and there that I would attend as many hearings as
possible during my stay in Montpelier.

Although most public hearings were inconclusive, occasionally they
could make a difference. Such was the case with *H. 477,* a bill sponsored
by a group of young House members which was designed to "decriminalize" the personal use of small quantities of marijuana.

Once again, the House Chamber was packed when *H. 477* came up
for a hearing, sponsored this time by the House Judiciary Committee.
Unlike Garry Buckley, the chairman of the House committee, Representative Tim O'Connor, didn't place a time limit on the speakers, although he did indicate he would alternate the testimony, the first four
witnesses being in favor of the bill and the subsequent four opposed,
until all of them had a chance to testify. The lack of a time limit
proved to be unfortunate because the House Chamber was brightly
illuminated and very hot, thanks to floodlights which had been in-
stalled all over the place in order to make an Educational TV film of
the hearing.

The young House members who sponsored the bill had worked hard
to line up an impressive array of expert witnesses, with each of the first

four speakers coming from out of state. One was a professor from the Harvard Medical School, and the three others were from Washington, D.C.: an elderly woman doctor, a former official in the Federal Bureau of Narcotics, and a spokesman for a group know as NORMAL (National Organization for Reform of Marijuana Laws). The witnesses presented reams of statistical data and other material in an effort to indicate that there was no compelling evidence to prove that marijuana was a dangerous drug. The four of them took almost an hour, which was much too long for the audience was seething under the hot floodlights. Obviously, facts and statistics are important to legislative deliberations, but they can be overdone, since many issues are settled on the basis of emotions and perceptions. There was an audible sigh of relief when the four witnesses finished, and Tim O'Connor called on the first opposition witness.

At this point a burly farmer, decked out in faded blue overalls and a bright red flannel shirt, came pounding down the aisle. He identified himself as a Vermonter.

"That's right, I'm a Vermonter. Born and bred in Vermont, and I don't want to sit here like a monkey all night under these hot lights and listen to a bunch of out-of-state 'experts' tell me how to run my own life."

It was a pretty potent political thrust, an effective appeal to Vermont traditionalism, which brought an appreciative murmur from many in the audience. Then the farmer turned full circle, and pointed directly at the last witness to testify, the spokesman from NORMAL: "Young fella," he bellowed, "I want to know who paid for your trip up here from Washington, D.C."

The spokesman rose hesitantly in his seat, and started to explain the various sources of NORMAL's financing. "We are supported by many different groups." He paused. "Let's see, some of our money comes from medical foundations, some from mental health associations, some from the Playboy Foundation . . ."

"The Playboy Foundation!" the farmer roared out. "Did I hear you say your trip up here to Vermont was paid for by the Playboy Foundation?!"

There was a momentary silence before the audience exploded. I realized right there on the spot that the marijuana decriminalization bill was dead as a doornail. Although the hearing went on for hours, no further witnesses were needed. The Vermont House was not about to vote out a bill to decriminalize pot when it was backed up by the resources of the Playboy Foundation.

That hearing signified a quick, decisive death blow for the marijuana bill, but other bills would go through hearing after hearing without any conclusive results at all. Such was the case with the bottle law. Each year, bills were sponsored to repeal, amend or strengthen the "bottle deposit" legislation, and whenever a hearing was held on one of them, the grocers would stream into town to express their outrage over loss of business in border stores, and loss of dignity because they were being turned into garbage collectors.

The verbal pyrotechnics at these gatherings really could approach the spectacular. One of my Dartmouth students, Kevin Fitzgerald, went to a bottle-ban hearing with me, and he couldn't believe so many people could be excited over this kind of issue. "Oh, no, this is very controversial," I told him, repeating Jack O'Brien's earlier observation on the Equal Rights Amendment. "Just you wait and see. This is very controversial."

The first speaker, an Enosburg Falls grocer, began the fireworks in a most dramatic, Lincolnesque fashion: "We, the people. That's right, ladies and gentlemen. You and me. We, the people, are in jeopardy. If Abraham Lincoln was alive today he would turn over in his grave. The road to hell is paved with good intentions." He waved his arm in a long, graceful sweep across the spacious legislative hall. "I wish the honorable legislators in this chamber who passed this dreadful law would hit that road."

A huge roar went up from the crowd (it was impossible to control a bottle-ban hearing despite repeated warnings from the chairman). Kevin was staggered. "I can't believe it," he shouted to me over the surrounding din. "Abraham Lincoln and *bottles*?"

But that's the way it went all night long. A continuous uproar over free enterprise, minutemen, the Green Mountain Boys, Abraham Lincoln, and a host of other heroic figures. The most moving comment of all, however, was spoken very softly by a quiet little grocer who sat down next to me after Kevin had called it a night. The grocer was about five feet, five inches tall; he was dressed in a plain black suit, with white socks and polished black shoes. He introduced himself as "Mr. Tony," the owner of a store in Brattleboro down in the southeast corner of the state.

"It's nice to meet you, Mr. Tony," I replied. "My name is Frank Smallwood. I'm a senator from Windsor County, just to the north of you, up near the White River Junction area."

"Senator Smallwood," he said in an earnest, pleading tone, "I'm a border grocer. The people in my area don't want to pay the higher prices on deposit bottles. They don't want to bring their bottles back to the store. Instead, they drive over to New Hampshire or down to Massachusetts where there's no deposit at all. I'm losing my business to out-of-state competitors. Why are you driving me out of business? Why does the legislature want to drive people like me out of business?"

I looked down at the floor and shook my head silently. I couldn't think of a helpful reply. The emotions on both sides of the bottle law were so intense that I couldn't think of any way to work out a reasonable compromise between the environmentalists who favored the bill and the grocers who were bitterly opposed. I didn't see much room to maneuver on this one. And unfortunately the tumultuous hearings in the House Chamber didn't provide any real answers at all.

2. Lobbying

While the general public focused a lot of energy on the big hearings, the State House lobbyists blanketed any and all events—hearings, committee meetings, floor debates. Whatever the occasion, the lobbyists were present if their interests were affected. Although I had taught political science for fifteen years, I didn't have any first hand acquaintance with lobbyists before my arrival in Montpelier. The only one I could ever recall meeting had lectured to one of my graduate-school classes at Harvard back in the early 1950's. I remember very distinctly that he had encouraged us to consider professional careers in lobbying if we were really interested in changing public policy in the United

States. After I watched the lobbyists at work in the Vermont legislature, I understood what he was talking about.

The State House lobbyists were an extremely varied lot. Some were
part-time, unpaid amateurs who drifted in and out on behalf of such
causes and organizations as Save Spruce Mountain, the League of
Women Voters, the Vermont Federation of Sportsmen, and Child
Advocates, a citizens' lobby which spoke on behalf of legislation bene-
ficial to young children. Many of them, however, were full-time resi-
dent lobbyists who represented such groups as the Associated Industries
of Vermont, the League of Cities and Towns, the Retail Grocers'
Association, the Farm Bureau, the Vermont Public Interest Research
Group, the State Labor Council AFL-CIO: the Vermont Truck and Bus
Association, the Wholesale Beverage Association, the Vermont State
Nurses Association, the Vermont Education Association, Legal Aid, the
Low Income Advocacy Council, the State Employees Association, en-
vironmental groups like Vermont Tomorrow; and on and on. In addi-
tion, some organizations retained nonresident lawyers who came to
Montpelier as the occasion demanded: John Carbine of Rutland for
the electric utility companies; Ralph Foote of Middlebury, a former
Lieutenant Governor who represented the Vermont Nursing Home
Association, among other clients; and Henry Black of White River
Junction, who seemed to have been a fixture around the State House
since the days of the original republic of Vermont back in 1777–91.

Also, the heads of the state executive agencies spent a lot of time
lobbying for their bills when the legislature was in session, and we
invariably had one or more agency secretaries or commissioners testifying on bills in committees and during public hearings.

Although the lobbyists represented a wide diversity of interests, most
of them had a number of characteristics in common. As a general rule,
they were articulate, hard-working, and extremely well informed in
their particular areas of expertise. This last attribute—information—
represented their chief weapon and gave them real clout. As far as
I could find out, the lobbyists didn't offer legislators any money or
other direct inducements; at least, they never offered me anything, not
even a sociable drink. Instead, they relied on information. They were

specialists, both in their subject matter and also in the dynamics of the legislative process and procedures. The reason they knew the procedures so well was because many of them concentrated on negative, or defensive, lobbying in an attempt to block a bill from passage. James Finneran, who represented labor, the truckers and the Vermont Wholesale Beverage Association in Montpelier, explained the reason for this to some of my students in terms of "Finneran's Law of Seventy."

When I invited Jim down to Dartmouth to speak to one of my classes, he showed up dressed to the teeth as the "perfect" lobbyist— dark-blue shirt, white polka-dot tie, dark-tinted glasses (to protect his eyes against the glare of the snow, he explained, although his visit took place in the month of May). Jim, a short, wiry, forty-three-year-old Irish import from Worcester, Massachusetts, with a master's degree in politics, was one of the more intriguing characters in the State House lobby corps. Because of his flashy dress, the press took great pleasure in portraying him as the lobbyist incarnate. He was a very dedicated professional, as he indicated when he described his Law of Seventy to my students.

"If a bill hits the floor, you don't have the foggiest idea how the vote will come out unless you do an awful lot of homework. It's a hell of a lot easier to kill a bill than it is to pass it.

"To kill a bill, all you need is a majority of a committee, but to pass it you need a majority of the House. To put it in mathematical terms, there are eleven menbers on most of the key House committees I deal with: Commerce, Highways, Natural Resources. If I can help just six of these eleven members to see the sweet light of reason, then I can kill a bill by keeping it bottled up in committee.

"But once it gets out on the floor, it takes seventy-six members to kill it, since there are one hundred fifty members in the House. The difference between six votes and seventy-six votes constitutes Finneran's Law of Seventy. Give me a choice, and I'd much rather kill a bill with six votes than try to get one killed with seventy-six votes. It's a simple matter of political arithmetic; the arithmetic of time and energy."

Although defensive lobbying played a prominent role at the State House in Montpelier, there were some instances where lobbyists got legislators to initiate bills which promoted their specific concerns. In his book on the United States Congress, *Member of the House,* Representative Clem Miller provided a classic account of how the walnut-growers launched a highly successful campaign to get the federal government to buy excess walnuts for diversion into the school lunch program in order to keep the price of walnuts stable.

We didn't have any walnut growers in Vermont, but a number of interest groups were quite active in trying to make things happen. The Vermont Public Interest Research Group, for example, worked closely with Representative Brian Burns, a Democrat from Burlington, to push a children's dental-care measure through the legislature. I cooperated with Child Advocates Inc., in preparing a child-abuse reporting bill which I sponsored, and also with the Vermont League of Cities and Towns on another bill to establish a comprehensive retirement system for local government employees. These groups were invaluable because they had the knowledge to translate ideas into the reality of statutory law.

Since there were over one hundred registered lobbyists in the State House, it was impossible to know them all. I met quite a few, however, and I was somewhat surprised by the fact that I developed a much more effective relationship with the economically oriented business lobbyists than with many of the environmental and public-interest spokesmen. The main reason for this was that the economic lobbyists would talk very straight and very directly. They had a down-to-earth, pragmatic grasp of what they were after, which made it easy for me to give them a simple Yes or No answer (if I agreed or disagreed with them). A number of the public-interest lobbyists, on the other hand, tended to be considerably more diffuse, to a point where it was often difficult to understand what they wanted. Also, when they portrayed themselves as representing "the public interest," some of them appeared to interpret this amorphous concept in terms of their own personal policy preferences which I was never certain really coincided with "the public interest" (whatever that was).

On the whole, however, the great majority of the lobbyists constituted an interesting assemblage of energy, experience, and expertise. They provided an important daily input into the legislative process as they hovered around the State House, pushing and hauling in an effort to see killed, or passed, the bills which they felt were important.

3. Telephone Calls

When Alexander Graham Bell invented the telephone back in 1876, he started a revolution in constituency communication. Every time I got back to my hotel room in Montpelier, there were at least two or three messages waiting for me *(Please call* ———) , and during weekends at home the phone seemed to ring all the time. The children would often answer, and I never knew what to expect when they would cover the phone with a hand and say, "Dad, it's for you. It's Mr. [Someone] from Hartland," a totally unknown name to me.

The most intriguing call I received during my two years in the legislature was not from a stranger, however, but from an old friend, Dan Fraser, the owner of Dan & Whit's General Store in Norwich. It all started late one afternoon when I picked up the phone myself:

"Hello, Frank. This is Dan Fraser. I've got a problem with the state, and I wonder if you could help me out."

"I'll be glad to try, Dan," I replied. "What seems to be the trouble?"

"It involves shrinking gasoline. I just found out I'm paying taxes on shrinking gasoline. I don't think that's fair. Do you?"

"Wait a minute, Dan," I responded. "I'm not sure we've got a good connection here. It sounded to me like you said something about shrinking gasoline."

"That's right," he repeated. "The state is taxing me on shrinking gasoline, and I want you to do something about it."

"Look, Dan, I've got to come down to the store a little later this evening to pick up a couple of quarts of milk. Why don't we talk this over then?"

"O.K., that's fine with me. I'll be here until closing. I really hope you can straighten this out because it's a helluva thing for the state to do."

After Dan hung up, I tried to imagine what in God's name he could be talking about. He was an interesting and shrewd Yankee; a Vermont native, born in Norwich. Over the years he had worked non-stop to build up his business to a point where his all-purpose store grossed over a million dollars a year. The place was open 364½ days annually (closed at noon on Christmas) to sell every kind of consumer product imaginable—food, clothing, hardware, gasoline, the works. Dan always kept a sharp eye out for anything that affected his operations, and during my tenure in the legislature he'd given me numerous earfuls on the bottle law, milk price controls, and a host of other complaints. But shrinking gasoline? This was a new one. He'd never mentioned this before during the course of our lengthy conversations.

When I arrived at the store that evening he was sitting up at his desk high above the paint and hardware section.

"Hi, Dan," I greeted him warily. "What's the problem with your shrinking gasoline?"

"Good of you to drop by," he returned my greeting while reaching up for a pile of bills that were stacked on top of his desk. "These are the accounts I receive from Purcell's Oil Company every time they deliver gasoline for the pumps in front of the store. We're keeping very close track of them this winter because of the gas shortage. Half the time we can't get regular deliveries so it's important to keep precise records in order to know exactly how much we have. Well, to get to the point, last month we began to notice that we weren't selling exactly the same amount of gas as was being delivered. We were losing between one percent and three percent of our deliveries each month."

Aha, I thought. Foul play. As a result of the gas shortage, they were getting short-changed on their deliveries.

"I couldn't figure it out," Dan continued. "Then I remembered reading something way back about gas shrinking if there was a temperature change. Yesterday morning when Purcell delivered a load of gas, I went out, jumped up on top of the truck, and dropped a thermometer inside. It was on a piece of string. The gas inside the truck had a temperature of fifty degrees. This morning I dropped the same thermometer down inside our tank under the ground next to the pumps. The temperature was only forty degrees. You know, it's pretty cold at this time of year, so the gas cools off in the tank under the ground."

Holy smokes. I couldn't believe it. This was really wild. The mysterious case of the frozen gasoline.

"Well, this morning I called up the motor vehicle department in Montpelier to tell them I thought I was losing gas because it shrunk in the ground. The fella up there—I can't remember his name—but the fella up there told me, 'Yup, that's right, gasoline shrinks if there's a drop in the temperature; for every one degree drop in the temperature, it shrinks six gallons out of a thousand.' Now that's my problem. Every time Purcell brings me gas I pay them nine cents for each gallon they deliver to cover the state gasoline tax. I'm supposed to get it back when I sell the gas, but I don't get it all back because the gas shrinks so I don't sell as much as I buy. Take last year." He paused while he shuffled through his papers. "Yes, here it is. Last year I bought 538,862 gallons of gas from Purcell. I figure at least one percent of that gas shrinked away in the ground, probably more. But even at one percent shrinkage, I paid a tax on 5,388 gallons that I never sold. At nine cents a gallon that's a total tax of $484.92. I figure the state owes me at least $484.92 in back tax refunds for gas I never even sold last year because it shrunk in the ground, and I want you to get it back for me."

I gasped in disbelief, trying to follow the tortuous trail of the shrinking gas from Purcell's truck, to Dan's tank under the ground, to the automobiles which filled up at the front of his store. Finally I responded with a question.

"Dan, I can see where you could lose gas in the winter due to a drop in the temperature, but what about the summer? If gas shrinks in the winter, then maybe it expands in the summer. If that's the case, you'd break even during the course of the year."

"Yes, you're right," he replied. " Gas does expand when the temperature goes up. According to the fella in Montpelier, you get back six more gallons in a thousand for every one degree rise in the temperature. But that doesn't do me any good at all. You see, in the summer Purcell takes its gas out of storage tanks sitting above the ground that are in the sun all day. The gas sits in the hot sun all day, and then it cools off again when they put it in my tank under the ground. Actually, I figure I lose more gas shrinking in my tank during the summer than in the winter. In the winter, they keep the trucks in a heated garage to get them started in the morning, but in the summer their gas is even hotter because it sits in the sun. Maybe you should pass a law that tanks can't sit in the sun. Maybe all the gas should be stored underground for safety as well as shrinkage."

I nodded sympathetically. He'd obviously done his homework on this one.

"Well, O.K. I can see where you've got a problem, but it's pretty complicated, and we aren't going to solve it here. I'll call the tax department when I go back to Montpelier next Tuesday to see what they think should be done about this."

"Fine," Dan nodded back. "That's what I hoped you would do. I appreciate your help."

It was the beginning of a long and arduous run-around. I called the tax department to explain the problem. At first they wouldn't believe me, but I assured them that gas was shrinking under the ground in Norwich, and probably everywhere else in the state. After numerous discussions, I finally suggested a potential solution; namely, that they should levy a tax on the gas that was sold out of the pumps, rather than on the gas that was delivered into the storage tank below the pumps. In this way, no gas could be taxed unless it was actually sold. They balked at this, indicating that they were unsure of the revenue implications for the state highway fund. In the end, they took the classic way out. They agreed to appoint a study committee to look into the problem, and report future recommendations. As far as I could find out nothing happened to the study, and the matter is still under investigation.

Dan Fraser was mad as hell. He wanted the $484.92 he figured the state owed him, and he wanted it in no uncertain terms. As I said, he was a native Vermonter. It was bad enough to pay any taxes at all, but he sure as blazes didn't want to pay taxes on something that didn't exist because it was shrinking away in the chilly, dark tank under the ground in front of his General Store.

4. Letters

If all forms of oral communication failed, constituents could always pick up their pens, and churn out a letter to air their grievances and express their opinions.

I received all sorts of letters on all sorts of issues from all sorts of people. Occasionally, I would receive a letter thanking me for something I had done in the legislature, but this was pretty rare. Most people didn't appear to utilize the U.S. Postal Service unless they had something on their minds, or something to get off their minds.

The most hostile letter I received involved an issue over which I had no jurisdiction whatsoever. It was written by an outraged woman from the Springfield area when the gasoline shortage became acute in the winter of 1974, and there was talk in Washington about staggering hours of sales, or possibly rationing gasoline:

> Dear Senator Smallwood,
>   Who the hell do you think you are to tell me that I can't drive my car on Sunday? Do you think this is Nazi Germany? We have certain rights in America, and one of them is the right to drive our cars on Sunday especially when Nixon flies his airplane all over the place all the time.

This particular letter really miffed me. I hadn't realized the founding fathers had guaranteed everybody a Constitutional right to drive their automobiles whenever they pleased, but I figured out some kind of reply because I always attempted to respond to letters. Since we had no real secretarial help in Montpelier, I decided it was easiest to send brief handwritten notes, and I spent quite a bit of time keeping up with correspondence in my hotel room in Montpelier or at home during weekends. Actually, this turned out to be one practice which actually produced complimentary letters back from constituents. A number of them indicated this was the first time in their lives they had ever received a handwritten note from one of their elected officials. They were very impressed with the personal touch, and they wanted to thank me for taking time to write.

This last observation indicates something very significant about the political communications process inward, from my constituents to me. I think a great deal of the importance of these communications resulted from the fact that they provided people with an opportunity to express their opinions, an outlet to air their concerns. Even if they were confused about whom to write (like the woman in Springfield on Sunday driving), at least they had a chance to get things off their chests. On numerous occasions, I'd write or talk to people to tell them that I simply couldn't agree with their views, and I was not going to vote the way they wanted me to vote. They would often express dissatisfaction, but then, once the issue had been resolved, some of them would thank me for taking the time to listen to them. Lewis Anthony Dexter describes this same situation in the U.S. Congress when he indicates, "Constituents and pressure groups are often satisfied with a fair hearing, not insisting on a specific conclusion . . . Few constituents deny their vote to a Congressman who generally listens to them just because he differs on any one issue."

Thus, many people seemed to be more interested in the opportunity to have their say, and to know that someone was listening to them, than they were in the final policy outcome of any particular issue. In essence, they were more concerned with the *process* of communication than with the substance, and if I gave them a sympathetic hearing, they were often willing to accept a final decision even if they didn't agree with it.

I think this concern with the participatory process helps to explain a key role our state and local governments play in the American political arena. Much of what goes on in Washington may be remote and incomprehensible, but the states and local communities are here and now; both more understandable and more easily accessible to those citizens who are anxious to voice their concerns. For better or for worse, we personified the political system in human terms by being close enough to our constituents to let them get at us if they cared to do so. Because the state and local governments are this close to the people, they play an extremely valuable role in our democratic system of government; a role which I suspect is destined to increase in significance in the future as we move into an ever more confusing world of big technological bureaucracy in Washington and in the world beyond. As another Dartmouth alumnus, Nelson Rockefeller, noted in his book *The Future of Federalism*, the founding fathers demonstrated a unique genius when they created "a political system that has more than one center of sovereign power, energy and creativity."

CHAPTER

12

★ ★ ★ ★

Reaching Out

To enjoy politics one must enjoy people.
Stimson Bullitt
To Be a Politician

WHILE MANY PEOPLE took the initiative in getting in touch with us, many legislators also made a major effort to reach out to the public to explain what they were up to in Montpelier. I engaged in a lot of this outreach activity; appearing on radio shows, issuing press releases, writing letters and the like. The most powerful form of outreach, however, involves personal visits with constituents so they can see who you are and decide for themselves whether or not you wear horns. In my case such appearances took a variety of forms which ranged from meetings with civic groups to trips to the local town dumps.

1. Group Meetings

Virtually every weekend during the legislative session, I was invited to attend one or more meetings scheduled in different parts of the county by various civic groups: Rotary Clubs, the County Board of Realtors, the Farm Bureau, the League of Women Voters, Southern Vermont Federation of Sportsmen, Chambers of Commerce, and the like.

The Springfield Chamber of Commerce meetings were the toughest of all because they were breakfast affairs, scheduled to begin at 7:30 A.M. Since Springfield was forty miles south of Norwich, I had to get up at six o'clock to grab a cup of coffee before heading off into the dark, cold winter mists. Fortunately, the Chamber invited us to address only one or two breakfast meetings each legislative session, so the different legislators in the county shared this particular vigil.

As luck would have it, however, I was asked to attend the kickoff breakfast of the 1974 series, which fell on Monday, January 7. This was the first day after the new national "Daylight Saving" time switchback that was instituted to save energy. A laudable goal, I thought, as I drove through the dark to Springfield. The local newspaper, the *Times Reporter* noted my plight with the headline YELLOW CANDLELIGHT FOR SEN. SMALLWOOD on a story which began with the words of Robert Lewis Stevenson: "In winter I get up at night and dress by yellow candlelight." A very nice touch.

As I attended more and more meetings, I developed a feel for the individual rhythm, tempo, and timing of the different groups. While the Chambers of Commerce gathered for breakfast, the Rotary clubs met for lunch, and the Board of Realtors favored more elaborate dinner sessions, always preceded by a drawn-out cocktail hour that could produce occasional disarray among members of the audience during an after-dinner speech. The League of Women Voters meetings were Sunday afternoons or weekday evenings, very carefully orchestrated, with a moderator in attendance to make sure that statements were brief and to the point. The meetings I enjoyed the most were sponsored by the sportsmen's clubs (which could turn out to be rather tumultuous Sunday night affairs) and by the county Farm Bureau, which were always held on Saturday nights in a small room on the second floor of the Woodstock Town Hall.

About twenty to thirty people, plus an assemblage of legislators, would show up for the Farm Bureau meetings. Roger Eastman, who operated a dairy farm in Weathersfield, chaired the meetings, assisted by Bob and Muriel Follett, also of Weathersfield, and former Senator Margaret Hammond of Baltimore. These gatherings were notable for their hard wooden chairs, excellent home-baked cakes and cookies, and for the refreshing, down-to-earth skepticism the participants employed to pick apart some of the more nonsensical legislation that was under consideration in Montpelier. A fairly sizable delegation of legislators would usually appear, John Alden, Herb

Ogden and me from the Senate, plus Representatives John Murphy, Henry Hicks, Sam Lloyd, Susan Webb, and others from the House.

One night we were all huddled together when Roger Eastman asked about a proposed flood-plain zoning bill which was under consideration. Sam Lloyd from Weston was in attendance, so he responded to the question since the bill was in his House Natural Resources Committee.

"It's a badly needed piece of legislation," Sam explained. "Everybody knows it's unwise to permit people to build homes and other structures on flood-plains where they can be swept away in a flood. The bill is designed to delineate flood-plain areas throughout the state, and to place building restrictions on these areas to prohibit construction."

"Does that apply only to new buildings, or to existing buildings as well?" Roger Eastman asked. "I operate a farm which is located on a flood-plain in Weathersfield Bow, down on the Connecticut River. There's no question that my fields are in a flood-plain, and so is my barn. Would this law affect my barn?"

"Oh, no," Sam re-assured him. "It only applies to new construction. Like any other zoning legislation, it contains a 'grandfather clause' that exempts existing structures. You wouldn't have any trouble at all with your barn."

Roger wasn't satisfied. "I don't know. I'm still not sure how it would work. Take my own case. What would happen if my barn burned down after this law was passed? Could I build a new barn in the very same place?"

Sam Lloyd looked puzzled, and I could see Henry Hicks whispering something to John Murphy; obviously there was some confusion on this point. After a moment Sam ventured a reply: "Well, in the event of such an unlikely occurrence, I think it would be all right to rebuild in the same location as long as you constructed a floodproof barn."

A buzz of commentary swept around the room.

"Did you say a floodproof barn?" Bob Follett asked. "What is a floodproof barn?"

"Well, I'm not sure that is the proper terminology." Sam Lloyd hesitated. "What I mean to say is that I am sure there would be some

way to handle such an emergency in the highly unlikely event that
Roger's barn actually burned down, or burned up. I mean for example,
it would probably be possible to construct a new barn on stilts, or
something like that."

At this point the room exploded in a babble of excitement. John
Murphy started to chuckle, and Herb Ogden was beginning to shift
uncomfortably in his hard wooden chair.

Then Henry Hicks stormed into the fray. "For God's sake, a barn
on stilts!" he exclaimed. "How would the cows ever get in and out
of the place? Even though I'm in the legislature, sometimes I think
we're all crazy up there in Montpelier. For God's sakes, I didn't know
we were considering a law to put barns on stilts."

I looked over at Sam Lloyd, who was pretty beleaguered at this
point, and decided to see if I could help restore some sense of order
to the deliberations.

"Look, we're talking about a unique situation," I came to his aid.
"Sam's right. We do need some kind of legislation to protect flood-
plains, and it's impossible to write each law to cover every conceivable
type of bizarre situation that might arise in the future. I'm sure, Roger,
that if your barn burned down, there would be some way that an
accommodation could be made to handle this kind of emergency."

Roger still wasn't satisfied. He was obviously worried that he
would end up with no barn at all unless we pinned down this matter
right then and there. "Let me ask you a question," he came back at
me. "Do you think it would be O.K. if I rebuilt my barn with a door
in the front, and another door in the back, so the water could run
down through the middle?"

There was another explosion of laughter. I smiled at Sam Lloyd,
and he nodded back in agreement. "Yes, Roger," I responded, "I'm
sure that would be O.K., as long as you made the doors wide enough
to accommodate the Connecticut River."

Another burst of laughter and applause.

"Smallwood," Henry Hicks boomed out, "I hope to hell you know
what you are talking about. I'm counting on the Senate to fix up
this bill, once the House gets through with it."

John Murphy chuckled again, and slapped his knees. The members
of the Windsor County Farm Bureau voted tentative approval of the

flood-plain bill, with the tacit understanding that something would be done to take care of Roger Eastman's barn in Weathersfield Bow in the unlikely event that it burned down at some unspecified future date.

2. Office Hours

In addition to attending various meetings throughout the county, I held office hours once each month in the Springfield Town Hall on Monday afternoons from two until five o'clock. I wasn't sure at first whether anybody would show for these, but about ten to fifteen people usually dropped by, so they proved to be worthwhile.

Many of the people who came in had specific complaints (they hadn't received a Social Security check, they had lost their driver's license and didn't know how to replace it, etc.), but a number stopped by to chat, and it was interesting to get their views on various bills that were being considered by the legislature.

During one of the afternoon sessions in late February, an elderly woman came in and introduced herself as Mary Peirce of Weathersfield. We began a pleasant conversation, in which she expressed her concern about all the changes that were taking place in Vermont. She then urged me to support any kind of environmental-planning legislation that would leave things the way they were without any further development at all. At last she got to the main point of her visit.

"Senator, we sponsor a wonderful program in the Weathersfield Center Church every summer. It's called 'Casseroles and Culture.' Once each month we have supper together—that's the casserole part; and then we go upstairs in the meeting room for a lecture and a slide show by an outside speaker—that's the culture part. I wonder if you would be willing to be one of the speakers this summer?"

"That's very flattering," I replied, "but I'm not sure what you would want me to speak about. Do you have any specific topic in mind?"

"Well, we have already scheduled a program for July, a slide show about a trip to Russia and Greece. I think our August program should be closer to home. I wonder if there's anything you could tell us about what's going on right here in Vermont, even right here in Windsor County?"

"As a matter of fact," I told her, "when I ran for the state Senate,

I took a lot of slides of the different towns I visited, and the people I met, during the campaign, and I made up a slide show for use in my classes back at Dartmouth. I must say that Windsor County is so beautiful that many of the slides turned out very well. I could give you a slide show of campaigning in Windsor County."

"That would be perfect," she exclaimed. "We could call it Electioneering in Windsor County. I think that would be just fine. As for a date, we'd like to schedule the supper for Friday, August 17th. Would that be all right with you?"

"O.K.," I nodded. "I must say this is the most farsighted planning I've ever encountered. Six months lead time. Very good. I'll mark it down now in my date book, but you'd better send me a reminder early in the summer, just in case I lose my book in the meantime."

"That's just fine. I'm glad I booked you up in advance. I think you will enjoy 'Casseroles and Culture.' It's a very successful program, and Electioneering in Windsor County should be very interesting."

I didn't see her again until Friday evening, August 17, when Ann and I drove down to the Weathersfield Center Church. This stately old red-brick meetinghouse, built in 1821, is framed by a long arcade of maple trees, planted in 1866 as a memorial to the 136 Weathersfield men who served in the Civil War (believed to be the highest proportion of any town in the Union states). There was a reasonably sizable crowd milling around the entrance when we arrived, including Armstrong Hunter, the editor of the local weekly newspaper, and a number of other friends I had met during my tenure in the Senate. After a few brief pleasantries, we all went inside to pass through the casserole line, before sitting down at long wooden tables, with spotless white paper tacked on top of each. I looked around the room, and couldn't help but notice that only half the tables were full. Apparently the subject of Electioneering in Windsor County didn't appeal to too many people.

Armstrong Hunter, sitting on my left, noticed my glance around the room.

"Frank, I'm sorry about the size of the crowd," he said. "It's O.K., about sixty or seventy people, but we usually have more. Actually, Aunt Mary Peirce who planned the program is fit to be tied. She wanted to get a big audience, so she ran some spot ads on the Spring-field radio station. Unfortunately, there was a mix-up, and believe it or not, you're talking tonight about electrical engineering in Windsor County." He smiled blandly.

"Armstrong, you must be kidding," I said aghast. "Did you say electrical engineering? No wonder Mary Peirce is upset. We arranged this six months in advance, and now we've got the audience here under false pretenses. What do you think I ought to do?"

"Oh, go ahead and talk about your campaign," he replied en-couragingly. "We did send out postcards announcing the topic as Electioneering in Windsor County. Half the people probably expect you to talk about one thing, and the other half expect something else. Under the circumstances, I think you can talk about anything you want. Russia and Greece again, just like last month, and at least half the people wouldn't know the difference."

After dinner I had a nice chat with Mary Peirce, who apologized for the radio snafu. I re-assured her that everything was fine before we went upstairs into the meeting room for a slide show on my Windsor County campaign escapades. Actually it went O.K., and everyone seemed to enjoy it. Thankfully, I didn't get any questions about electrical engineering, a subject that was then, and still remains, an utter and complete mystery to me.

3. Speeches and Public Appearances

I attended a lot of political gatherings and made a lot of speeches, but the ones I enjoyed the most were those which involved Allen Foley. Al, who had encouraged me to run for the state Senate, was a seventy-three-year-old retired professor of American history at Dart-mouth who had become known from coast to coast as a specialist in Vermont humor, having written a book on the subject.

When Al got up to speak he couldn't resist the temptation to tell "just one" of his numerous anecdotes, which meant we were off to the races. To the delight of his audience, he would launch into story after story, each always very tart and dry, in keeping with the Vermont Yankee tradition. I remember once he explained how to handle government red tape by telling about an old-timer up in Vermont's Northeast Kingdom who sat down one evening by a lamp to fill out a government form that was overdue. Like many of us under similar circumstances the old man was not in a pleasant frame of mind to start with, and staring him in the face at the head of a box in the top righthand corner of the printed form were the words in bold type: DO NOT WRITE HERE.

Before going any further the old gentleman took a firm grip on his pen and wrote in the box, in equally bold letters, I WRITE WHERE I GODDAM PLEASE.

One of my special favorites involved two elderly Vermonters who were attending a rally when a local politician got up on the stump and took off on a particularly long-winded oration. One of the Vermonters, who was hard of hearing, turned to his compatriot and asked, "What's he talkin' about?" "He don't say," was the abrupt answer.

The audiences always roared at Al's stories to a point where it was difficult to get back to any serious discussion of political issues. It was a pleasant break from the normal speech-making routine. I always looked forward to attending meetings with Al Foley.

4. Town Visits

I made a lot of visits to different communities during my stay in the Senate, but one group of sites which I saw more frequently than I had anticipated as part of my citizens' outreach efforts were the town dumps scattered throughout Windsor County. Over the course of many years, sizable numbers of Vermonters had built up a strong sense of attachment to their dumps—especially on Saturday mornings, when traffic could be pretty heavy. At these times, the dumps served as sort of quasi-social/political centers along the lines of the agora, or central marketplace, in the ancient Greek polis. As a matter of fact, one central-Vermont radio station, WDEV, had even built a Saturday morning program around this tradition which they called "Music to Go to the Dump By."

Unfortunately, my senatorial visits to the dumps were not designed to gain any votes through casual weekend conversations. Instead, they were completely utilitarian, as I attempted to help various town managers and local selectmen feel their way through a maze of new environmentally oriented state regulations that severely curtailed the old, time-tested dump practices. First, to control air pollution, the state banned any burning in town dumps. Next came a tough new set of water-pollution regulations that created some real problems for towns like Ludlow and Cavendish, where groundwaters from the dumps were seeping into the Black River. The most difficult problem of all, however, was plain economics.

My dump visits all came about after I was asked to draft a statewide recycling bill for the Senate Natural Resources Committee. I based the bill on a plan which was recommended by a special group of solid-waste management consultants from Cambridge, Massachusetts. Once the bill was drafted, I wrote a column on the new plan for the local newspapers which pointed out (according to the consultants) that Vermonters were burying more than 190,000 tons of marketable waste materials in their town dumps each year which had a potential annual cash value of $2.5 million. Well, this statistic really caught on like wildfire. Vermonters are still thrifty enough not to look down their noses at 2.5 million bucks, so my newspaper column was picked up by the wire services and flashed to other papers throughout the state. Overnight I became Vermont's instant expert on dump management, a subject I hadn't touched at all during my student days at Dartmouth and Harvard.

After the news articles appeared, town officials constantly invited me over to wander around their local dump to see if I could provide some guidance on future policies. Their major difficulty grew out of the fact that many towns faced large economic expenditures if they were going to fix up their dumps to meet the new state environmental regulations. However, they didn't want to get involved with big capital outlays if Vermont was going into a new statewide recycling program that would replace the local town dumps with a modernized system of regional landfills.

My basic difficulty resulted from the fact that I couldn't really tell them what to do, since I was not sure the recycling bill was going to pass the legislature. (Actually, it never did pass; it got caught up in the bottle-deposit controversy, and too many legislators were afraid we would abandon the new "bottle ban" law if the state went into a major recycling program.) Anyway, I would go out to look over the various town dumps, where I hemmed and hawed because I didn't know what to tell the selectmen about public-policy trends in this particular area. Usually I would steer a safe middle-of-the-road course, and end up advising them to make modest interim expenditures to improve their dumps until we had a clearer fix on the status of the proposed recycling bill.

There wasn't an overwhelming amount of glory in all of this, but it constituted a unique aspect of my public-relations responsibilities which I really couldn't ignore. As a matter of fact, it even earned me a paragraph in the 1973 Norwich Town Report:

> The state has given us tacit approval of the way the Town is currently handling its rubbish. Senator Smallwood continues to advise against any large expenditure for a dump as he feels that the state will eventually come up with an over-all plan.

It was the only time I was ever singled out for reference in the Norwich Town Report during my entire tenure in the Senate.

13

★ ★ ★ ★

The Working Press

Politics is the most important thing in life—
for a newspaper.

Ibsen
An Enemy of the People

ALTHOUGH I spent a lot of time on the road making face-to-face contacts, it was necessary to rely on the news media (electrical engineering
and all) to reach out to most of the people in the county. When Plato
and Aristotle originally designed their ideal political communities,
they restricted their units' size in order to promote easy personal interaction (Plato called for a commonwealth of 5,040 households in the
Laws, while Aristotle limited his polis to "the largest number that can
be taken in at a single view" in *Politics*). Since there were natural
limitations on how far the voice could carry, or the eye could see, both
philosophers restricted their communities, geographically and in total
population, to facilitate citizen contact.

The modern technology of communications has changed all that.
Today, by means of press, radio, and television, we have extended
our ability to communicate over vast distances to vast audiences in a
manner which would have been incomprehensible to the ancient
Greeks. The news media, due to their potential outreach, play a unique
role in the political process. They constitute an independent, auton-
omous arm in contemporary American politics which provides the
link between the public and its elected representatives.

The number of news outlets in Vermont had burgeoned since the
time the state's first newspaper, the *Gazette,* was published back in
1780, to a point where today there are eleven daily papers, twenty-three
weeklies, eighteen AM radio stations, five FM stations, two major in-
state commercial TV stations, plus a statewide educational television

network. That's a lot of news media to serve 460,000 people, and one veteran State House observer told me that the Vermont legislature had more press coverage per capita than any other state legislature in the nation.

During the course of my stay in Montpelier, I got to know many of the State House reporters fairly well, although we always managed to maintain a discreet, arms-length relationship with each other—which was probably healthy. Occasionally we'd have a cup of coffee together, but that's about as far as it went. I guess the words "congenial distance" constitute a pretty good description of my relations with the press corps. I always tried to answer their questions directly, when and if they approached me, but since I was a freshman senator not privy to very much inside information, the reporters never leaned very hard on me, and I certainly never tried to lean too hard on them.

After I watched the press corps in action for a while, I began to speculate on some of the different aspects of political reporting. The first involved the reporters' perceptions of their own roles. Many of them were pretty young, in their late twenties or early thirties. I knew the pay wasn't terribly good, and the hours were horrendous, as they ran around the State House from early morning to late at night covering debates, committee meetings, public hearings, and everything in between. I couldn't help but wonder what motivated them to keep up such a grueling schedule. A second area of speculation related to the kind of criteria they employed to determine whether a story was newsworthy. When the legislature was in session, there were literally a hundred different events they could have covered in any given day. I was intrigued as to what priorities they used to report one event and ignore another. Finally, I wondered what role the reporters may have played in pushing particular points of view they may have favored.

During one Dartmouth seminar we were discussing the role of the press in politics when George Hannett, one of my students, indicated that he would like to tackle this topic in a research paper. I introduced George to Tom Slayton, a Vermont Press Bureau reporter, who, in turn, introduced him to the other State House reporters. George was able to conduct fairly extensive interviews with most of them. In his study, he concluded that the members of the Montpelier press corps held three different perceptions of their roles as reporters of the political process.

The first was that of a neutral observer. This involved the explicit assumption that the press played a purely objective role that was limited to conveying the facts, leaving interpretations to the reader, and "letting the chips fall where they may."

The second was that of a "public watchdog." This was a more aggressive interpretation of the press as a guardian of the public interest, with an emphasis on process rather than policy. Specifically, it assumed that the press had a responsibility to be vigilant against public corruption and malfeasance; that it should test the veracity of public statements; and that it should expose secrecy at any and all levels of the governmental process.

The third role was that of a policy advocate. This was the most aggressive interpretation of all, and it implied a direct attempt to influence legislative events, either by focusing attention on neglected policy areas, or by highlighting and interpreting specific issues which the reporters felt had major policy implications.

The overwhelming majority of reporters advised George that they regarded themselves as "neutral observers," with some admitting they performed "watchdog" functions from time to time. Very few felt that they played a direct role in the policy process. In short, they tended to view themselves as objective, detached, impartial professionals. However, virtually all the reporters did agree that they made a number of very subjective choices each legislative day regarding which events they would cover and which they would ignore. After reading George's paper I began to follow the press coverage more closely, and developed the following rough outline of some of the key considerations reporters used to identify political news.

1. Personality criteria. Many events were automatically covered by virtue of the source providing the information. Here position in the hierarchy was all-important. If the Governor held a press conference, it was covered no matter what was said. There was automatic news value in terms of the source: the fact that the Governor had made a statement. The same was true of the Speaker of the House or key committee chairmen.

Another group who received priority attention were certain types of political personalities who made "good copy." I questioned the reporters about this, and they experienced difficulty specifying precisely who made good copy, though they seemed to gravitate instinctively towards certain individuals who were pithy, readily quotable, or excitingly aggressive in pushing their points of view.

2. *Scope of issue.* A second important criterion that dictated priority coverage was impact in terms of widespread readership. Specifically, any issue that promised to affect large numbers of people was news. A major new tax proposal, for example, would invariably receive heavy coverage (whether or not it had any chance of passage) because of the size of the potential audience that might be affected. The larger the potential impact, the higher the degree of coverage.

3. *Symbolic issues.* The most intriguing criterion of all involved exciting or "politically sexy" issues. These were very hard to pin down, although a top priority appeared to be conflict and controversy. If two or more individuals or groups got into a fight, this was a newsworthy event. Other glamour issues were likely to involve the more fallible aspects of the human condition: scandals, tragedies, and the like.

Less emphasis was placed on such human emotions as humor (government is serious business), or quieter achievements, especially if they involved complex legislation. The glamour issues tended to emphasize the more symbolic policy matters that could be easily coded into powerful (and conflicting) emotional reactions (*e.g.,* the big, bad lobbyists versus the good, little guys).

4. *Chance issues.* Occasionally the reporters stumbled across an issue as the result of a chance encounter, a tip, or some other accidental source. When this happened they tended to pursue the issue aggressively, particularly if it promised to provide an "exclusive" which would give them a leg up on the opposition.

5. *"Planted" news.* Many reporters admitted reluctantly that they could be manipulated by public officials who leaked news, planted

rumors, or sent up "trial balloons" to serve their own interests. The reporters didn't like to be used in this way, but they indicated that they often had little choice since they were never sure whether the story constituted hard news, and they didn't want to risk being beaten by their competitors.

All these five priorities were employed in a frenzied atmosphere of competing time deadlines, which constituted a key element in the newsgathering environment. Although the reporters would co-operate occasionally by pooling stories, most of their work was carried out as part of a competitive business enterprise that was designed to sell a specific product: political news. Under the circumstances, I felt the reporters did a good job, at least as far as I was concerned. I was mis-quoted seriously only once during my two years in the legislature, when a reporter attributed a comment to me that I never actually made. Later he offered to print a retraction, but we both decided this didn't make any sense. If people missed the original story, there was no sense asking them to pick up the same mistake in a corrected story the second time around.

In addition to the full-time State House reporters, a few of the smaller weekly papers provided part-time selected coverage. I felt the best of these was the *White River Valley Herald*, which ran a weekly legislative column by Kathryn Wendling of Pomfret. The young editor of the *Herald*, Dick Drysdale, was also the only weekly editor who set a policy of publishing key Senate roll-call votes—a practice which I admired very much.

In retrospect, the different reporters who scurried around the State House pursued a very demanding schedule under a lot of pressure. They made an important contribution to the political process.

While the reporters I encountered worked hard to maintain an air of objectivity, they were never sure how their stories would be used in the next day's paper. The news-disseminating business is a complex system, and a lot of city editors, managing editors, and the like took over the management of this system once the news left Montpelier. These individuals made crucial decisions regarding a story's place-ment, length, and headlines, which determined whether it constituted page one news, or should be relegated to page sixteen (if it appeared at all).

At this point there was no question in my mind that many of the papers pushed their own particular policy preferences in the way they presented the news. Actually there was nothing new about this. In his study *Yankee Politics in Vermont,* Frank Bryan describes a classic policy controversy that took place between the Rutland *Herald* and the Burlington *Free Press* back in 1936 over the question of whether federal funds should be used to construct a Green Mountain Parkway along the north-south spine of western Vermont. The issue was finally put to a public referendum, and after analyzing the editorial leanings in headlines and picture captions in both papers, Bryan concluded that "newspaper coverage was at least a re-inforcing variable" in the contest. The editors of a rival paper were more blunt in their assessment of the situation: "The Parkway difference of opinion is not really and truly a referendum. It is a battle between the Burlington Free Press and the Rutland Herald. A vote for the Parkway is a vote for the Free Press. A vote against the Parkway is a vote for the Herald." The Parkway issue was finally defeated in the referendum, after receiving its strongest voter support in the Burlington-Chittenden County area and its strongest voter opposition in Rutland County and its environs.

What was true back in 1936 was still true four decades later. Particular papers tended to present strong views on issues they favored and opposed. The *Vermont Sunday News,* for example, was a bastion of conservatism on virtually every public issue it deemed worthy of presentation. The Rutland *Herald,* on the other hand, was particularly aggressive on environmental issues where it pushed hard in its news coverage for a strong "bottle ban" law and a strong state land-use plan.

The *Herald's* treatment of the state land-planning effort was a classic case of headline dramatics, as it led its readers through a series of cliff-hanging episodes by means of its daily news coverage. During the 1973 legislative session, the paper ran page one headlines on the fate of the Capability and Development Plan that rivaled *The Perils of Pauline.* In January and February these headlines advised that the plan was "fading" and "gutted." In March the plan was "knifed" and "stabbed again" before it finally emerged from the House "alive, if not well." In April, when the plan hit the Senate, it was "dying," "dead," and "killed." Finally, in the last week of the session, the plan miraculously "passed." It's difficult to know if this tortuous trail of horrendous headlines had any impact in whipping up public support for the plan, but since the measure appeared to have nine lives anyway, such support may not have been necessary.

Of all the headlines that appeared, my favorite involved Senator Robert Gannett, my good friend from Windham County. Just at the end of the 1974 session, the House passed a bill known as the "Little Davis-Bacon Act" that was referred to the Senate General and Military Committee. The bill, which was designed to mandate a state prevailing wage for construction trades (along the lines of the federal Davis-Bacon Act), constituted a pretty controversial and potent measure. I was unsure how the committee planned to handle the issue, since there were only a couple of days left in the session, and I figured they might want to hold hearings before they reported it on the floor. Hence my surprise when I picked up the newspaper next morning and saw this headline:

GANNETT AX-WIELDER

ON PREVAILING WAGE

As soon as I walked into the Senate Chamber that morning, I went over to Bob's desk and held out my hand. "Ax-wielder, old buddy," I bubbled cheerfully, "vere haf you bean and ven did you get to Montpelier?"

Bob nodded his head in his quiet way and chuckled. " 'Ax-wielder Gannett,' that really beats all," he smiled. "We were coming out of the committee room last night when a reporter caught me in the hall. He asked about the bill, and I told him that the House version failed to define its key term—'prevailing wage'—properly, so we wanted to discuss this with the Commissioner of Labor and Industry before we decided whether to report it out of committee. Since time is so short, the reporter must have concluded that any delay would be fatal, and I guess I became the hatchetman as far as the Little Davis-Bacon Act is concerned. But 'Ax-wielder Gannett'—what a moniker to hang on me!"

That's the way it went with the news—a hero one day, an ax-wielder the next. Which raises an interesting question: Did it really make any difference? What impact, if any, did the news media have in shaping public opinion?

Most political science studies indicate that the press exercises only minimal influence in elections compared to party preference or the political allegiance of one's parents. But what about influencing public attitudes with respect to specific policy issues? Here again, studies indicate the impact may be only nominal. To return to the 1936 Green Mountain Parkway controversy, Frank Bryan's analysis could find "no relationship between newspaper coverage and the vote on the Parkway. . . . Newspaper influence was not an important factor in that vote, a finding supported indirectly by much of the literature of political science and public opinion which reports that the press generally has a minimal effect on election results."

My own experience in the state legislative arena tended to confirm this hypothesis. Although a lot of constituents would tell me that they had seen my name in the paper, they could rarely remember what I had done or even what the story was about. Indeed, some of my constituent communications appeared to be transmitted in a circuitous, grapevine manner that I could never fully pin down. On one occasion I made a strong statement on the floor of the Senate against the restoration of the death penalty in Vermont, and my statement received very heavy coverage on the front pages of the newspapers and via radio and television. The very next day a group of constituents from Windsor County made a visit to the State House, and—you guessed it—not one comment on my position on the death penalty, either pro or con. Instead, they had heard "by the grapevine" that I had serious reservations about instituting a mandatory hot-lunch program in Vermont schools, and they wanted to know how an "enlightened" legislator like me could take such a position.

While it's debatable exactly what effect the press had on public opinion, there's no doubt in my mind that the newspapers did very definitely influence the legislative process in one key respect: namely, many of the legislators themselves followed the papers very closely. As a result of their own reading habits, they believed the press to be equally important to the general public, to a point where their own actions were influenced by press coverage. Every morning the majority of the legislators who stayed at my hotel buried their noses in the daily newspapers in an effort to absorb every word (especially their own names appearing in print). Because the legislators read the papers so diligently, they appeared to act on the assumption that everyone else in Vermont was just as diligent in reading the papers; an assumption which hardly appeared to be grounded in any concrete evidence. Be that as it may, the legislature seemed to develop a dependence on the press that often bordered on fixation, and in this respect, therefore, the press played a very powerful role in shaping legislative opinion.

Yet in the final analysis, the situation appeared to be reciprocal, because if the legislature depended on the State House reporters, these same reporters also depended on the legislature to generate their daily news stories. In this manner, we became strangely dependent upon each other.

This interdependence was really driven home to me one day in August when I visited the State House to attend a meeting of a summer-study committee which was conducting its business after the legislative session had adjourned. At the conclusion of the meeting I went to the cafeteria for a cup of coffee. It was somewhat startling to see the place completely vacant, totally devoid of any of the normal frenzied chatter that took place from morning to night when the legislature was in session. I was sitting there all alone, sipping my coffee, when a delegation of the Montpelier press corps entered the room in the persons of three newspaper reporters and two members of a portable-camera crew from a Burlington television station.

It was like Old Homecoming Day when they descended on me en masse: "Frank Smallwood! Good to see you. What are you doing in Montpelier on a beautiful summer day like this?"

"I'm here for a meeting of the summer-study committee on nursing homes," I replied.

"Damn, that's not really news," one of them said. "Boy, this place is some drag in the summer, a real dullsville. Nothing at all seems to be happening. There's no news at all to report."

"How about it, Frank?" one of them cut in. "Do you want to make a statement about something? It's really a slow day. Can you think of anything at all you'd like to say?"

I mulled over the offer. It was pretty tempting. I was serving as chairman of the Governor's Commission on Higher Education and could make a comment on that. I was also serving on a legislative study committee on small business, and could undoubtedly say something about that. It was pretty heady to realize that I could make a statement about virtually any political issue, and, as long as it was reasonably intelligent, it would almost certainly get newspaper and television coverage throughout the state. But in the end I decided that I didn't have anything terribly important to offer the press corps. "Sorry folks," I said, "but I'm afraid that no news is good news."

"Not for us it isn't," they muttered as they circled back out of the cafeteria, and headed down the hall.

It was a strange type of dependency relationship. We relied on the news media, but the news media relied on us as well. I sipped my coffee and thought about a line from one of Ibsen's plays that we used in an introductory course in government back at Dartmouth: "Politics is the most important thing in life—for a newspaper." And for many politicians as well, I concluded. Yet I wondered how long I was destined to remain one of them in light of the growing demands on my time, and the startling realization that there was nothing particularly special I really wanted to say when the press had invited me to give them a story.

PART IV

□ □ □ ⊠

Reflections

14

★ ★ ★ ★

Legislative Boxscore

When all is said and done, legislation seems imbued with a will of its own.
Clem Miller
Member of the House

DURING the winter months of 1973 and 1974 the Vermont General Assembly met for 195 days to consider 755 bills. If statistics mean anything, our batting average was a healthy .365, since we enacted 276 of these bills into law. In addition, we handled a heavy load of confirmation actions in the Senate, and joined the House in passing 81 Resolutions (ranging from an expression of sympathy over the death of a Vermonter in a Boston airplane crash in July 1973, to an expression of agreement with a federal law which specified that "the United States Flag is considered to be a living thing and should be treated with utmost respect").

One of the most interesting aspects of these two sessions related to the fact that public perception of their over-all "success" or "failure" appeared to rest upon the passage, or defeat, of a very small number of "high-visibility" bills. If we enacted a few of these big spectaculars into law, the entire session was considered a success; if not, the entire session was a failure. We passed 127 bills in the 1973 session, including a few pretty big ones, so we were hailed in newspaper editorials for "a proud record" (*Valley News*), "strong legislative finish" (Rutland *Herald*), and "happy ending" (*Vermont Standard*). The following year we passed another 149 bills, but not many blockbusters, so we were dismissed as a mediocre "footnote in history" (Burlington *Free Press*).

This press fixation on "big" bills appeared to reflect, and guide, general public reactions. Most of the people I talked to outside the legislature didn't have the faintest clue regarding 90 percent of the bills we were considering. If they knew anything at all about the legislative session, their concerns invariably focused on a handful of highly publicized bills that received major press coverage. In addition, selected groups would follow special-interest bills very closely. The sportsmen's clubs, for instance, knew about every fish-and-game bill under consideration. However, they were the exception to the rule. As far as John Q. Public was concerned, he couldn't have cared less about the bulk of the more routine bills. The validation of the Corporate Charter of the Brattleboro Lodge of Elks *(Public Act No. 212, 1973 Adjourned Session)* simply didn't ring any bells for him.

Because the big-bill focus was so prevalent, I decided to make up my own boxscore of some key bills I was closely involved with during the 1973–74 legislative sessions. Since appropriations measures and other important "housekeeping" bills are passed every session, I have eliminated these in an effort to focus on more unique one-time bills. This is a purely personal listing, and while I'm sure other legislators would come up with different priorities, I particularly enjoyed working on the following for the reasons cited:

1973 SESSION:

1. Capability and Development Plan. This bill represented the important second step in our effort to enact a comprehensive state land-use plan, which would guide future growth and development in Vermont.

2. Capital-gains tax on land sales. Another environmental bill, pushed by the Governor, which levied a state capital-gains tax on profits derived from speculative short-term land sales.

3. "Right-to-know" law. An open-government bill, sponsored by Senator John Alden, which provided for better public access to meetings of governmental bodies at the state and local levels.

4. Equal Rights Amendment to the United States Constitution. (Taking part in ratifying a constitutional amendment was a unique experience.)

5. Children's dental care. The political dynamics surrounding the passage of this worthwhile preventative health care bill were fascinating.

6. Re-apportionment of the State Senate. An agonizing exercise in internal legislative politics, which was finally pulled out of the fire by a last-minute compromise engineered by Senator Bill Doyle.

1974 SESSION:

7. Emergency energy powers. There was a lot of haggling over how much authority to grant the Governor to deal with the energy shortage in Vermont in the winter of 1974, but this measure indicated that the legislature could respond to a crisis when necessary.

8. Registration of nursing homes. The Health and Welfare Committee slaved long and hard over this complicated issue before we finally discovered a workable compromise.

9. Municipal Employees' Retirement Act. A personal favorite I introduced during the first week of the first session, which finally passed on the last day of the second session thanks to some strong pressure by the Vermont League of Cities and Towns.

10. Child-abuse reporting law. Another personal favorite, which I sponsored in an effort to strengthen reporting procedures in this area. Hardly an earth-shaking measure, but one which gave me a great deal of satisfaction.

In spite of the above successes, there were a number of major areas where we appeared to be paralyzed, simply unable to act at all. The field of education was especially disappointing. We couldn't move on reforming the state-aid-to-education formula or on establishing a mechanism to co-ordinate the planning of education beyond the high school, due to the lack of any kind of consensus agreement as to what should be done in these areas. We also ducked out completely on a statewide recycling program which continually got snarled up in the pitched battles over the container-deposit ("bottle ban") legislation.

Other areas where we were unable to generate enough solid support to move aggressively involved state transportation planning; elimination of the poll tax; inability to pass a state land-use plan (which was actually destroyed in a morass of uncreative bureaucratic haggling within the executive branch) ; and failure to make any practical long-range reforms in the local property tax, especially reforms that might help save the dwindling number of Vermont farms. Indeed, it was interesting that we didn't really make any dramatic moves in the agricultural area during my two years in Montpelier despite repeated lip service to land-use taxation and the like. The farm bloc in the legislature simply was not strong enough to push any major bills through the General Assembly.

Despite our failures, we passed a number of other measures—among them constitutional amendments, creation of industrial development and housing financing agencies, floodplain zoning, and minimum wage laws—that add up to a respectable record of accomplishment.

¶WHEN I first arrived in Montpelier, and was groping around the Senate Chamber in an effort to find my desk, I was aware that there were certain cohesive influences—the leadership structure, procedural rules, social norms, and the like—that tended to hold a legislative body together. At the conclusion of my tenure in Montpelier, I realized that there are also certain patterns and dynamics within the legislative process, itself, that play a major role in the formulation of public policy. Although Clem Miller indicated in his fascinating personal diary, *Member of the House,* that "legislation seems imbued with a will of its own," there are certain internal forces that help to shape the dynamics of the legislative process. Five of these forces were extremely important in the Vermont legislature.

1. Words and Symbols

First, and most obvious, the basic building-block in legislative politics—indeed, in all politics—is words. A deluge of hundreds, then thousands, then hundreds of thousands of words: words, words, and more words. While the bulk of these appear in the form of daily oral onslaught in committees, in hallways, and on the floor, the real focus of this verbal outpouring is the written word, that finely honed print that appears, and/or disappears, during the enactment of statutory law. Many times the fiercest oral pyrotechnics were generated by the smallest written words. It makes a great deal of difference whether a bill reads "the commissioner may . . ." or "the commissioner shall . . ."

This fixation on words highlights another basic characteristic of the legislative process, and that is the use of symbolic language to code political issues. In part, symbols are used quite simply to manipulate opinion, a point that Harold Lasswell emphasized in his *Politics* when he explained that symbols constitute powerful psychological stimuli to mobilize support for, or opposition to, specific political causes. Many people think that symbols are only used to type political personalities ("liberals," "moderates," "conservatives," and the like), but this is only half the story. Symbols can also be employed to label political issues as well, and many different issues were simplified into symbolic language to elicit responses for or against specific bills.

Thus in the Vermont legislature the container-deposit law became the "bottle ban"; the solid-waste management program was labeled "recycling"; a public access bill was referred to as "right-to-know"; and a child dental-care measure was magically transformed into the "tooth fairy" bill. All such labels tended to give these measures a higher degree of visibility, and even glamour, in terms of eliciting public endorsement.

On the other side of the coin, some code words were employed in an effort to whip up antagonism against specific bills. The term "super agency" was always dragged out to oppose bills designed to consolidate administrative services through the creation of a new state bureau, like a transportation authority or a higher-education planning commission. Similarly, another negative symbol, "statewide zoning," was employed very effectively to kill a proposed state land-use plan.

2. Intuition and Common Sense

While the most obvious rationale for the use of symbols grew out of their practical utility to influence political behavior, they also served an economizing function. This resulted from the fact that the legislature was overloaded with much more business than it could digest rationally. Consequently, major issues were often simplified into sym-

bolic language to reduce the decision-making process to more comprehensible and manageable proportions. In essence, complex issues
were packaged into simpler code words in an effort to keep the legislative process in focus. This necessity not to "lose-sight-of-the-forest-
for-the-trees" highlighted a tendency on the part of many wary veteran
legislators to exercise a healthy degree of skepticism against accumu-
lating too much data on specific bills, especially if ultrasophisticated
technology was used in an effort to collect such data.

My most disastrous encounter with this cold hard fact of legislative
life emerged from the one (and only) time I attempted to put the
Dartmouth computer to work in an effort to analyze one of the trickiest
policy problems we faced—the re-apportionment of the state Senate.
Under a United States Supreme Court ruling, it was necessary for us
to re-draw the district (county) lines for the Senate in accordance with
the "one-man, one-vote" principle that the Court had set down in
Baker v Carr and subsequent cases. The Vermont Senate had bogged
down completely in this issue during the 1972 session, so a State
Apportionment Board had taken over the job of trying to draw up a
new set of Senate electoral districts for presentation to the 1973 legislature. Instead of trying to work within the borders of the existing
counties, the board had gone off on a tangent and proposed 30 new
single-member Senate districts that zigzagged all over the state.

The result was a crazy quilt that satisfied no one. Windsor County,
for example, was chopped up into four new districts with my home
town of Norwich being placed in a district that zoomed up the Connecticut River to the town of Newbury (Orange County), thirty-five
miles to the north. Herb Ogden's town of Hartland was placed in a
district that resembled an inverted swastika; John Alden was dumped
into a third separate district; and the Town of Springfield was pulled
out of the county entirely to be lumped with the neighboring community of Bellows Falls. Since all fourteen of Vermont's counties were
emasculated in a similar fashion, none of the senators liked the
Apportionment Board's proposed scheme.

Nevertheless, the board stuck by its guns, and one of its major
arguments was that this was the only way the state could be re-apportioned into Senatorial districts of 14,800 people each in accordance

with the Supreme Court's criterion. I began to think about this, and it struck me that there must be more than one way to re-apportion the state Senate in order to follow the Court's directive. Enter the Dartmouth computer.

I got in touch with Joel Levine, a faculty colleague who was a member of the college's math-social science program. After explaining the problem to him, I asked if there wasn't more than one way to re-apportion Vermont's 246 towns and cities and still meet the Court's requirement that each of the thirty senators should represent a district of approximately 14,800 people.

"Obviously the answer is Yes, Frank," Joel replied. "It's really a pretty simple problem of combinatorics. Actually, it may involve a variation of a tiling problem, or perhaps even a grid approach. No, I think combinatorics is most applicable. Yes, that's the best way to approach it. Simple combinatorics."

"Well ——" I hesitated, not having the slightest clue of what he was talking about. "If you use that approach, how many different ways do you think Vermont could be re-apportioned?"

"That's a very interesting question," he answered thoughtfully. "Let me mull it over, and I'll get back to you later today."

Joel came to my office that same afternoon to advise that, after making a rough estimate of the problem, he had concluded that there were a great many different ways to re-apportion the state Senate in accordance with the Court's decision.

"That's great, Joel. That's what I was hoping you would say. I knew the Apportionment Board was off base on this. How many ways do you think it could be done?"

He frowned in thought. "Well, I would estimate there are at least six million different ways."

"Six million! Did you say there are six *million* different ways to divide up the senatorial districts and still meet the one-man, one-vote criterion. Six million?"

"Oh yes," he replied. "Actually, I think that may be a conservative estimate."

"Gadzooks, that's astounding; really astounding. I can hardly believe it. Hey, there's a problem: no one else will believe it either. Is there any way you could indicate how there are six million ways to do this that people would understand?"

Joel frowned again, and after a long pause indicated that he could program Dartmouth's Kiewit computer to print out maps of the different ways the re-apportionment could take place.

"That would be great, Joel, but you can't print six million maps. Is there some way you could limit the number of maps, and still get the point across?"

Further deep thought before he finally lit up with a knowing smile. "I've got it"—he snapped his fingers—"let's take just one town in Vermont as an example, and see how many different ways it could be combined with adjacent towns to meet the necessary population of 14,800. Yes, that's what I can do. But I'll need to know two things. What town do you want me to use, and how much deviation from the 14,800 total will the Court permit?"

After considerable discussion we decided to focus on the Town of Woodstock, smack in the middle of Windsor County, and to allow for a plus or minus deviation of 5 percent from the desirable 14,800 population total. Joel indicated that it would take a while to program the computer and print out the maps, but he hoped to complete the job within a few days.

A week passed without any further results. A check with Joel indicated there had been some bugs in the mapping program, but he hoped to have the job completed shortly. Two days later he staggered into my office loaded down under an incredible mass of computer print-outs.

"Good God, Joel!" I blinked in alarm as he dumped the load on my desk: "What have we got here?"

"Over 2,500 computer maps," he replied matter-of-factly. "There are over 2,500 ways the Town of Woodstock can be combined with adjacent towns to meet the plus or minus 5 percent deviation."

It was incredible. I picked up the top of the mound of print-outs and the whole stack of paper began to unfold its accordion pleats. All the maps were attached together and folded into flat sheets, sort of like toilet paper from a metal box in a public restroom—but much bigger, about the size of paper towels—all folded together in an enormous stack of paper.

I looked at District Plan Number 10. Woodstock was located at the bottom in a square of nine towns: total population 15,192, deviation +368 (+2.5 percent). Plan Number 15 was a long rectangular map with Woodstock in the middle of a string of eight towns; total population 14,709, deviation −115 (−0.8 percent). Joel and I turned the pile over, and started at the opposite end. Plan Number 2435 was shaped like a camel, with Woodstock at the top hump of an eleven-town district; total population 15,035, deviation +211 (+1.4 percent).

"Joel, this is really incredible," I finally murmured. "I had no idea there was this much work involved. I really feel badly to have asked you to take this on."

"Think nothing of it," he replied cheerfully. "Once I got the program set up right, the computer did all the work. I simply designed the program, and the computer took over. Once it got moving, it just cranked out the maps on its own."

"Well, I still think it's incredible. There's only one problem. How am I going to get this stuff to Montpelier? It's too big to fit into a suitcase."

"Cut it in half, and put it in two suitcases," he laughed. "It certainly should convince anyone that there's more than one way to re-apportion the Vermont Senate."

After Joel left I called Senator Bill Doyle to tell him about the maps. Bill had been working like crazy in the Government Operations Committee on the re-apportionment issue. He was terribly excited, and indicated that he would arrange to have me testify before the committee after he had checked it out with the chairman, Senator Orzel. Ten minutes later Bill called back and said that it was all arranged to have me testify on the following Tuesday morning.

It actually did take two suitcases to carry the computer print-outs to Montpelier. Since the Government Operations Committee was scheduled to meet at 10:30 in the morning, Bill and I went down off the floor at ten o'clock to set up the maps. Bill's eyes almost popped out when I opened the first suitcase and dumped the stack of print-outs on the table. We began to unfold the maps until soon the table was filled, whereupon we cut off the print-outs at Plan Number 35 and started to stick more maps around the walls of the committee room. We ran out of wall space in no time at all. There was still a huge pile of print-outs on the corner of the table and I hadn't even opened the second suitcase.

"Good Lord, Frank, we can't put up all these maps in here," Bill groaned. "There simply isn't enough room."

"Well, we could always go out the front window, down the State House lawn, up over the State Office building, and into the Winooski River," I suggested.

Bill roared with laughter. "We'd be arrested for littering. I think we've put up enough maps anyway. You can just open the second suitcase to show the committee the rest of them."

By this time the floor session had adjourned upstairs and the senators were wandering down to their various committee rooms. Andy Orzel poked his head in the doorway, and looked dumfounded when he saw the computer maps spread out all over the place. "What in God's name is this stuff on the wall?"

"Maps, Andy—computer maps," Bill Doyle explained. "They're back-up evidence for Frank's testimony this morning on the re-apportionment issue."

"But what do all these maps prove?" Andy wanted to know.

"That there's more than one way to re-apportion the Vermont Senate," I put in. "These maps indicate that there are more than twenty-five hundred ways to re-apportion the town of Woodstock alone."

"Woodstock? What's Woodstock got to do with this?" Andy demanded as senators began crowding at the door to watch the commotion. "Of course there's more than one way to re-apportion the Senate. That's the problem we've been trying to resolve all along. There's a Republican way and a Democratic way. Do these maps tell us anything about how many Republicans live in these towns and how many Democrats?"

"No," I told him. "But that wasn't part of the computer program. We didn't include any party variables in the print-outs. They were programmed for a different purpose."

Andy threw up his hands in dismay. "Frank, you really don't need to testify this morning unless you want to. We'll take your word for it that there's more than one way to re-apportion the Senate—that's what the Republicans and the Democrats have been fighting about for the past two years. So would you and Bill mind taking these maps off the wall? Let's begin our business without all these distractions."

I called Joel Levine to let him know what had happened. He chuckled with delight, but was sympathetic. "To tell you the truth, Frank, I doubted if the Senate was going to let a computer intrude into the re-apportionment issue. But it was a damn fascinating analytical problem in combinatorics. I really enjoyed working on it. Let me know if I can be of further help."

That was the end of the Great Computer Print-out, and it illustrated a very important point about the public-policy process. The old-time Vermont legislators had been around long enough to develop their own intuitive approach to complicated issues. They attempted to rely on an interesting mixture of horse sense, personal judgment, and political instinct to unravel the more complex problems. Certainly there was more than one way to re-apportion the Vermont Senate—a Republican way and a Democratic way. It was as simple as that. You didn't need 2,500 computer maps to belabor the obvious.

It was an interesting exercise in the application of practical common sense to the art, not science, of policy formulation. In the last analysis, the re-apportionment of the Senate was resolved by a political compromise, as was the case with most other issues. The final plan stuck as closely as possible to county lines, but the Republicans gave up one seat when a portion of the Rutland County district was shifted north to the Democratic Burlington-Colchester area. In retrospect, I guess that's why Andy Orzel was so upset. He was the senator from Rutland County who eventually got burned by the re-apportionment plan.

3. Incremental Decision-making

Another basic characteristic of the legislative process involved its reliance on incremental decision-making. By "incremental" I mean that completely new policies rarely burst full-blown onto the floor of the legislature. Instead, the overwhelming bulk of our labors involved amending existing laws in order to make marginal modifications in the status quo. And of course this practice could lead to real snafus if we weren't careful.

For one thing, we had to exercise extreme caution in repealing all relevant sections of an existing law whenever we dealt with incremental amendments or else we would end up with two different laws on the books which said two different things. Senator Art Gibb was extremely conscientious in checking out relevant repeals for the Natural Resources Committee, and he constantly warned me, "Watch the repealers, Frank, they can get us into an awful mess of trouble if they're not handled properly." He was right. During one previous session, the legislature had inadvertently changed all felonies into misdemeanors because they hadn't followed the repeals of old law closely enough when they had passed a new criminal code.

My most frustrating encounter with incremental decision-making grew out of S. *124,* a bill we considered in the Health and Welfare Committee to license nursing homes. When the draft first came into the committee, it appeared to be the essence of simplicity. It consisted of a one-sentence amendment to 18 v.s.a. 2002 (1) that changed the designation from "home for the aged" to "residential or custodial facility," and defined such facility as "a building, or part thereof, used for the lodging or boarding of three or more persons who are incapable of self-preservation because of age, or physical or mental limitation."

Well, believe me, these words were like quicksand. The deeper we dug into this issue, the deeper we got bogged down into a morass of state and federal laws and regulations that made no sense at all. Being a nurse, Madeline Harwood, our chairman, was anxious to push the bill through quickly although it had come into the committee pretty late in the 1973 session. However, after several preliminary hearings we realized that we had opened Pandora's box on this one. We agreed, therefore, to keep the bill in committee in order to hold hearings during the summer recess to see if we could get it in shape for the 1974 adjourned session.

All this took place before the nursing-home scandals broke wide open in New York and other states, so the committee worked virtually unnoticed during the summer months. We held six summer hearings in Montpelier, and although nursing-home operators and Health Department personnel showed up from all over the state, we received no press coverage to speak of. As the committee sat through hearing after hearing, it became obvious that the problem in Vermont involved no major scandals. The great majority of the nursing-home operators appeared to be a pretty decent bunch of people. Instead, they, and the elderly people who occupied their facilities, were trapped in an incredible maze of contradictory laws which had grown out of previous bouts of incremental decision-making.

Our legislative staff assistant checked back over existing Vermont statutes and discovered that they had been amended so many times over the course of the past century that eight separate definitions of nursing-home facilities were being used by different state agencies. In one bureau they would be referred to as "nursing homes"; in another they were called "homes for the aged"; in another, "custodial homes," —and so it went. It became clear that the state laws had been patched together over the years with so many different amendments that we didn't even have a clear definition of kinds of facilities we were attempting to deal with.

The federal laws and regulations were even worse. The Department of Health, Education and Welfare defined the facilities in terms of Level I, Level II and Level III care, and provided a different kind of subsidy payment for elderly welfare patients in each type of facility. An even more difficult set of requirements grew out of the national Occupational Safety and Health Act (OSHA), which established so many different regulations with respect to fire escapes, sprinkler systems, and the like, that they threatened to drive many of the smaller homes out of business. When we juxtaposed the federal requirements with the state requirements, the entire system became a bureaucratic nightmare.

The committee finally received so much testimony, and became so confused on this issue, that we decided to visit some of the different kinds of nursing homes in Burlington to see at first hand what was going on out there in the real world of real people. It was one of the most moving, and at times depressing, excursions I ever made in my life. We saw a great many old people who were simply staring at the walls or ceilings with the blank expression that indicated life had passed them by. We also saw some happier patients, and met a lot of nurses and other supervisory personnel who really cared about what they were doing. The most startling encounter of all took place in a Catholic nursing home that had been converted from an old parochial school. The place was spotlessly clean, and as soon as we walked through the door it was obvious that this was an operation characterized by care, concern and love.

A cheerful nun met us in the entry hall, and escorted us through different rooms painted in fresh, lively colors. I was really impressed, and felt that I was experiencing the bright spot in a difficult and trying day. Then, when we were walking through the second floor of the home, the nun motioned to me and Senator Russell Niquette to come over and look into a corner area. We both poked our heads through the doorway of an unoccupied triangular-shaped room.

"I wanted you to see this because there's a rather sad story that goes along with this room," the nun explained. "We had a wonderful old lady who lived in this room for seven years. She really loved the place because it had three corner windows, and she could look out over the back yard and watch the changing of the seasons. Then one day a government inspector came in here and told us we would have to move her out of the room."

Russ Niquette looked at me with a puzzled frown. "That seems strange, Sister," he said. "What was the problem?"

The nun sighed. "The room was too small. The government regulations required one hundred square feet of usable floor space per bed, and the room was only ninety-seven square feet."

I looked over at Russ, whose face seemed drained of color. After a moment I picked up the thread of the conversation. "Could you tell us, Sister, what happened to the lady after you had to move her out of the room?"

"That's the saddest part of the story," the nun said. "She died a short time after we moved her out of here. We think it was the move that really did it. This was her home. She had lived here for seven years. She just couldn't adjust to a new room after all that time."

A wave of real despair swept over me. I didn't know what to say, so I didn't say anything at all.

We visited a couple of other homes that afternoon, but I couldn't get the nun's face out of my mind. Russ Niquette was as depressed as I was. The rest of the trip was pretty gruesome. We talked to operators of smaller nursing homes who were afraid they would go out of business if they had to comply with all the OSHA requirements. Then we visited a second-story place, after climbing up a long rickety flight of stairs. It was dirty and dreadful. Obviously some kind of regulation was needed for this type of facility, but how could we pass reasonable regulations that made sense in terms of the human beings who were caught up in all this chaos? The law can be a very blunt instrument.

We ended up at Russ Niquette's house in Winooski. None of us knew what to do. I was worried that if we tried to license every home in the state, many of them wouldn't be able to meet the state requirements, and a lot of elderly people would be thrown out into the street. On the other hand, if there were no regulations at all, abuses could take place and some people could be badly mistreated. I couldn't see any solution at all. Madeline Harwood was as concerned as I was, and Bill Daniels didn't have any instant answers to this one. Finally, Russ Niquette spoke up.

"I've been in the legislature for a long time, and I must admit that this is a very, very complicated problem," he said, passing his hand over his brow. "The more I think about this, the more I feel that we have to do two different things here. First, we've got to pass legislation that classifies these different types of homes in an orderly fashion, so we know what we are dealing with here. We can't have eight different definitions, each with a different set of regulations, and make any sense out of this at all."

Russ paused before continuing his train of thought. "The second thing I think we should do, once we have classified the different homes properly, is to set up a dual system of regulations. We should license the larger homes where all sorts of medical treatment is taking place, so that they can be adequately monitored by the Department of Health. However, I'm not sure we have to license all the smaller boarding homes where no direct medical supervision is required. I think we should treat these types of facilities in a different manner."

"But what would you do with the smaller homes?" Bill Daniels interrupted. "Would you have any regulations at all to govern their activities?"

Another long pause before Russ responded. "Maybe we could register them," he replied.

"What would that mean?" I cut in.

"Well, it would mean that each one of them would have to sign up with the Agency of Human Services so we would know how many of them were out there and where they were located. But it wouldn't be necessary to license each one of them, and make them conform to all the OSHA regulations and other requirements that could simply drive them out of business. In essence, we would wipe all the old statutes off the books, and start from scratch. We would reclassify all the facilities, putting them in two different categories: licensed homes and registered homes. The licensed homes would be subject to all the stricter regulations, but the smaller registered homes would be subject only to informal inspections by state authorities, particularly in the event that the Health Department received some kind of specific complaint that they weren't being operated properly."

Of course this wasn't the perfect solution, but it was one hell of a logical improvement over the existing system. We all went back to Montpelier to consult with the people in the Agency of Human Services who agreed that the proposed scheme made a lot of sense. Thus *S. 124* became a "strike-all": we knocked everything out of the original bill, and rewrote it from scratch. We worked our heads off before we were satisfied. It wasn't until the middle of the 1974 session that the Health and Welfare Committee asked me to report the bill on the floor of the Senate. It was one of the longest floor reports I delivered in my two years in Montpelier. I explained the background of the bill, talked about our trip to Burlington, indicated how Senator Niquette had thought up the licensing-registration formula, and concluded by explaining that this might not be an ideal solution to a difficult problem but it represented a very real improvement over the present system. The bill passed both the Senate and the House without much debate, and was voted into law as *Public Act 153, 1973 Adjourned Session.*

The measure didn't create much of a public stir, but it was one of the most satisfying experiences I had during my tenure in the state Senate. A year later nursing-home scandals broke out all over the country, and became one hot political issue in many other states. However, the situation was relatively calm in Vermont. Our new legislation was already safely tucked away in *Vermont Statutes Annotated,* Title 18.

4. The Personal Touch

While some of the laws we passed grew out of the type of lengthy, laborious studies that characterized the nursing home bill, others sprang up miraculously out of chance encounters. Such was the case with *S. 175,* a bill I sponsored to strengthen the state's law governing the reporting of suspected child abuse cases.

Strange as it may seem this bill arrived in the Vermont Senate by way of California. It all started when I received a letter in the summer of 1973 from Professor Ruth Lovald of Goddard College in Plainfield, Vermont. She indicated that she had just returned from a conference on children's care on the west coast where she had met an old friend of mine, Connie Starbird of Sausalito, California. Ruth said in her letter that she had told Connie that Vermont didn't have a very good child abuse law, and Connie had suggested that she write to me about this because she knew that I was serving in the Vermont legislature. After I spent some time looking into the matter, I concluded that Ruth was right, the existing law wasn't very strong, so I consulted with her and some of the staff people in the State Health Department, particularly Karen Davis, about what should be done to improve the situation. The result was *S. 175* which was introduced for first reading on opening day of the 1974 session.

The bill was designed to accomplish three objectives: first, to provide a broader definition of child abuse to include mental as well as physical injury; second, to broaden legal immunity for persons who reported such potential abuse in good faith, by protecting them from suit for libel or defamation; and third, to set up a better procedure by which the Department of Social and Rehabilitation Services could investigate and follow up on the reports which it received of child abuse. When I drafted the bill I assumed it would be assigned to the Health and Welfare Committee, but instead Jack Burgess sent it off to the Judiciary Committee, presumably because of the legal-immunity provisions relating to prosecution. I began to get restless after the bill sat in Judiciary for a month without any action at all. It was at this point that the personal touch came into play again, but this time it was within the legislature itself, rather than from a correspondent in California.

I approached Bill Daniels, who served on Judiciary, to see if he could help get the bill moving. It was just after he had delivered his floor report on the funeral directors, so he was pretty down, but he agreed to see what he could do. Bill Doyle was also a member of Judiciary, and he indicated he would pitch in too. A couple of days later Garry Buckley, the committee chairman, walked over to my desk to ask me if the bill was important. The informal grapevine had obviously reached him.

"It's not the most earth-shaking bill in the world," I told him, "but I think it's a very worthwhile measure. I'd appreciate it if you could try to move it out."

"O.K., Sport," he replied. "We're really jammed up with a pile of bills, but if you think this one is important, we'll give it a whirl."

Two days later I was invited into the committee to explain the background of the bill. It immediately became obvious that one provision wasn't going to fly—the broadened definition of child abuse to include both physical and mental injury. The committee wouldn't buy the mental-injury part at all; two members expressed concern that it sounded like a bill that tried to tell parents how to raise their children. However, the rest of the bill looked good. I agreed to drop the provision about mental injury to get it out of the Judiciary Committee, and the bill was reported for second reading on February 15, midway through the session. It passed the Senate and moved into the House, where it was again referred to the House Judiciary Committee for further study.

Another month went by. Nothing happened. It was now mid-March and the adjourned session was scheduled to end April 2. It was time to reach out again to see if I could get things moving. If the bill didn't make it through the adjourned session it was completely dead, since all proposed legislation became null and void at the end of the second session, and the issue would have to start over from scratch in the 1975–76 General Assembly.

I called on Tim O'Connor, the House committee chairman, to see if he could take some action on the bill. He was sympathetic, but indicated that the committee was really overloaded and he couldn't make any promises so late in the session. Fortunately, though, I had three friends on the committee; I talked with them, and they indicated they would see what they could do. The bill was finally moved out to the floor of the House during the last week of the session. Representative Louise Swainbank, who reported out the bill, did a very good job. There was some flak from the old-timers who expressed concern that we were spoiling the younger generation, with one grizzled veteran wanting to know if this bill meant that parents couldn't spank their children anymore. The debate was relatively mild, however, and the bill passed the House without too much trouble. It appeared on the statute books as *Public Act 237, 1973 Adjourned Session*.

While a number of groups had expressed an interest in this issue, the outside pressure wasn't strong enough to assure its passage. Its supporters included the Governor's Commission on Children and Youth, plus a number of children's lobby groups, but these organizations simply didn't have the firepower to push a bill like this along in the closing days of a session. Unless a bill was a real blockbuster that carried its own momentum, the crucial factor at this stage of the legislative process was personal intervention on the part of individual legislators.

Since a number of House members had come to my rescue on my child-abuse bill, I was happy when I had an opportunity to reciprocate when Representative Judy Rosenstreich of Waterbury Center came to me for help during the waning weeks of the session on two bills she had sponsored. Both came in to the Senate Health and Welfare Committee when the clock was ticking down towards adjournment. One

dealt with charges for the care and treatment of mental patients at
the Waterbury State Hospital, and the other was designed to modern-
ize the laws relating to the commitment of children to the custody of
the state. There was no question that both bills were worthwhile, but
the real issue was whether they would be lost in the shuffle as the
legislature rushed to adjournment. We finally voted them both out of
the Health and Welfare Committee midway through the final week
of the session, and they appeared on a very crowded calendar for
Thursday, two days before we were scheduled to head for home.

I reported both bills, but we didn't get around to acting on them
until late Thursday evening, a little before eleven o'clock. I looked up
at the balcony, where only two visitors were sitting, apparently about
to fall asleep, plus Judy, who was looking down intently in the hope
that there wouldn't be some last-minute snafu that could have spelled
disaster at that stage of the session. However, both bills passed second
reading without any questions at all. Most of the senators were so
bone-tired that they weren't about to raise a ruckus over hospital
charges or commitment of children. I winked up at Judy when the
second bill passed and she returned a grateful, if weary, smile. It
reminded me of the opening day of the 1973 session when I had looked
up at Ann and Susan in the balcony. On that occasion, however, there
had been an element of electricity and excitement in the air. In this
particular instance, the two-year session was coming to an end, and
all that the battle-scarred troops really wanted was a good night's
sleep.

5. The Multiplicity of Roles

Anybody who has been involved in the legislative process for any
reasonable period of time is eventually forced to recognize the fact
that a legislature is basically a "reactive" body which tends to respond
to most key problems on an after-the-fact basis. As Jimmy Breslin notes
in *How the Good Guys Finally Won,* a legislature "is not a place of
positive action. It is an institution designed only to react, not plan or
lead."

One of the basic reasons for this is that a legislature consists of a variety of voices which are, more often than not, attempting to sound off on a hundred different themes at once. Under the circumstances it is difficult for such a divergent body to get out ahead on very many major policy issues. A striking case in point involved the energy shortages that hit Vermont during the winter of 1974. Not one major bill dealing with the energy crisis was seriously debated during the 1973 legislative session, but we were deluged with such bills during the 1974 session. In essence, we were reacting to the crisis after it had hit us so hard that it could no longer be ignored.

This type of reactive approach creates a lot of problems and undoubtedly helps to account for the fact that legislative bodies in general, and state legislatures in particular, suffer from a generally poor public image. It's questionable, however, whether this is a fair appraisal. As political scientist Alan Rosenthal has observed, state legislatures are likely to be characterized "as weak sisters to administrators and governors. Yet probably more than any other American institution, state legislatures have recently undergone significant change."

Another political scientist, Ira Sharkansky, makes a similar point in *The Maligned States* when he observes that "one of the ironies of American politics is that the states receive so much negative publicity. They do not deserve to be whipping boys. The states are sources of strength." I agree with this observation. Despite all our problems, Vermont was ahead of the United States Congress in many areas of political innovation and creativity. Although we engaged in our share of frustrations, we were also making some very real strides in getting on top of many key issues, such as environmental planning, campaign-finance reform, open government and "right-to-know" legislation, and the like.

Part of the difficulty in evaluating the effectiveness of the state legislatures results from the fact that we fail to make such evaluations on the basis of what a legislative body is designed to accomplish. When the average citizen thinks about the legislature, he is likely to conclude, "Oh yes, that's where they make the laws." So far so good. But making laws is only one part of the legislative process. Actually, a legislature is designed to perform a multiplicity of roles, which is a point made by

Professor Duane Lockard, who once served in the Connecticut Senate, when he observes that a legislature is "vitally important as an agency that reflects the views of different elements of the state, that allocates resources between the public and private sector and also within the government, that provides some kind of overview of the bureaucracy, and that mediates conflicts between competing forces."

When viewed in this light, the legislature performs a wide variety of different functions in our political-governmental system. First, it carries out a legitimizing role (creating and ratifying legislation by enacting statutory law). Second, it performs a distributive role (allocating revenues and tax burdens). Third, it performs a political role (mediating conflict and reconciling different pressures from divergent special interest groups). Fourth, it performs a representative role (reflecting constituency views and dramatizing issues so that they become the subject of open public debate). And finally, it carries out the role of watchdog (overseeing the executive branch).

Because of this multitude of roles, the legislature is a political body, and, in the words of political scientist Malcolm Jewell, "politics is the key to understanding the American state legislature." In effect, it serves as a lightning rod to which all the conflicting pressures of American society are drawn, and its primary job is to de-fuse these pressures so that the political system can function intact without blowing wide apart.

Hence, when all is said and done, the legislative process is a very complicated, but vitally important, way to air political issues in a manner that enables the public to be brought into the democratic decision-making process. It's difficult to judge how well fifty divergent state legislatures perform their multiple roles because they differ so widely in size, salaries, staffing, and many other areas. Vermont has one hundred fifty members in its House, while its eastern neighbor, New Hampshire, has four hundred; Alaska and Nevada, on the other hand, have only forty. By the same token, Vermont pays its legislators a very modest $4,500 per biennium (maximum salary, depending on the length of the sessions), while New Hampshire pays a miserly $200, and California a whopping $53,490.

In most recent evaluations of state legislative performance, Vermont has come out somewhere in the middle. In a study conducted by the Citizens Conference on State Legislatures, Vermont was ranked nineteenth among the fifty states in functional effectiveness, twentieth in accountability, and thirty-fourth in information. However, other rankings were lower with the state near the bottom (forty-seventh) in lack of "representativeness" in legislative membership (due to our frugal salaries, which restrict the diversity of people who can afford to serve as state legislators). Despite this last ranking, I found that the Vermont legislature contained a remarkably capable group of members who performed their duties with a high degree of dedication and commitment.

In the final analysis, we certainly made mistakes, and I could hardly claim that we were super-efficient in all we tried to accomplish. Instead, we engaged in our fair share of what Charles Lindbloom has described as "the science of muddling through." Yet although representative democracy is hardly the most efficient form of government, it's the best system we have been able, so far, to devise. As Rep. Robert S. Babcock, a former Lieutenant Governor and University of Vermont political scientist, observed in describing a recent legislative session, "No one will believe this, but we found that most politicians were incorruptible, diligent and very competent." I didn't observe anything in my two years in the Vermont State House that would prompt me to challenge that basic fact of political life.

CHAPTER

15

★ ★ ★ ★

The Personal Dimension

Politics is an all-or-nothing venture.
Stimson Bullitt
To Be a Politician

A MONTH AFTER the 1974 legislative session adjourned Ann and I spent a long weekend at the Trapp Family Lodge in Stowe. It was mid-May, and the mountain scenery was breathtaking, with the long, rolling Worcester Range spread out before us to the east, and Camel's Hump jutting up sharply to the south.

We took long walks through the upland woods and meadows to look at the delicate wildflowers: trillium, hepatica, and the soft green fiddlehead ferns that were beginning to reach up along the steep, rocky streambanks. The woods were serenely quiet except for the rustling of numerous scarlet tanagers, which we spotted all through the low forest cover, despite the fact that they usually fly very high during their northward spring migration through Vermont.

In addition to providing a chance to get away from it all, our walks gave us time to talk about my future plans; to decide whether or not it made any sense for me to continue in the political arena. It didn't take us long to realize that I simply would not be able to carry the load of increasing, and increasingly varied, commitments I was undertaking.

My first year in the legislature, when I was on sabbatical leave from Dartmouth, had been almost a breeze. But the second year was completely different, a real nightmare, as I returned to full-time teaching. So forget the theories about the part-time citizen legislator. As far as I could see, there is no such animal: when the political life is pursued with any reasonable degree of diligence, it becomes an all-consuming business.

By the second winter my family was edged out completely as I spent more and more time attempting to reconcile two full-time careers. Every day became a blur of conflicting demands: meeting classes, grading student papers, preparing lectures, serving on college committees, following up constituency chores, studying bills, answering letters, giving speeches, appearing on radio shows, meanwhile with the telephone ringing, ringing, ringing all day long.

Something had to give, and I thought about the options long and hard. Since virtually my entire professional career had been devoted to education, I concluded that I could make more of a difference working with students and teaching, and seeing more of my family, than by attempting to pursue the spiraling demands of a fledgling political career.

Although the choice was obvious, my decision was made somewhat reluctantly. On the positive side, I felt the long hours in Montpelier had certainly been worthwhile. I made a host of new acquaintances from all over the state, and there had been some solid accomplishments—not too many, perhaps, but enough to give me a sense of satisfaction: the child-abuse reporting law; the bills we had studied so hard and rewritten in the Health and Welfare and Natural Resources committees; and my proudest single achievement of all, the sponsorship of a new law that established a comprehensive statewide retirement system for local government employees in Vermont. I was very pleased when the League of Cities and Towns awarded me their Certificate of Service, although I really should have presented the award to them since it was their lobbying effort which pushed the bill through to final passage.

There had also been disappointments, but they are an integral part of the political process. The essence of politics, especially legislative politics, is compromise, which means that no participants can gain (or lose) everything they may be after.

Most important of all, I learned a great deal about the dynamics of practical politics; and also a great deal about myself in relationship to the demands that grow out of the political life.

From the outset it was obvious to me that there are certain basic human traits that appear to be desirable in any political personality: a basic sense of fairness and integrity, a reasonable degree of intelli-

gence, an ability to laugh and maintain a sense of balance in the face
of conflicting pressures. These factors certainly are important, yet
there is another equally important set of requirements that I completely underestimated: the personal time and energy demands that
we place on our public servants in a democratic system of government.

To state it as bluntly as possible, anyone who is interested in making a major commitment to politics had best be prepared literally to
give up all else if this commitment is to be fulfilled. As Stimson Bullitt
observed in *To Be a Politician,* "politics is an all-or-nothing venture."
There's no way—at least I found no way—to pursue the political life
on a casual, leisurely, half-time basis. Unexpected demands pop up
all over the place, often at the most inconvenient time. Drop everything, Frank, there's some new crisis out there somewhere that will
take the rest of your afternoon (and probably your evening as well).
The pressures of political life are so chaotic and so unpredictable that
plain, hard physical stamina becomes of overriding importance to
anyone who hopes to pursue a political career. What I'm talking about
here is simple raw energy. You can be bone-tired, but if constituents
want to see you on something that they think is important, you'd
better be ready to draw on some hidden inner reserves in an effort to
respond to their needs. The political life is a tiring, grueling, continuous depletion of personal energy reserves. This is the first, and most
significant, insight I gained about the political process.

A second basic fact that emerged very early is that a great deal of
your physical and mental energy is expended on routine business that
may not appear to be of any particular earth-shaking importance.
The point here is that you are a public servant. Certain issues may
not be terribly important to you, but if they are important to your
constituents, you'd better listen and pay attention. Although some of
the bills we considered in committee bored me nearly to death, they
represented legitimate concerns on the part of selected segments of the
public, and there was no way I could conscientiously ignore these
concerns. In short, a great deal in the political process does not—repeat
does not—involve the big glamorous policy issues. Most of the work
is sheer routine and hardly awe-inspiring. If you are not prepared
to face this fact, stay away from the political arena.

Third is the matter of privacy, or, more accurately, lack of privacy.

Once you have entered the public arena, a great deal of your business becomes public business. If you're on some kind of an ego trip and like to read your name in the newspapers, it's great; but if you really want to pack off and get away from it all, that's a different matter. There's very little room for personal privacy in the world of politics. This is another of the basic facts of political life.

Finally, you've got to have a pretty thick skin, and a sense of inner direction that is strong enough to guide you through some turbulent waters. It's not so much that everybody is trying to cut up everybody else all the time; the knives weren't that sharp, at least in Vermont. Rather it's the ability to reach specific conclusions in areas of considerable uncertainty; the ability to reconcile yourself to the reality that much of what you do will inevitably be misinterpreted and/or misunderstood; the ability to recognize that you have to provide leadership in helping people to understand and face complex issues that they would like to oversimplify. Dartmouth's former president John Dickey used to tell me that one of the key tests of leadership was "the capacity to be undismayed in the face of adversity and uncertainty." I was a little fuzzy on the concept when he first explained it to me, but I understood it much, much better after I finished a stint in the political arena.

I thought about all these things quite often during the summer of 1974 after I had announced that it would be impossible for me to run again for the Senate, and a new group of candidates was out there in the hustings, fighting over that third Windsor County seat now open in the state legislature. It was an interesting exercise in personal introspection, one which really came into full focus on election night of 1974, when a local radio station asked me to serve as a political analyst to interpret the results that would be rolling in throughout the evening. I experienced a strange feeling as I sat in the studio all night, poring over wire-service listings of vote totals and realizing that I was no longer part of the returns. A lot of familiar names appeared on the tally sheets. Tom Salmon was re-elected Governor in the Democratic near sweep of Vermont, while incumbents John Alden and Herb Ogden were returned to office for Windsor County, and the third Senate seat was captured by Republican John Howland, the business leader who had kindly invited me to deliver my "garbage truck" speech to the Rotarians two years earlier.

When I returned home after midnight I sat in the living room for a long time reaching back over the two years I had spent in Montpelier. There were some satisfying accomplishments and agonizing defeats. But mostly there were the memories of all those people out there: the help and encouragement I had received from Bill Doyle and John Alden in my 1972 campaign; the thoughtful considerate leadership of Ed Janeway, Jack Burgess, John Boylan and Art Jones; the great funeral debate between Bill Daniels and Graham Newell; Jack O'Brien's fiery temper; Andy Orzel's reaction to the pile of 2,500 computer maps, long afternoon meetings in the Health and Welfare Committee with Madeline Harwood, Dotty Shea, Bob Bloomer, and Russ Niquette; the face of the nun in the Burlington nursing home; Art Gibb's work on "repealers"; Bob Gannett's floor reports; Herb Ogden's quick, dry wit; Garry Buckley's booming voice; the meetings with the House Democratic Breakfast Club; the Florida trip to the Eagleton Conference with Judy Rosenstreich; the warm friendships I made with Republicans like Fred Smith, Ellery Purdy, Sandy Partridge, and Ward Bedford, and with Democrats like Esther Sorrell, Dick Soule, Bob Brannon, and Tom Crowley.

And there were all those constituents with a thousand and one different concerns: Dan Fraser's shrinking gas; Roger Eastman's floodproof barn; Mary Peirce's invitation to speak in the old Weathersfield Center Church about "Electrical Engineering" in Windsor County, the senatorial visits to the town dumps.

Finally, I thought about the different lobbyists I had met, plus all the people working in various state agencies. In many ways, the relationship between the legislature and the executive branch is an adversary one since the agencies were invariably asking for more funds than we were able to appropriate. Yet, despite Jack O'Brien's constant railing about "executive welfare," Vermont benefits from the talents of some very capable public servants—people like Health Department employee Karen Davis, who helped with the child abuse bill; or Tom Davis, the Secretary of Human Services; or Paul Philbrook, the beleaguered Commissioner of Social Welfare.

It was an incredible experience meeting all these people—just as I suspected it would be when I first told my family I had decided to throw my hat into the ring, and my son David had asked me, "What hat? You don't wear a hat, even in the winter." Unfortunately David had been wrong. I tried to wear too many hats at the same time, and I found that I no longer could keep them all on at once.

I'm glad I had an opportunity to participate in the political process. It was a great adventure. I'm sure I will think about my old colleagues quite often in the years ahead, especially when I'm meeting my Dartmouth classes at nine-thirty on cold winter mornings at the very moment when some future Lieutenant Governor is banging down the gavel in the majestic Senate Chamber in Montpelier, and announcing in solemn tones, the "Orders of the Day."

Appendix

Governor: Thomas P. Salmon, Democrat, Rockingham (Bellows Falls); lawyer.

Lieutenant Governor: John S. Burgess, Republican, Brattleboro; lawyer. President of the Senate.

Secretary of State: Richard C. Thomas, Republican, Montpelier.

Attorney General: Kimberley C. Cheney, Republican, Montpelier; lawyer.

State Treasurer: Frank H. Davis, Republican, Burlington; lawyer.

Auditor of Accounts: Alexander B. Acebo, Republican, Barre City; business administration.

VERMONT SENATE 1973-74

John T. Alden, Republican, Windsor County; insurance. Vice chairman, General and Military Committee.

H. Ward Bedford, Republican, Addison County; retired farmer. Chairman, Finance Committee.

Robert A. Bloomer, Republican, Rutland County; lawyer. Vice chairman, Judiciary Committee.

John H. Boylan, Republican, Orleans-Essex counties; retired railroad store-keeper. Vice chairman, Appropriations Committee.

Robert J. Brannon, Democrat, Franklin-Grand Isle counties; farmer. Vice chairman, Agriculture Committee.

T. Garry Buckley, Republican, Bennington County; real estate and insurance. Chairman, Judiciary Committee.

Reginald G. Cooley, Republican, Orange County; owner, asphalt paving company.

Thomas M. Crowley, Democrat, Chittenden County; insurance. Vice chairman, Committee on Highway Traffic.

Robert V. Daniels, Democrat, Chittenden County; professor, University of Vermont.

227

William T. Doyle, Republican, Washington County; professor, Johnson State College.

Robert T. Gannett, Republican, Windham County; lawyer.

Arthur Gibb, Republican, Addison County; Angus cattle breeder. Chairman, Agriculture Committee.

Madeline B. Harwood, Republican, Bennington County; registered nurse. Chairman, Health and Welfare Committee.

Edward G. Janeway, Republican, Windham County; dairy farmer. President Pro Tempore of the Senate; chairman, Appropriations Committee.

Arthur H. Jones, Republican, Orleans-Essex counties; electrical engineer. Chairman, Natural Resources Committee.

Gerald I. Morse, Republican, Caledonia County; retired poultry farmer.

Graham S. Newell, Republican, Caledonia County; professor, Lyndon State College. Vice chairman, Education Committee.

Russell F. Niquette, Democrat, Chittenden County; lawyer. Vice chairman, Health and Welfare Committee.

John J. O'Brien, Democrat, Chittenden County; retired sports promoter. Chairman, Committee on Highways and Bridges.

Herbert G. Ogden, Republican, Windsor County; cidermill operator.

Andrew J. Orzel, Republican, Rutland County; town clerk. Chairman, Government Operations Committee.

Sanborn Partridge, Republican, Rutland County; educator. Vice chairman, Government Operations Committee.

Ellery R. Purdy, Republican, Rutland County; retired teacher. Chairman, Education Committee.

Dorothy P. Shea, Republican, Washington County; homemaker. Chairman, General and Military Committee.

Frank Smallwood, Republican, Windsor County; professor, Dartmouth College.

Donald L. Smith, Republican, Washington County; apple orchardist. Chairman, Legislative Council, Committee on Highway Traffic.

Frederick P. Smith, Republican, Chittenden County; banker.

Esther H. Sorrell, Democrat, Chittenden County; homemaker.

Richard C. Soule, Democrat, Franklin-Grand Isle counties; insurance. Vice chairman, Institutions Committee.

Fred Westphal, Republican, Lamoille County. Chairman, Institutions Committee; vice chairman, Finance Committee.

Bibliography

AIKEN, GEORGE D., *Speaking from Vermont.* New York: Frederick A. Stokes Company, 1938.

ALBRIGHT, PAUL, ed., *The Book of the States,* Vol. XX. Lexington, Ky.: Council of State Governments, 1974.

ALLEN, IRA, *Natural and Political History of the State of Vermont.* London: J. W. Myers, 1798.

ARISTOTLE, *Politics,* in *The Basic Works of Aristotle,* R. McKeon, ed. New York: Random House, 1941.

BABCOCK, ROBERT S., "Vermont Politicians Serve the Public," *Burlington Free Press,* November 9, 1975.

BARBER, JAMES D., *The Lawmakers.* New Haven, Conn.: Yale University Press, 1965.

BEARSE, RAY, ed., *Vermont: A Guide to the Green Mountains,* second ed. Boston: Houghton, Mifflin, 1966.

BERINI, SYLVIA R., ed., *Vermont Legislative Directory and State Manual: 1973-74.* Montpelier, Vt.: Secretary of State, 1974.

BRESLIN, JIMMY, *How the Good Guys Finally Won.* New York: Viking Press, 1975.

BRYAN, FRANK M., *Yankee Politics in Vermont.* Hanover, N.H.: University Press of New England, 1974.

BULLITT, STIMSON, *To Be a Politician.* New York: Doubleday and Co., 1938.

CITIZENS CONFERENCE ON STATE LEGISLATURES, *The Sometime Governments.* New York: Bantam Books, 1971.

CRANE, CHARLES E., *Let Me Show You Vermont.* New York: Knopf, 1950.

EMENHISER, J. DON, ed., *The Dragon on the Hill.* Salt Lake City: University of Utah Press, 1970.

FENNO, RICHARD F., JR., *Congressmen in Committees.* Boston: Little, Brown, 1973.

FLINT, WINSTON A., *The Progressive Movement in Vermont.* Washington: American Council on Public Affairs, 1941.

Gazetteer of Vermont Heritage. Chester, Vt.: The National Survey, 1966.

HARD, WALTER, JR., ed., *Green Mountain Treasury: A Vermont Life Sampler.* New York: Harper & Bros., 1961.

HILL, RALPH N., *Yankee Kingdom: Vermont and New Hampshire.* New York: Harper & Bros., 1960.

JEWELL, MALCOLM E., *The State Legislature, Politics and Practice.* New York: Random House, 1962.

LASSWELL, HAROLD, *Politics: Who Gets What, When, How.* New York: Meriden Books, 1958.

———, *Power and Personality.* New York: Viking, 1948.

LINDBLOM, CHARLES, "The Science of Muddling Through," in *Public Administration Review,* 19 (Spring, 1959).

LOCKARD, DUANE, "The Legislature as a Personal Career," in D. G. Herzberg and A. Rosenthal, *Strengthening the States: Essays on Legislative Reform.* New York: Anchor, 1972.

———, *New England State Politics.* Princeton: Princeton University Press, 1959.

MADISON, JAMES, *The Federalist Papers,* Federalist No. 51, 332. New York: Mentor, 1961.

MILBRATH, LESTER, *Political Participation.* Chicago: Rand McNally, 1965.

MILLER, CLEM, *Member of the House: Letters of a Congressman.* New York: Scribner, 1962.

NUQUIST, ANDREW E., *Town Government in Vermont.* Burlington, Vt.: Government Research Center, University of Vermont, 1964.

———, *Vermont State Government and Administration.* Burlington, Vt.: Government Research Center, University of Vermont, 1961.

PLATO, *Laws,* in *The Works of Plato,* B. Jowett, trans. New York: Tudor, n.d.

RIEGLE, DONALD, *O Congress.* New York: Popular Library, 1972.

ROCKEFELLER, NELSON A., *The Future of Federalism.* Cambridge: Harvard University Press, 1962.

ROSENTHAL, ALAN, *Legislative Performance in the States.* New York: Free Press, 1974.

ROSSITER, CLINTON, *Parties and Politics in America.* New York: Signet, 1960.

SHARKANSKY, IRA, *The Maligned States.* New York: McGraw-Hill, 1972.

Vermont Statutes and Legislative Journals: 1973–74. Montpelier, Vt.: Secretary of State, 1973, 1974.

WENDLING, KATHRYN A., ed., *Vermont Citizens Guide.* Burlington, Vt.: League of Women Voters of Vermont, 1972.

WHEATON, WILLIAM L., ed., *Vermont Facts and Figures, 1973.* Montpelier, Vt.: Vermont Department of Budget and Management, 1973.

WOLFINGER, R. E., ed., *Readings on Congress.* Englewood Cliffs, N.J.: Prentice-Hall, 1971.

Subject Index